The Global Challenge

The Global Challenge

BUILDING THE NEW

WORLDWIDE ENTERPRISE

**Robert T. Moran and
John R. Riesenberger**

McGRAW-HILL BOOK COMPANY

London · New York · St Louis · San Francisco · Auckland
Bogatá · Caracas · Lisbon · Madrid · Mexico
Milan · Montreal · New Delhi · Panama · Paris · San Juan
São Paulo · Singapore · Sydney · Tokyo · Toronto

Published by
McGRAW-HILL Book Company Europe
Shoppenhangers Road, Maidenhead, Berkshire SL6 2QL, England
Telephone 0628 23432
Fax 0628 770224

British Library Cataloguing in Publication Data

Moran, Robert T.
  Global Challenge: Building the New
  Worldwide Enterprise
  I. Title II. Riesenberger, John R.
  658.4

  ISBN 0–07–709022–5

Library of Congress Cataloging-in-Publication Data

Moran, Robert T.
    The global challenge: building the new worldwide enterprise / Robert T. Moran and
  John R. Riesenberger.
      p.   c.m.
    Includes bibliographical references and index.
    ISBN 0–07–709022–5
    1. International business enterprises—Management. 2. Comparative management.
  3. Executive ability. I. Riesenberger, John R. II. Title.
  HD62.4.M663   1994   94–10893
  658′049–dc20   CIP

1234 BL 987654

Typeset by Computape (Pickering) Ltd, North Yorkshire
and printed and bound in Great Britain by Biddles Ltd, Guildford and King's Lynn

Contents

Foreword

Many global managers have been facing the challenge of running businesses on a worldwide basis and have essentially had to learn from experience.

For many years, there was little academic support for this effort. Business schools were far behind in teaching global management. When globalization became the in-word of the 1980s, the confusion over the interpretation of the new craze was quasi-general, ranging from extreme centralization of business decisions to total adaptability to local market requirements. However, it has become clear that a new set of realities has been emerging, and significantly impacting how companies need to be managed for success. It is no longer conceivable that a company, whatever its size, can ensure its long term viability by confining itself to its domestic market, however large that market may be.

The Global Challenge: Building the New Worldwide Enterprise is the first book I have come across that fully and remarkably addresses the subject of global management in practitioners' terms. Not only does it cover the background, evolution and current state of global management, but it brings a particularly helpful focus to the importance of human resources and organizational structures. The greatest barrier companies face in their attempt to compete on a global scale, is their own ability to recruit, develop and keep managers who have the capability of being effective in cultures different from their own—managers who are able to deal in a multi-dimensional environment and in structures that are inevitably complex.

This book offers practical recommendations on how to assess and improve global organizations. It is a 'must-read' for current and future global managers.

Jean-Pierre Rosso, President and Chief Executive Officer
Case Corporation

Acknowledgments

We wish to acknowledge several individuals and institutions.

- Richard and Marie Riesenberger for their guidance, love and support.

- Christopher Bartlett and Sumantra Ghoshal for their research and inspiration for this book.

- Peter Seaver and Ley Smith for their approval and support for this project.

- Jan Patterson, Sylvia Krieg, Yvette Livingston, Tammy Waidelich and Cheryl Rooney for literature searches; Janna Hensley for illustrations, and Jan Patterson for contributing to the section on Competency Two.

- Individuals from our Institutions—American Graduate School of International Management (Thunderbird) and The Upjohn Company—who encouraged and supported our writing efforts in numerous ways.

- Kate Allen and Phil Ruppel of McGraw-Hill UK and McGraw-Hill US for agreeing we had something worth saying on the subject of globalization.

- Philip Kotler, Christopher Bartlett, Gary Hamel, Jean-Pierre Rosso, Sten Langenius and J. T. Battenberg III for reading our manuscript and for their positive comments.

- Judith E. Soccorsy and Cherri Glowe for their editing, administrative and organizational skills.

Introduction

In Tom Peters's and Robert Waterman's 1981 best seller, *In Search of Excellence*, the acronym KISS—Keep it Simple Stupid—was read and discussed by millions. This perspective of Peters and Waterman was one of the essential attributes of excellent companies in resisting the pressure to complicate, and instead keeping things simple. Another management writer said it differently: 'Good management is the art of making difficult things simple, not simple things difficult.'

Such is the overriding purpose of this book. Our goal is to write about difficult things—competition, global changes, vision, structure, strategy, organizational change, competencies required to succeed in a complex business world—in a style that is simple, practical and useful, yet, when appropriate, grounded in theory and sound academic and business practices.

We hope to turn readers 'on' not 'off' to the challenges, opportunities and pitfalls of working in the changing global environment that is the reality of today and probably tomorrow as well.

Our overriding goal is to help readers confront the problems of globalization that they experience and to discover some ideas, models, paradigms and frameworks they can apply to their organizations with beneficial results.

Some of the material may not be new to readers, such as sections of Chapters 2 and 3. In this case, we recommend skipping ahead to Chapters 4 and 5 where, we are convinced, most readers will find new insights.

This book has undergone several iterations and most chapters have had many rewrites. Notwithstanding, the book is incomplete and imperfect for what we hoped to accomplish. Both authors, however, learned from each other and from the many books and materials they shared.

Robert T. Moran
John R. Riesenberger

Part I

Part I (Chapters 1–4) focuses on those external sociological and economic forces that have contributed to the rapid escalation of the globalization of business competition.

The problem and the challenge

Denial, in varying degrees, is a fact of life in most systems. Examples are many. In families, children deny that their parents are alcoholic; women deny that their husbands are abusive. In business organizations and academic institutions, similarly, 'realities' are suppressed, 'feelings' are stuffed, and intellectualization exercises force new realities into old paradigms.

> 'People deny reality. They fight against real feelings caused by real circumstance. They build mental worlds of shoulds, oughts, and might-have-beens. Real changes begin with real appraisal and acceptance of what is. Then realistic action is possible.'
>
> These are the words of David Reynolds, an American exponent of Japanese Morita psychotherapy. He is speaking of personal behavior, but his comments are applicable to the economic behavior of nations, as well.[1]

Denial in its various forms is a global problem. The following humorous parody illustrates the denial of a country's competitiveness problem and a misdiagnosis. This example is American, but it can easily apply to most countries.

THE AMERICAN WAY

The Americans and the Japanese decided to engage in a competitive boat race. Both teams practiced hard and long to reach their peak performance. On the big day they both felt ready.

The Japanese won by a *mile*!

Afterward, the American team was discouraged by the loss. Morale sagged. Corporate management decided that the reason for the crushing defeat had to be found, so a consulting firm was hired to investigate the problem and recommend corrective action.

The consultant's findings: The Japanese team had eight people rowing and one person steering; the American team had one person rowing and eight people steering.

After a year of study and millions spent analyzing the problem, the consulting firm concluded that too many people were steering and not enough were rowing on the American team.

So, as race day neared again the following year, the American team's management structure was completely reorganized. The new structure: four steering managers, three area steering managers, one staff steering manager and a new performance review system for the person rowing the boat to provide work incentive.

The next year the Japanese won by *two* miles!

Humiliated, the American corporation laid off the rower for poor performance and gave the managers a bonus for discovering the problem.[2]

In this oversimplification, in the first race the Americans were overconfident and denied they had a competitiveness problem. In preparation for the second race, there was a serious misdiagnosis. Gary Hamel states it well:

> To fully understand our competitive advantage/disadvantage, we have to go deeper, and look at our 'genetic coding'—i.e., our beliefs, our managerial frames. It is these beliefs that restrict our perceptions of reality and degrees of freedom. To be successful, a company needs 'genetic variety.' Our challenge must be to get outside our restrictive managerial frames.
>
> If you want to enlarge your managerial frames, you must be curious about how the rest of the world thinks—and you must have humility. The real competitive problem is not that our institutional environment is hopelessly unhelpful, but that our managerial frames are hopelessly inappropriate to the next round of global competition.[3]

Market share shifts: a global competitiveness problem?

We expect this book to assist individuals in correctly diagnosing their organizations' global competitiveness problems and, more importantly, to place persons with the necessary global competencies in the positions required to make globalization work. We begin with an overview of market share shifts in some key industries. Drawing upon reports and analyses by Lawrence Franko[4] and Andrew Kupfer[5] we note growth and decline patterns in the following industries.

Aerospace

The United States still dominates approximately 75 per cent of the world's aerospace manufacturing. US aerospace exports in 1991 were $43 billion, and this industry is categorized as a growth industry, with demand for airplane seating capacity expected to double in the next two decades.

The European Airbus consortium is expected to continue to grow at least as fast as the industry. Airbus currently has over 100 customers and controls 30 per cent of the commercial jet market. A recent study reports that Airbus has received $26 billion in government subsidies.[6]

Japan will become a significant player in the industry in the coming decade. Japanese manufacturers are currently developing manufacturing processes for engines, fuselage parts and electronic equipment. Japanese companies have entered into joint ventures with General Electric, Pratt & Whitney and Rolls-Royce to develop and manufacture jet engines.

The United States will maintain its dominance, but market share is expected to erode due to projected reduced military expenditures in the coming decade.

Automobiles and trucks

Although America's share of the manufacture of motor vehicles remained constant at about 36 per cent during the 1980s, a significant portion of this is due to non-US automobile companies' production in the United States.[7] Japanese car manufacturers have increased their share of US auto market sales from 20 per cent in 1985 to 30 per cent in 1990. Two-thirds of America's current trade deficit with Japan, $50 billion, can be attributed to motor vehicle importation. Actual US market share of sales of the top 12 global automotive manufacturers has dropped from 83 per cent in 1960 to 38 per cent in 1990.[8]

Telecommunications equipment

European and Japanese telecommunications companies are growing at rates that exceed those of US organizations. France's Alcatel now outsells AT&T's equipment division (formerly Western Electric) in global telecommunication sales.

Component manufacturing for US telecommunications firms has largely shifted to lower-cost Asian countries. Northern Telecom (Canada) has been very successful in capturing specific markets from AT&T during the last decade. Growth during the coming decade will include large new markets in newly developing economies. Japanese and European manufacturers will be well positioned to capitalize on these markets.

Metals

Japanese and German steel giants have captured the marketplace. No American manufacturer is listed among the top 12 companies. Although the production of steel in the United States remains at about 33 per cent of total production, most of the mills have either been purchased by non-US companies or entered joint venture agreements with them. The joint ventures have provided technological knowledge transfer and capital to refurbish the factories and install more efficient processing capabilities.[9,10]

Computers

Japan's share of the top 12 global computer companies has grown from 0 to 23 per cent during the last 30 years. American market share has fallen from 95 to 70 per cent during the same time frame. European corporations remain a distant third, and will likely encounter considerable manufacturing competition from Japan and other Asian countries. American firms' expertise in software development, work stations and innovation will keep it a major contender in the coming decade.

Production of computers has shifted dramatically to Japan and other Asian countries. US production has declined from 64 per cent in 1980 to 45 per cent in 1989. A considerable percentage of the components for these US-produced machines is derived from manufacturers outside the United States. If these figures were taken into account, the production share of the United States would be considerably lower. Japanese production increased from 22 to 36 per cent in the same time frame, and European production increased from 5 to 18 per cent.

Food and beverage

The food and beverage industry is one of the most local, decentralized industries in the world in terms of both production and consumption. The preference for locally produced and prepared products is anticipated to remain fairly constant, and industry growth will show only marginal increases, based on the projected slow population growth in the coming decade in the developed countries of the world.

Europe and the United States each produce about 40 per cent and Japan about 17 per cent of the capacity of the 14 nations studied by Kupfer. If European unity becomes a reality in the agricultural sector and governments eliminate subsidies, we could see a renewed challenge for markets from the European Union. The opening of Eastern European markets will serve both as a source of less expensive food and as a new customer base for global food corporations such as Coca-Cola and Nestlé.

Chemicals

The three largest firms in chemical production, BASF, Hoechst and Bayer, all reside in Germany. America's DuPont, Dow and Monsanto also rank in the top 12 chemical companies. Japan's presence is small in domestic production. Total US production still remains number one, but this is in large part due to the sizeable production by European firms in the United States. The balance of both domestic production and sales has remained fairly constant during the last decade with some positioning changes, e.g. Imperial Chemical Industries moving ahead of DuPont after the divestiture of Conaco.

The biggest challenge for the industry in the coming decade will be environmental issues. If European governments provide funding for environmental controls, it could give European companies a competitive advantage over American-based corporations.

Forest products

Sweden has taken the lead in European paper and forest products sales. Franko reports that sales by Stora and Svenska Cellulosa have moved Swedish sales to the top 12 global forest products firms, from 0 per cent in 1970 to 18 per cent in 1990. The United States still dominates, with 62 per cent market share of sales of the top 12 companies, a decline from 81 per cent in 1970.

The US share of country production in US/Japan/Europe markets has increased during the last decade from 46 to 49 per cent. Major US companies such as International Paper and Georgia-Pacific have invested heavily in productivity improvements in the last decade—over $8 billion in new, high-efficiency production lines and mills. Over 60 per cent of US pulp production was exported in 1991.[11]

Increased competition from new forest products companies in South America are expected to begin to show gains by the end of the decade.

Pharmaceuticals

From 1980 to 1989, US domestic production of pharmaceuticals showed growth from 40 to 43 per cent, versus Europe's market decline from 38 per cent in 1980 to 35 per cent in 1989, and Japan's flat production of 22.3–21.8 per cent during the same period.[12]

Global sales volume of the top 12 pharmaceutical houses showed a decline in US market share from 55 per cent in 1980 to 49 per cent in 1990. No Japanese firms were placed in the top 12 in 1990.[13]

As deregulation progresses in Europe, the Japanese should benefit from the more homogeneous regulatory environment. Increased pressure for pricing controls in the US market will adversely affect US manufacturers to a greater extent than others because a greater percentage of total sales is tied to the US market.

Banking

During the past 30 years, Japanese and American banks have virtually switched positions in global sales. Japan's market share of the top 12 banks has moved from 0 per cent in 1960 to 66 per cent in 1990; America's decline has shown a staggering drop, from 61 per cent in 1960 to 0 per cent in 1990. It is interesting to note that only one US bank, Citibank, still ranks in the top 25. Citibank wisely built the most effective foreign market presence while the opportunity existed.[14]

Industrial and farm equipment

Japan and Korea have grown from 0 per cent market shares to 23 and 17 per cent, respectively, of the top 12 corporations during the last three decades. American corporations have slipped from 37 to 26 per cent during the same time. European market share has also plummeted, from 55 to 35 per cent.

Furthermore, equipment manufactured in the United States has declined during the last decade from 43 per cent in 1980 to 37 per cent in 1989. European production has remained essentially flat at 39 per cent, but production in Japan has grown, from 18 to 24 per cent. The importation quotas on foreign-made machine equipment into the United States has resulted in foreign firms establishing US production facilities to meet US market needs. US production would be considerably lower, and retail prices would also fall, if these import quotas were removed.[15]

Global performance

American, European and Asian companies are facing a major challenge in maintaining global competitiveness. Many speakers and writers about competitiveness during the past few years have suggested that a large number of companies around the globe need a 'wake-up call'. This may be an overused and banal expression, but consider the following facts.

Hadjian and Tritto[16] report that in 1992, of *Fortune*'s list of the largest 500 industrial corporations in the world,

- One-quarter (125 of 500) lost money.

- Total sales rose only 3.6 per cent (equal to inflation).

- The number of employees fell for the fourth consecutive year.

Furthermore,

- Of 128 Japanese companies on the list, 21 reported losses and many of those that made money showed declines from the previous year.

- Of 162 American firms on the list, 60 showed losses, but a major factor was a one-time accounting adjustment required for health care liabilities owed to retirees (SFAS 106). Statement of Financial Accounting Standards 106 (SFAS 106) is a rule imposed by the Financial Accounting Standards Board in 1992, requiring firms to set aside additional funds for healthcare liabilities for retirees.

- Europe's economy continued to worsen. For example, five of the six Italian companies on the list reported losses; Volvo of Sweden cited its greatest losses ever.

Joseph E. Pattison[17] identified some of the dimensions of America's global failures whose roots may go back many years to a time when the US 'domestic economy was so large that one didn't need worry about the economy outside US borders':

- In 1970, six of the ten largest banks in the world in terms of assets were American, four were European and none were Japanese. In January 1993, eight of the ten largest banks in the world were Japanese and the remaining two—Crédit Agricole and Crédit Lyonnaise—were French.

- From a profile of 433 chief executive officers (CEOs), the *Wall Street Journal*[18] identified four characteristics of managers from the United States, Europe, Japan and the Pacific Rim (Table 1.1). The respondents in this survey were 93 executives from the United States and Canada, 100 from Europe, 100 from Japan and 40 from various Asian countries. Another finding of the survey was that many CEOs believe that globalization is important, but do not know how to make it work.

- In overall competitiveness, the World Competitiveness Report 1992[19] ranked the United States behind Japan, Germany, Switzerland and Denmark.

- Exports exceeded imports in the United States in the first part of the 1980s; now imports exceed exports, with the largest trade deficit occurring between 1985 and 1987.

- European Union (EU) unemployment was expected to rise above 18 million in 1993. Almost three-quarters of a million people are seeking asylum in the EU every year. Leaked information from the European Ad Hoc Group on Immigration suggest that stern measures would make it extremely difficult for Third World citizens to enter the EU.[20]

It is estimated that:

- Japanese car companies will manufacture 800 000 cars per year in Europe by the year 2000.

Table 1.1 Characteristics of managers (%)

	USA	Europe	Japan	Pacific Rim
No foreign experience	14	3	1	2.6
Travel abroad once or twice per year	23	1	15	18
Travel abroad more than twice per year	56	80	78	75
Worked abroad	32	47	19	46

- Japanese car companies will sell 50 per cent of all new cars in Europe by the end of the decade.[21]

Is globalization the answer?

Between 1987 and early 1992, over 2400 business articles addressing 'global' issues appeared in the literature. Of these, over 1000 were devoted to 'multinational' concerns of organizations, and the majority of the remaining articles focus on 'globalization', which has come to be the most frequently used word to describe the corporate strategy of the 1990s. What is it, and will globalization help solve the competitiveness problem?

At a recent seminar, all 20 senior executives of a global firm based within the United States were asked to define globalization and then to describe briefly their organization's globalization strategy. Definitions of globalization differed, and their thoughts on organizational strategy had little in common.

'By the year 2000, 50 per cent of our business will be overseas', said the CEO of a large US company recently. 'We are globalizing.' The audience cheered. But there seemed to be a serious communication gap between the CEO and his people. The CEO provided no clear statements about globalization, and no instructions as to how to become a global company. Many asked what they were supposed to do differently.

To achieve successful globalization, a skilled global workforce and leadership team are needed, but it is difficult to identify and develop the competencies required to make globalization work. The task is further complicated by a lack of consensus and understanding of globalization, even among managers within the same company.

This problem is illustrated by Stephen H. Rhinesmith's *Training and Development Journal* article, 'An agenda for globalization', which looks at Intel, the leading integrated circuits manufacturer:

> Ask Andy Grove, the scion of Silicon Valley and founder of Intel, whether Intel is a global corporation. He will answer emphatically, 'yes.' Ask Dov Frohman, director of Intel's Research Center in Israel, the same question and he will just as emphatically answer 'no.' Ask Sharon Richards, cross-cultural coordinator for Intel and she will answer 'yes' in strategy, but 'no' in the skills and attitudes of the people and the corporate culture of the company. Who's right? All three are—and that's the first problem with globalization. Nobody—even in the same company—seems to have the total picture of how to make globalization work.[22]

Studies of other organizations support the observations of Intel managers. In their survey of 93 managers from all organizational levels in some of the world's leading companies, Global Partners of Boston[23] discovered that 71 per cent of executives believed their global strategy was widely understood; interestingly, only 33 per cent of middle managers said they understood it. This gap between strategy and implementation appears to be wide.

A few years ago, the attitude of many American managers and executives was simple: the domestic economy of the United States was sufficiently large, so there was little need to be involved in markets outside our borders. This misconception was not shared by the British, French, Japanese and others.

From the perspective of structure, Christopher Bartlett and Sumantra Ghoshal clearly state the challenge in their book *Managing Across Borders*.[24] In the evolution of organizations, from domestic to international, to multinational, to global, to transnational, the authors believe that the transnational corporation has the efficiency of a global structure and at the same time the ability of a multinational structure to respond locally.

The following analogy may be simple but appropriate. In many countries the bicycle (domestic or export production only) has been replaced by the automobile. However, there are different kinds of automobiles. In the United States most automobiles have automatic transmissions. In Japan automobiles are smaller, have right-hand steering wheels and are fuel-efficient. In Europe cars are driven by stick-shift gear boxes and are relatively small. Because of these differences, drivers need different skills for different operating environments.

So it is with different organizational structures. Depending on the organization's structure, the control–work flow dynamics interaction will be different, and the *competencies* of the executives and the managers required to impart the vision and implement the strategy to all employees will be different. All three basic organizational structures have positives and negatives. The *goal* is to shift the negatives to positives to achieve the *ideal* combination of decision-making and knowledge transfer, that is, to capitalize on the strengths of the structure and overcome the negatives to become an ideal or optimal structure for the situation.

In this context, it is our opinion that businesses have been successful in identifying which positions in their organization are critical for success. Identifying their best people and the top performers in their organization has also been accomplished to a high degree in many companies. However, we believe that most organizations have difficulty articulating just what competencies, abilities or qualities these individuals possess that make them top performers. In terms of globalization competencies, we expect to address this dilemma and provide some answers.

Stephen Rhinesmith states:

> It is now clear that global change will be a way of life in the 1990s and beyond. The forces of technology, political freedom, territorial dispute, ethnic rivalries, economic competition and entrepreneurial ingenuity are stronger than all the

centuries of social, political, and economic fabric that have woven the world into its current form.

At the center of these changes, as always, will be people. Employees, managers, and leaders of organizations struggling to adapt to the new world rushing toward them—and away from them.[25]

After clearly describing the 'contexts within which a global organization operates' and the 'three levels of globalization within each organization', Rhinesmith states there are 'six mindsets for global perspectives' and 'six competencies for global effectiveness'. From this it appears that all global managers should be trained alike to develop the required competencies.

It is our belief that traditional organizational structures have inherent strengths and weaknesses in decision-making, knowledge transfer and attitudinal leadership. We will identify the inherent strengths and weaknesses in each structure and the interactive and cultural competencies required to overcome those weaknesses and fully benefit from the strengths. This book will not necessarily recommend changing structures (don't throw out the baby with the bath water), because if only the structure is changed, the problems not addressed transfer to the newly created structure. Likewise, the mere correction of problems and weaknesses will result in the creation of others.

The necessity to differentiate competencies can be illustrated in the following exercise, written by John Riesenberger, about centralized, decentralized and shared decision-making. It was first presented during a seminar with graduate students in international management. In the case there are three positions: the corporate marketing perspective, the subsidiary perspective, and the perspective of the CEO. The dilemma of determining 'who is right?' and 'what to do?' becomes quickly apparent when one analyzes their assigned position in the case. The more difficult questions of 'who decides? or 'is compromise the right choice? or 'should corporate headquarters or the subsidiary make the choice?' are less clear. The implications for individual financial bonuses and promotions also become apparent. There is no right answer. However, questioning the complex issues regarding corporate, subsidiary or shared decision-making responsibilities is the goal. Hopefully, students will learn that 'think globally, act locally' is not always the way to solve the dilemma. Chapter 5 will clearly demonstrate this.

The corporate perspective

- You are one of several corporate marketing directors and you reside at corporate headquarters. Your responsibilities are *global*, and you are charged with making sure that each subsidiary follows the Global Marketing Plan for Product #1: 'The Global Toaster'.

- You are a top candidate for a key promotion, but your selection is highly dependent on your getting all subsidiaries to 'follow the plan'.

- You are having problems with several subsidiary product managers.

- Your company switched to a centralized corporate staff only a year ago. Before this change, subsidiaries operated with almost total autonomy.

- The product manager from one of the subsidiaries called to say that she wanted permission to change three specifications: color, cord length and guard width.

- You are charged with persuading all subsidiary product managers to follow the Global Plan. Your promotion depends upon it. Economies of scale and global advertising are key elements to profit maximization.

- You are paid 'to win'. Your vice president is counting on you to get all subsidiaries to comply.

Table 1.2 lists selected product characteristics of the Global Toaster.

The subsidiary perspective

- You are the product manager for toasters for a subsidiary of a multinational company. Your company has 'gone global' with a centralized corporate staff only about a year ago. Before this change, subsidiaries had greater autonomy.

- Your country general manager, Mr Shultz, is from the 'old school'.

- Your subsidiary has a small assembly plant for making toasters. It can also fabricate certain parts.

- Your in-country market research indicates that in your marketplace certain product characteristics are preferred over the corporate 'standard'.

- You and Mr Shultz *resent* the 'corporate mandate' and know, from local market research, that you can sell more units by doing the following:

  1. Change color panels to *chrome*.

  2. Extend length of plug cord by 15 cm.

  3. Bread is sliced thicker in your country; widening the inside guards by 10 per cent would better accommodate the bread.

Table 1.2 'Global Toaster' specifications

Size	35 × 15 × 20 cm
Weight	1 kg
Color	White, beige
Inside guard width	2.5 cm
Cord length	90 cm
Plug type	Variable, depending on government requirements
Heating coils	Global type #2
Frame	Aluminum
Economies of scale	Only achieved with all units the same

- Mr Shultz is counting on you to get permission for all three variations.

- You are a candidate for promotion, and your promotion depends on maximizing the sales and earnings from this product.

The CEO perspective

- You are the CEO of XYZ Home Appliance Corporation. Your company has maintained a 'multinational approach' to business for many years and has 'gone global' with a centralized corporate staff about a year ago. Before this change, subsidiaries had greater autonomy.

- Your decision to 'globalize' was to take advantage of the usual benefits of such activities as well as the defensive benefits of such decisions.

- Today, behind a one-way mirror, you will observe the interaction of one of your corporate marketing directors and one of your subsidiary product managers as they discuss strategy implementation of one of your products.

- Your corporate goal is to maximize earnings and market share. You realize the importance of economies of scale and global branding, and you also understand the importance of local responsiveness.

A role-playing of these positions clearly demonstrates that the 'competencies' required of each is different.

A new kind of paradigm

As the economies of countries are becoming more global, and as change and innovation become more the norm than the exception, managers are challenged to create more flexible organizations and to shift their ways of thinking about organization, structure and strategy. Hirschhorn and Gilmore[26] state that the boundaries that arise in new organizations are more *psychological* than *organizational*. To understand the new evolving environment accurately, managers must recognize their personal response to the changes.

It is our belief that business is undergoing a paradigm shift. Simply put, in the old paradigm an organization required experts in traditional functional business skills such as marketing, accounting, management, finance, etc., to ensure its success. The new paradigm requires organizations and managers continuously to be part of a seemingly endless adaptive process involving both functional and cross-functional expertise. Global managers and leaders need skill to deal with the unexpected, the ambiguous. The paradigm shifts required of business organizations will be described throughout this book.

Peter Drucker[27] has been teaching and writing for years that managers need to manage skillfully. Against the claims of management that a change in corporate culture will get results, Drucker states that changing the habits and the behaviors of managers will get results, and that effective leadership should be based on consistent performance in the changing environments where managers must function.

Contribution of this book

Our expected contribution to the globalization literature and the globalization efforts of organizations is to enable readers to:

1. Understand the external environmental forces that are causing today's global competition in most industries.

2. Understand the critical importance of developing a global strategic vision and the strategic thinking process used to amplify it. (This will be covered in Chapter 3.)

3. Understand the need for centralization, decentralization and shared decision-making in global organizations.

4. Identify how knowledge and learning occur throughout worldwide organizations.

5. Identify firms' basic formal organizational structures and their inherent strengths and weaknesses.

6. Identify core competencies and weaknesses as they apply to *control* and *work flow* in various structures.

7. Identify competencies required in the new paradigms, and see the necessity to shift from old to new paradigms. (These will be described in Chapters 10–13.)

8. Identify what quality initiatives will be essential to excel in the remainder of this decade.

In the course of the book, readers will not only need to assess their own company, but also to acquire the skill needed to diagnose the critical competency strengths and weaknesses of competitors.

Notes and references

1. M. Crichton, *The Rising Sun*, Ballantine Books, New York, 1992.
2. Recently sent to the authors after a seminar. Author was listed as anonymous.
3. Gary Hamel, 'Pushing the envelope of global strategy and competitiveness', 12 February 1993. A summary of remarks by Gary Hamel for the Executive Focus International 1993 Executive Forum.
4. Lawrence G. Franko, 'Global corporate competition II: Is the large American

firm an endangered species?', *Business Horizons,* November–December, 1991, pp. 14–22.

5. Andrew Kupfer, 'How American industry stacks up', *Fortune,* 9 March 1992, pp. 30–46. A review article of ten-year activity.

6. Ibid. Gellman Research Associates studied the issue of government subsidies for Airbus for the US Commerce Department, p. 32.

7. Ibid., p. 42.

8. Franko, op. cit.

9. Ibid., p. 20.

10. Ibid., p. 42.

11. Ibid., p. 38.

12. Ibid., p. 46.

13. Ibid., p. 20.

14. Ibid., p. 19.

15. Ibid., pp. 41–2.

16. Ani Hadjian and Lorraine Tritto, 'Another year of pain', *Fortune,* 26 July 1993, pp. 188–234.

17. Joseph Pattison, *Acquiring The Future.* Dow Jones-Irwin, Homewood, Ill., 1990.

18. Reported in an article by George Anders, 'Going global: vision versus reality', *Wall Street Journal,* 22 September 1989.

19. As stated in *Challenges,* World Competitiveness Report, Council on Competitiveness, 1992.

20. Reported in Anne-Elizabeth Moutet, Paola Buonadonna, Tony Paterson, Chris Pommery and Chris Endean, 'Fortress Europe?', *The European,* 11 July 1993, p. 6.

21. As reported in Kevin Eason, 'Japanese accelerate into Europe', *EuroBusiness,* June 1993, pp. 18–24.

22. S. Rhinesmith, 'An agenda for globalization', *Training and Development Journal,* February 1991, pp. 22–8.

23. As reported in the Summary Report, 'Global strategy and implementation: What makes leading global companies successful?' Global Partners, Boston, Mass., January 1992.

24. C. A. Bartlett and S. Ghoshal, *Managing Across Borders,* Harvard Business School Press, Boston, Mass., 1989.

25. Stephen Rhinesmith, *A Manager's Guide to Globalization,* Business One Irwin, Homewood, Ill., 1993.

26. L. Hirschhorn and T. Gilmore, 'The new boundaries of the boundaryless company', *Harvard Business Review,* May–June 1992, pp. 104–15.

27. Peter Drucker, *Managing for the Future: The 1990s and Beyond.* Truman Talley Books/Dutton, New York, 1991.

> To maintain a leadership position in any one
> developed country, a business—whether
> large or small—increasingly has to attain and
> hold leadership positions in all developed
> markets worldwide. It has to be able to do
> research, to design, to develop, to engineer
> and to manufacture in any part of the
> developed world, and to export from any
> developed country to any other. It has to go
> transnational.
>
> PETER F. DRUCKER
> *Managing for the Future*

The new world economy

Why are people uptight about their jobs today? Why is the rate of turnover of CEOs and senior executives escalating? Why are so many corporations (including major blue-chip firms) downsizing their organizations? These dramatic and disastrous activities are occurring because of the evolutionary changes sweeping the global economy.

Readers who believe they have a firm grasp of the environmental forces causing these changes may wish to skip Chapters 2, 3 and 4 and move directly to Part II of the book. Part II focuses on the core characteristics of the optimal, worldwide organization, describes the strengths and weaknesses of 'traditional' corporate structures and offers advice on what must be accomplished to excel in the current economic sea of change.

Impact of increasing global competition

Bruno Jonker and the other 19 remaining Dutch clog factory owners are experiencing severe competitive pressure from Far Eastern imports. Manufacturers from these countries have significantly undercut the prices of local Dutch manufacturers, and have captured a significant market share of the miniature clogs that are popular with tourists. They have also made inroads into the market of 2 million pairs of full-size clogs sold each year in the Netherlands. To preserve pride and save the ancient Dutch craft of clog making, the Dutch government is subsidizing a training program to encourage young people to learn the craft of making wooden footwear.[1] In essence, cheaper imports are reducing the sales of Dutch-produced clogs resulting in lower domestic sales. This means that fewer Dutch people are needed in this craft. So the problem is one of cheaper imports, not lack of labor.

Companies, regardless of how small, specialized or locally unique they are, are experiencing heightened competition from non-domestic rivals.

Revolution in the global marketplace

The decade of the 1990s is witnessing a staggering transformation of political and economic change. The move to capitalism by Eastern Europe and the Confederation of Independent States and the rapidly emerging economies of Asia will challenge the current order. Japan, and the formation of regional trading blocs the North American Free Trade Association (NAFTA), the European Union (EU), the Asian Free Trade Association (AFTA) and others—will create a new world economy like nothing we have seen before.

Why is global competition escalating rapidly?

In this chapter we will examine the rapid escalation of 12 environmental forces that are changing the competitive marketplace for most industries. The decade of the 1990s is witnessing a shift to a marketplace that is characterized by ever-increasing global competition.

Corporations—small, medium, and large—are all being affected. The fact is, global competition will significantly impact most organizations and industries during this era. Corporations must learn how to survive and prosper in a global environment that is characterized as highly dynamic and unstable.

The phases of evolution

Phase One: 1945–1975

The 30 years following World War II marked an era characterized by high demand and growth. Economies of the free world flourished and the standard of living improved in most developed societies. Corporations focused on economies of scale and mass production to meet an insatiable market demand. Emphasis was placed on quantity and the efficient use of raw materials, labor and capital.

Phase Two: 1975–1985

A fundamental shift occurred between the early-1970s and the mid-1980s. Increased production capabilities led to equilibrium and an eventual surplus supply in many industries. This fundamental shift changed corporate competitive advantages to those of increased quality, low cost and technological advances. Economies whose corporations were geared for premium quality, superior technology and low-cost production prospered. Governments began to provide incentives for global companies including lower tariffs, tax incentives and incentives to build new factories in their countries. Global economic growth began to slow.

Phase Three: 1985–2000

The new political and economic order (Fig. 2.1) is unfolding rapidly. The emergence of regional trading blocs poses economic advantages for member states but will prove damaging for inter-bloc trade. The era of economic growth between 1945 and 1985 has been replaced by an era characterized by volatility and constant change. Those organizations that accept these changes as opportunities, and develop appropriate global strategic visions, organizational structures and core competencies to effectively capitalize on this new environment, will emerge as the victors.

Old paradigm	New paradigm
1. Governments focused on national barriers to entry	1. Governments are developing 'regionalization' alliances such as the EU, NAFTA, AFTA, etc.
2. Local technical standards hampered economies of scale	2. Trend toward homogeneous technical standards will favor economies of scale
3. Expensive and limited telecommunications favored domestic firms	3. Increased telecommunications options at lower costs encourages globalization
4. High cost and slow delivery of products favored local production	4. Lowered costs and increased speed of delivery have stimulated global commerce
5. Barriers to entry, distance and lack of exposure favored heterogeneous demand for products	5. Global exposure to products through commerce, travel, advertising and TV have encouraged a more homogeneous demand for certain products
6. Competition remained largely local	6. Competition from non-domestic competitors is increasing
7. Exchange rates were relatively stable and controlled	7. There is increased exchange rate volatility due to global market demands
8. Technological research remained largely local	8. The increasing rate of technological change has encouraged firms to invest in R&D in multiple markets

Fig. 2.1   The evolving paradigm for the New Economic Era: the marketplace

Performance: global versus domestic-only companies

A recent Conference Board Study examined the ten-year performances (1979–89) of all US companies publicly quoted on the US stock exchanges with sales exceeding $10 million. This database represents over two-thirds of total worldwide US manufacturers' sales and the vast majority of US manufacturing firms with more than 500 employees.[2] From this analysis, it was possible to determine key characteristics of 'outstanding' firms.

The following definitions were used for the purposes of this study:

- *Multinational.* This applied to firms that had either foreign sales offices or foreign production plants.

- *Domestic.* All others were considered domestic even if they export or engage in some form of international alliance, e.g. licensing, joint ventures, etc.

Results

- Only 38 per cent (742 of the original 1928) companies survived the decade under the same corporate identity.

- Of the 742 survivors from 1979, 60 per cent (444) were 'multinational'.

- Only 40 per cent (298) of the survivors were 'domestic only'.

- The 'multinational' firms in the study were 50 per cent more likely to survive the decade versus 'domestic'-only firms.

- The annual sales growth of the surviving multinational firms was a staggering 8.8 per cent versus an annual sales growth of only 5.5 per cent for 'domestic' firms.

- Profitability in the surviving 'multinational' firms was 9.4 per cent annually versus only 7.1 per cent for 'domestic' firms.

- 'Multinational' firms significantly increased their involvement with joint ventures and licensing agreements during the decade.

- 'Non-domestic' research and development activity increased seven-fold (from 3.7 to 25.6 per cent) during the decade and was a key determinant of success.

Outstanding corporations

'Outstanding' firms are defined in this Conference Board Study as those firms that ranked in the top 20 per cent of both sales growth and profitability over the decade (see Fig. 2.2).

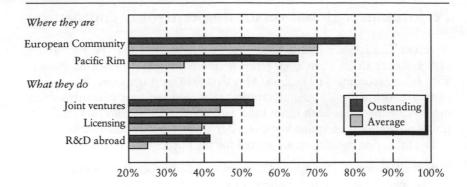

Fig. 2.2   What outstanding firms do differently
Note: Based on all firms in the top quintile of performance, in terms of both growth and profitability (Reprinted with permission from The Conference Board Report, no. 977, *Global Presence and Competitiveness of US Manufacturers*, 1991).

Of the firms ranked 'outstanding' in this study, 80 per cent (30 of 37) were multinationals. These 'outstanding' firms are typically involved in more product lines and have larger market shares than the average firm.

Influence of environmental forces on globalization

Evidence indicates that firms engaged in commerce beyond their domestic borders are more successful than those that remain within their borders. What external environmental forces have influenced this shift? What things should my business organization be thinking about strategically as it plans ahead? Where is my industry and my corporation headed, and how can we best prepare for the future? What environmental forces are influencing this change, and how can we best utilize them for future success?

The environmental forces that are changing the competitive nature of our industries can be summarized as 12 key influencers: eight proactive forces and four reactive forces (Fig. 2.3). Our understanding of both our industry's and our company's stage of evolution in each of these forces will prepare us to develop a *global strategic vision* designed for success. In this chapter we will examine each of these 12 environmental forces.

The Global Executive Survey

The authors conducted a survey of senior executives of many of the world's largest companies. This research focused on gaining insight into

Proactive environmental forces

1. Global sourcing
2. New and evolving markets
3. Economies of scale
4. Trend toward homogeneous demand for products/services
5. Lowered global transportation costs
6. Government interaction: tariffs, non-tariff barriers, customs and taxes
7. Increased telecommunications at reduced cost
8. Trend toward homogeneous technical standards

Reactive environmental forces

9. Increased competition from non-domestic competitors
10. Increased risks due to volatility in exchange rates
11. Trend of customers evolving from 'domestic only' to global strategies
12. Increased pace of global technical change

Fig. 2.3 Environmental forces influencing an organization and its industry's degree of globalization

(1) contemporary thinking concerning identification and learning of skills necessary in the globalization process and (2) an analysis of the impact of the 12 environmental forces on globalization. A discussion of needed competencies for the globalization process will be reviewed in Chapters 10–13.

Forty-nine valid surveys from senior executives were utilized in our analysis (Fig. 2.4). Readers should note that the survey was carried out in 1993. Each executive was asked to evaluate how important, for his or her industry, each of the 12 environmental forces was five years ago (1988), how important it is currently (1993) and how important it will be five years on (1998). Survey participants rated each factor on a scale from 1 (low importance) to 5 (high importance).

For compilation of the bar charts, all those who responded with a 4 or a 5 to the importance questions were included. For example, if 13 per cent of respondents marked the number 4 for importance of economies of scale and 12 per cent marked the number 5 for the same question, the bar chart would show that 25 per cent thought this question was high in importance.

The bar charts clearly show a *rapid escalation of importance in all 12 environmental forces during the last five years* and an even *greater degree of importance five years from now!*

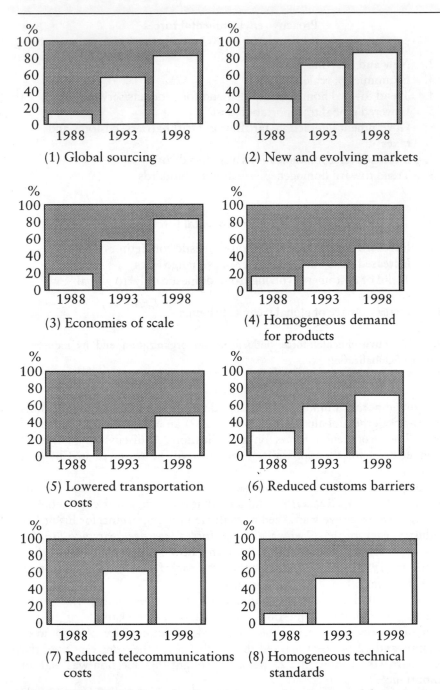

Fig. 2.4 The Global Executive Survey: impact of environmental forces (percentages of respondents stating that the factor specified was of high importance) (*Continues*) (*Source:* Moran and Riesenberger).

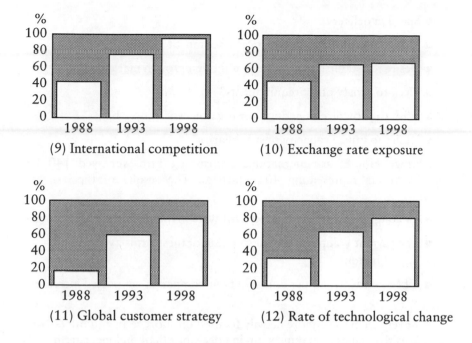

Fig. 2.4 The Global Executive Survey: impact of environmental forces (percentages of respondents stating that the factor specified was of high importance) (*Concluded*) (*Source:* Moran and Riesenberger).

Proactive environmental forces

1. Global sourcing

Raw materials and components

The competitive nature of worldwide commerce has resulted in companies seeking new sources of raw materials and components. Among the factors influencing the decision to move from a domestic to a non-domestic supplier are:

- No qualified domestic source
- Superior quality
- Lower cost
- More advanced technology
- Superior technical service
- Increased number of sources

- Speed in delivery
- Non-domestic sourcing practices of competitors
- Desire to establish a presence in a foreign growth market
- Need to satisfy offset requirements[3]
- Wish to provide competition for the domestic supply base
- Desire to utilize capacity of subsidiaries[4,5,6]

Harbridge House, an international consulting firm, surveyed 140 US manufacturers representing 40 industries. The results of their survey found:

- Of companies surveyed 74 per cent were involved in global sourcing.
- The current volume of global sourcing of these firms averaged $2–$3 billion.
- Of respondents, 60 per cent said their companies supported increased sourcing.
- Buyers seem to be more heavily focused on short-term and price-sensitive issues in making sourcing decisions than on longer-term, strategic issues such as supplier evaluation, teaming and overall economic trends.
- The reason cited most frequently for purchasing abroad was the lack of a qualified domestic source. Price, costs and superior technology were next in importance. Quality ranked in fifth place.
- Sixty-seven per cent of respondents were satisfied completely, or for the most part, with foreign sources.[7]

Ford's new 'World Car'
The Ford Motor Company launched its new 'World Car' in Europe in the spring of 1993. The CDW27 program, from which came three cars, known as the 'Mondeo' (in Europe), the Ford 'Contour' and the Mercury 'Mystique' (in North America), consumed nearly $6 billion in its development. A unique approach in global teamwork in design, sourcing of parts and assembly have created a new paradigm in automobile manufacturing.

Global sourcing of design expertise led to the decision to assemble one global engineering team, which at its peak totaled 800 people, to develop the car for both Europe and the United States. Europe was chosen as the design headquarters because of Ford Europe's expertise with the compact passenger car class. Design of automatic transmissions and air conditioning were assigned to the North American group because of their high volume and expertise. Four-cylinder engines, manual transmissions and suspensions were designed in Europe.

'World sourced' components play a key ingredient in the success of the Mondeo. All five-speed transmissions are produced in Europe for all global markets, and all automatic transmissions are made in the United States for all global markets (Fig. 2.5).

Ford purposely sought out global suppliers of parts. The estimated annual volume of these models will exceed 700 000 units and will include sales in North America, South America, Asia and Europe.

Many major components, although sourced from one global supplier, are manufactured in both North America and Europe. This dual manufacturing enables Ford to take advantage of reduced transportation costs and 'local content' requirements.

Ford's Mondeo was named 'European Car of the Year' for 1993.

Labor costs

In recent years many domestic firms have been faced with the choice of abandoning their domestic markets or moving manufacturing to lower-cost countries. Lower labor costs can provide a competitive advantage for companies whose products are labor-intensive. Dramatic examples of this can be seen in the rapid rise of Japan and South Korea in the 1960s and 1970s because of their low labor rates. As these countries have prospered, their wage scales have escalated and they have moved into production activities demanding greater skills; now they, along with other developed countries, have begun to move their low-skilled labor-intensive production activities to countries such as Thailand, Malaysia, Indonesia, Vietnam, Mexico and Brazil (Table 2.1 and Fig. 2.6). Similarly, European firms are capitalizing on lower wage scales in many Eastern European countries.

Batam is one of the 13 667 islands that comprise Indonesia. Because of Indonesia's low labor costs, many multinational corporations are establishing labor-intensive subsidiaries in the islands.

> For a glimpse of Indonesia's future export prowess, take a 45-minute boat ride from Singapore to Batam. You'll see AT&T, Seagate, and Smith-Corona among the scores of multinationals that are investing a total of $1 billion over the next couple of years in an industrial park carved out of jungle. The cost of Indonesian workers, including fringe benefits, is about $136 a month—one-third the Singapore rate—and Batam is a duty-free haven. The island has its own water supply, electric power, and microwave links to the world via the Singapore phone system.[8]

The low labor rates in Mexico have given rise to the establishment of a large number of low-skilled manufacturing jobs transplanted from the United States:

> More than 1,900 U.S. companies already have created some 453,000 Mexican jobs by moving assembly operations from the U.S. to Mexican plants known as *maquiladoras*.

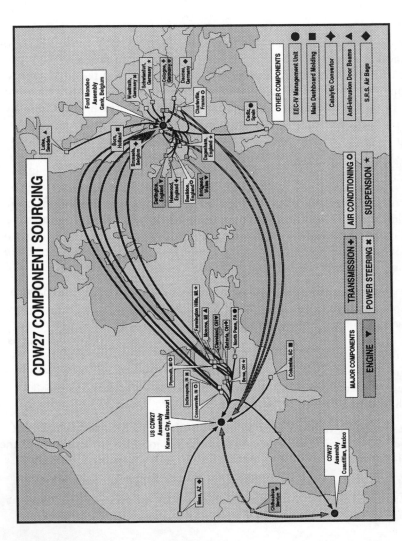

Fig. 2.5 Global sourcing: Ford Mondeo/Contour/Mystique (Reprinted with permission of the Ford Motor Company)

Table 2.1 Hourly compensation costs for production workers in manufacturing, 1992

Country or area	Hourly compensation (US$/hour)
Germany	25.94
Sweden	24.23
Switzerland	23.26
Norway	23.20
Belgium	22.01
Netherlands	20.72
Denmark	20.02
Austria	19.65
Italy	19.41
Finland	18.69
Canada	17.02
France	16.88
United States	16.17
Japan	16.16
United Kingdom	14.69
Spain	13.39
Ireland	13.32
Australia	12.94
New Zealand	7.91
Taiwan	5.19
Portugal	5.01
Singapore	5.00
Korea	4.93
Hong Kong	3.89
Mexico	2.35
Trade-weighted measure average for Asian NIEs (Korea, Taiwan, Singapore and Hong Kong)	4.84

Source: International Comparisons of Hourly Compensation Costs for Production Workers in Manufacturing, Report 844, US Department of Labor, Bureau of Statistics, US Government Printing Office, Washington, DC, April 1993.

Hourly costs

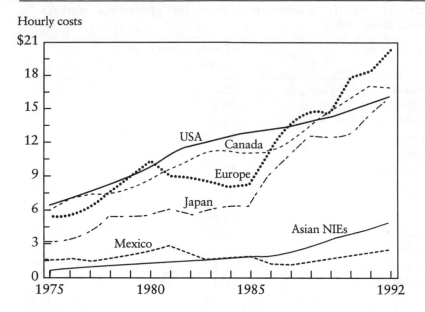

Fig. 2.6 **Hourly compensation costs for production workers in manufacturing,
1975–1992** (*Source: International Comparisons of Hourly Compensation Costs
for Production Workers in Manufacturing, 1992*, Report no. 844, chart 1, p. 2, US
Department of Labor, Bureau of Labor Statistics, US Government Printing Office,
Washington, DC, April 1993).

With or without free trade, however, the exodus is to some degree inevitable.
For example, typewriter maker Smith Corona announced in July it would move
its Cortland, NY, manufacturing operations south of the border, wiping out 875
New York jobs. Although the move will cost $15 million, the company expects
to save that much annually in labor and other costs.[9]

2. New and evolving markets

New and evolving markets provide opportunities for corporations to fuel
growth. Successful companies that have dominated their own and other
major developed markets will need to carefully evaluate where future
growth is likely to come from. Firms with mature product lines must look
to emerging economies and the future opportunities they hold for
enhancing sales and earnings. Domestic markets are increasingly facing
slower growth in many consumer products because of demographic
changes and heightened local competition. Research and development
costs continue to escalate.

'Companies aren't going to spend precious resources on one-country projects', says J. Richard Leaman, Jr., Scott Paper Co.'s Vice-Chairman.

All this means the profits are off-shore, in each other's backyards as well as in Latin America and fast-growing Asian countries. Unilever, the world's top ice-cream seller whose brands include Good Humor in the U.S., does a brisk business in Thailand, with a new plant there. But it's careful not to run afoul of local beliefs: It keeps out its Wall's Freaky Foot, a favorite ice-cream item in Europe, because to the Thais, the association with dirty feet is too strong.[10]

Gillette, the world's largest razor blade manufacturer, currently controls more than 50 per cent of the developed world's market share. Growth in the future will come from new markets. In August 1992 Gillette purchased majority control of China's biggest razor blade manufacturer. It has recently taken control of a big blade maker in India and has just completed building a new factory in Russia.[11]

Duracell International controls 79 per cent of the $3.2 billion US retail market for consumer alkaline batteries. However, Duracell's US sales growth is expected to slow to 5 per cent in 1993. Robert Kidder, CEO, has focused on expansion and growth overseas as the solution. Duracell opened new markets in Eastern Europe and Asia in 1992 and has formed a joint venture with an Indonesian distributor. Duracell predicted that more than 50 per cent of its 1993 revenues would flow from non-domestic sales compared with only about 33 per cent in 1992.[12]

Manufacturers of mature products such as Coca-Cola are relentless in their pursuit of new markets. In a recent interview prior to his retirement, Donald R. Keough, president and chief operating officer of the Coca-Cola Company, emphasized:

> Somebody asked me a couple of years ago, 'Why do we spend so much time talking about the business outside of the United States?' and I said, 'That's because that's where most of the people live.' It's that simple. Five percent of the world's population lives here [United States] and yet we still do 34% of our worldwide volume here. It is not knocking the great market of the United States to make the judgment that we'll be a bigger global company when that number is 25% or when it's 20% or 15%. It's simply a fact of income.[13]

3. Economies of scale

Survival in the 1990s cannot be taken for granted. Thriving requires unique approaches that result in new competitive advantages beyond the incremental growth acceptable in the past. Today, the marketplace demands goods of superior quality that are produced in the most cost-effective manner possible. Economies of scale provide one tool for reducing costs. Average production costs fall as the output of the product expands. Economies of scale are not limited to manufacturing. Michael Porter notes:

Scale economies can be present in nearly every function of a business, including manufacturing, purchasing, research and development, marketing, service network, sales force utilization, and distribution. For example, scale economies in production, research, marketing, and service are probably the key barriers to entry in the mainframe computer industry, as Xerox and General Electric sadly discovered.[14]

4. Trend toward homogenous demand for products/services

In many areas of fashion, food and industrial products, the world is growing towards similar likes or requirements. The increasingly global appeal of McDonald's hamburgers, Coca-Cola, consumer electronics, Benetton clothes and cappuccino, and the trend toward homogeneous technical standards are creating many 'global products'. Perhaps the greatest influencers in these trends has been the dramatic increase in affordable accessibility to telecommunication links and transportation during the past four decades. More than 20 years ago, Marshall McLuhan predicted that sophisticated media and high-tech communications would mold our planet into a 'global village'.[15]

Of all products and services available today, perhaps medicine is among the most homogeneous in demand. Medical practice around the world is becoming increasingly homogenized. As European unification approaches, it is common to find that a medical opinion-leader in London is often on as much of a first-name basis with his counterparts in France, Germany or Spain as with those in the United Kingdom.

> Many of these opinion leaders speak fluent English, the *lingua franca* of medicine, attend the same conferences, read the same specialist journals, and often know their medical counterparts, and even marketing personnel, within the major pharmaceutical companies. Importantly, these luminaries, in turn, can affect the thinking and prescribing habits of the collective might of the primary care physicians in their respective countries. Similarly, an advertisement for an antipsychotic agent for schizophrenia placed in the *British Journal of Psychiatry* will be seen by, and potentially influence, psychiatrists throughout Europe.[16]

Japanese consumer electronics, records and discs are essentially globally standardized products. Although each may contain some local adaptations, the majority of these goods are universal. Japanese consumer manufacturers have excelled at selling homogeneous electronic appliances by creating products with key features that possess broad appeal. Their emphasis on high quality, economical price and visual appeal as the most important product features have contributed to their success.

Companies can standardize the worldwide *content* of a product as well as the worldwide *mix* of products. As an example, candy manufacturers such as M&M, Mars, Cadbury and Nestlé sell a similar mix of products in many countries, although the product content may vary from country to country appealing to local tastes.[17]

As customers become more globally involved and enter multiple markets, their needs for more homogeneous, standardized products and services increase. This movement toward homogeneous demand further increase the competitive advantage of companies by reducing inventory, purchasing and production costs. Black and Decker, a manufacturer of electrical power tools, provides a good example:

> Before Nolan Archibald became CEO of Black & Decker in 1985, the company was a collection of highly independent subsidiaries, where British, French, and German country managers developed and sold their own products in their own countries. For example, the company made over 100 different motors worldwide. Not surprisingly, Black & Decker had tremendous overhead that was not offset by any efficiencies or economies of scale. When Archibald came on board, he instituted the development of standardized products that could be sold around the globe. By 1989, Black & Decker made only 20 different motors and was planning to reduce that number to five.[18]

The Gillette Company has dominated the global shaving industry for nearly 30 years. The secrets of its success focus on a homogeneous demand for shaving equipment, technological innovation and superiority, superior quality, and low-cost, highly efficient manufacturing expertise. Gillette is currently the number one blade manufacturer in the United States, is the leader in Europe with a 70 per cent market share, and maintains 80 per cent of the Latin American market.[19]

5. Lowered global transportation costs

Transportation costs of raw materials, components and finished goods play a key role in a firm's decision to either export or establish foreign subsidiaries. Transportation costs are also calculated as an important component of the total cost of products. The heavy weight and large size of some products result in transportation costs that prohibit shipment and require local production. For other products with low weight and high intrinsic value, such as consumer electronics, the economics of centralized manufacturing and low transportation costs make it preferable to manufacture centrally.

Transportation costs are generally high in industries where the final product is significantly lighter or smaller than the materials used in its manufacturer. These industries, such as steel, tend to be highly decentralized and located near the sources of materials. It is generally less expensive to ship the finished products than to transport the raw materials to a central location.

Companies in which the raw materials are significantly lighter in weight than the finished product tend to be ideally suited for manufacture at the location of the customer. Coca-Cola and Pepsi-Cola find it far more cost-effective to ship their syrups around the globe and provide for the local addition of water and bottling.

The global transportation costs of many commodities have fallen significantly since the early 1960s. These lower costs make both exportation and importation of products more cost-effective. The development of containerization, large-scale tankers, increasing volume and fuel-efficient jumbo jets have all contributed to the efficiencies of transportation costs. Total air cargo is expected to double by the year 2005.[20]

6. Government interaction: tariffs, non-tariff barriers, customs and taxes

Governments have played an active role in protectionist trade restraints for many decades, and continue to do so today. These practices take many forms including tariffs, non-tariff barriers, restrictions on imports and exports, customs duties and tax policies. Their purposes are to protect in-country social, political and economic interests. Such activities have also served as major sources of revenue in the past for leading countries and still serve so today for many newly developing countries (Table 2.2). Individual country or regional trading bloc policies are currently impacting on corporate strategies to expand their export and/or subsidiary operations.

Tariffs
Tariffs are taxes levied on products as they either enter or exit a country's borders. Their focus is usually either *protectionist* or *revenue-generating*.

In principle, most governments agree that free trade among all nations would increase global competitiveness and that the forces of competition would result in higher quality, lower prices and greater global availability of products. The General Agreement on Tariffs and Trade (GATT) was established after World War II to encourage free trade among nations through the lowering/elimination of trade barriers. GATT's 99 member countries have successfully reduced tariff revenues from a high of over 40 per cent of government revenues in the 1940s to only about 5 per cent today.

Newly developing countries continue to rely heavily on tariff revenues as a major source of governmental income. These *revenue tariffs* are generated by both imports and exports of products. The most highly developed countries have the lowest reliance on tariffs as a source of revenue.

The future of GATT remains uncertain. The fall of tariff restrictions has been paralleled by a rise in non-tariff barriers which GATT is ill-equipped to handle. The decision of major powers to develop bilateral negotiations with other nations has also weakened GATT's influence. The emergence of

Table 2.2   Taxes on international trade and transactions as a percentage
of government revenues

Country	%
Guinea	74.39
Solomon Islands	56.42
Lesotho	51.75
Belize	51.10
Iran	45.48
Seychelles	45.36
Cayman Islands	43.18
Yugoslavia	31.28
India	28.42
Thailand	19.11
Malaysia	17.97
Ecuador	14.34
Peru	10.75
Chile	9.87
South Africa	8.74
South Korea	8.19
Venezuela	8.15
Poland	6.23
Hungary	5.80
Mexico	5.13
Canada	3.50
Australia	3.28
Spain	2.07
Israel	1.83
Singapore	1.65
United States	1.46
Japan	1.33
Kuwait	1.26
Sweden	0.54
United Kingdom	0.06

Source: Government Finance Statistics Yearbook 1992, Vol. XVI, International
Monetary Fund, Washington, DC, 1992, pp. 42–3.

regional trading blocs like the EU, NAFTA and AFTA also threaten
GATT's future.

Non-tariff barriers
Non-tariff barriers have emerged in recent years to influence trade patterns
significantly. Such activities as import quotas, voluntary export restraints

(VERs), local content requirements, predatory 'dumping', local technical standards, government procurement policies and export subsidies through tax incentives are methods used by governments to restrict/encourage the flow of products into and out of their countries.

Thailand is one of the many developing Asian countries that is encouraging multinational firms within its borders to stimulate growth and exports. Exports increased over 23 per cent in 1991. By offering tax breaks, simplified customs regulations and other incentives, the Thais have attracted many multinational investors. Over 1500 Japanese companies have established operations in Thailand; between 1989 and 1991, a new Japanese factory opened every three days.[21]

Impact of the European Union integration

Regional trading blocs will provide benefits for member countries but will adversely impact non-member economies according to two recent analyses. The Cecchini Report commissioned by the EC Commission (EC)[22] estimates that the impact of the abolition of customs formalities, open public procurement, liberalization of financial services, increased competition and the economies of scale will:

- Increase EU GDP by 4.5 per cent (Fig. 2.7)

- Decrease consumer prices by 6.1 per cent

- Increase employment by 1 800 000

A recent Organization for Economic Cooperation and Development (OECD) report, however, indicates an estimated unemployment rate approaching 23 million for Europe in 1994. Conditions appear to be degenerating, at least in the short run.

A recent report by the US Congressional Budget Office[23] evaluated the long-term effects of the development of the European Union. Utilizing two different statistical methods, the impact they predict is indicated in Table 2.3.

Multinational corporations

The impact of tariffs and non-tariff barriers to trade has resulted in increased export activities for many firms and an increase in subsidiary formation for others. This trend is likely to continue and to escalate in the coming decade. Domestic-only firms will face greater local competition from imports and subsidiaries of foreign companies. In many cases, a good offense is preferable to a good defense. Domestic-only firms need to explore how they can capitalize on the opportunity for new markets through global trade. Global trade will increasingly become a means not only of expansion, but of survival.

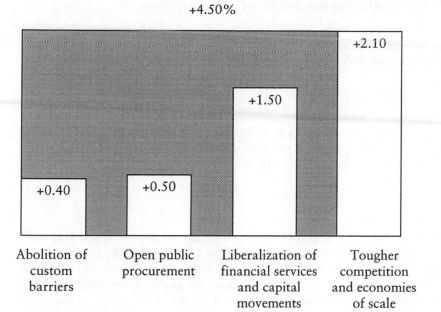

Fig. 2.7 Additional growth likely to be generated through achievement of the 1992 objectives (% of GDP) (*Source*: 'The Economics of 1992' (Cecchini Report), in *European Economy*, no. 35, March 1988).

Table 2.3 Development of the European Union long-term effects: US Congressional Budget Office Estimates (%)

	1993	2000
Europe		
Real GDP	3.0 to 4.9%	5.4 to 6.0%
Net exports	(−6.3) to 15.8%	34.5 to 48.8%
United States		
Real GDP	0.1 to 0.2%	0.0 to 0.2%
(v. 1980)	(2.3) to 1.9%	(2.1) to (9.8%)

Source: How the Economic Transformations in Europe Will Affect the United States, Congress of the US Congressional Budget Office, Superintendent of Documents, US Printing Office, Washington, DC, December 1990.

7. Increased telecommunications at reduced cost

Dramatic advances in telecommunications technology, increased demand for services, falling prices arising from privatization and global competition have played important roles in the globalization of commerce.

Privatization

Government privatization of telephone companies has resulted in the early stages of development of a global industry. It is estimated that between 1991 and 1995 at least 19 governments plan to privatize Postal Telephone and Telegraph companies (PTTs) with an estimated value of greater than $150 billion.[24]

Global competition

Many telephone companies have attempted to provide their domestic customers with a premium service at low cost. Worldwide advantages of scale have led these firms to pursue global markets because of the high capital investments required. In the five-year period from 1986 to 1990, telephone companies were involved with over 300 foreign ventures in more than 60 countries. Western European and US telecommunications companies invested over $11 billion in such ventures in 1989–90.[25] Robert Allen, chairman and chief executive officer of AT&T, remarks, concerning the company's strategic focus,

> There is a booming potential market overseas, and we are there in the thick of it . . . I intend that AT&T will seize those opportunities—not miss them. They are the heart of our business. We have 22,000 people in 40 countries and have about 25 overseas partners and alliances.[26]

Dr Paul Stern, former chairman of the board, president and chief executive officer of Northern Telecom, has a similar philosophy:

> It is a major corporate objective to gain business at a greater rate internationally.[27]

Global competition has resulted in price competition with significant savings to global consumers. More than 1000 telecommunications companies have opened in Japan since government approval was granted in 1985. To remain competitive, Nippon Telegraph and Telephone was forced to slash long-distance rates by 50 per cent between 1984 and 1990.[28]

Infrastructure investment

It is estimated that telecommunications companies invested over $108 billion in infrastructure investments in 1992—a 6 per cent increase over 1991. Greatest increases occurred in the Far East/Pacific Rim region with a rise of almost 14 per cent. The construction budgets in Western Europe rose 9 per cent, with significant investments in Eastern Germany.[29]

Increased demand for services

Cable, cellular and satellite usages are expected to increase exponentially in the coming decade. Several new multi-billion-dollar fiber-optic cable systems are currently under construction or are planned for completion by 1996. These new fiber-optic cables link the United States to Japan, Japan to multiple Asian countries and Europe to the United States. Upon completion, transpacific capacity will increase from 120 000 to 600 000 calls per year; transatlantic capacity will increase from 217 000 to 1.1 million calls per year.[30]

Motorola is gearing up for what it anticipates will be a wireless communications world by the year 2000. It is currently designing a $3.4 billion network of 66 high-orbit satellites that will enable users to communicate data and voice by cellular telephone from any location on earth. Motorola anticipates that more than 26 million people will use wireless communications by the year 2000. Chris Galvin, senior executive vice-president and assistant chief operating officer of Motorola's Paging and Wireless Data Group, recently commented that:

> Fundamentally, people like to communicate in their time frame, in their dimension, in their space . . . Our research indicates that one-half of all semiconductors will go into portable devices by the year 2000.[31]

8. Trends toward homogeneous technical standards

The establishment of technical standards has played an important role in commerce by providing consumers with products that meet certain minimum common standards of quality and performance. Technical standards can be double-edged swords in that they can restrict or exclude competition the more diverse those standards are from country to country or region to region.

A simple item such as the electrical plug is an excellent example of diverse technical standards that varies between countries within Europe and the rest of the world. Europe will be moving toward a uniform design of plug; this will create significant economies of scale and will increase rivalry among manufacturers, resulting in lower costs to consumers.[32]

The more homogeneous the technical standards are, the greater the degree of competition that will be created. The lack of major differences in technical standards between countries was of great help to Japan's Canon as it entered the photocopier market in the 1970s. Canon was successful in developing a single global photocopier that required minor modifications for individual countries. The airline industry has had highly uniform technical standards. International airports have runways that meet similar standards for the largest aircraft, and English is the universal language used by controllers and pilots around the world.[33]

ISO 9000

The International Organization for Standardization (ISO) was founded in Geneva, Switzerland, and is regarded as the premier decision-making body for the development of quality guidelines that provide global consistency and precision. The ISO has developed a set of technical standards known as ISO 9000, which determines whether companies provide services and products that comply with its quality procedures.

To date, over 50 countries have adopted the ISO 9000 Quality Standards as their own national standards. A growing number of corporations now require suppliers to become ISO-certified. The trend is escalating rapidly. Companies that follow the ISO guidelines and are certified have shown to improve quality and performance:

> By last year, ISO compliance became part of hundreds of product safety laws all over Europe, regulating everything from medical devices to telecommunications gear. Such products account for only 15% of EU trade. But German electronics giant Siemens requires ISO compliance in 50% of its supply contracts, and is nudging other suppliers to conform. That eliminates the need to test parts, which saves time and money.
>
> ISO even applies to service companies. At London's Heathrow Airport, British Airways PLC was racking up numerous complaints of lost cargo and damaged goods. Once ISO was imposed, BA discovered, among other problems, that its training didn't prepare handlers for new, automated unloading methods. Now, workers are updated whenever changes occur. In the first year, complaints dropped by 65%, and time spent fixing problems fell 60%.[34]

Japanese and American adoption of ISO 9000 guidelines is critically slow and has endangered the potential of many firms from these countries to continue global activities:

> Meantime, the rest of the world's delay in ISO compliance could keep foreign products out of the EC, if only temporarily. More than 20,000 facilities in Britain and a few thousand more in the rest of Europe are already ISO-certified, compared with the U.S.'s 400 and 48 in Japan. The U.S. has the most to lose, since 30% of its exports go to Europe. DuPont, for one, only began its ISO drive in 1989 after losing a big European order for polyester films to an ISO-certified British firm.[35]

European standards

The European Union is developing harmonized, European-wide standards which will replace multiple national product standards. Compliance with these product standards will be a critical condition, if not a legal requirement, for the sale of products in Europe. The impact of this action will be to reduce barriers to trade for countries within the EU. Manufacturers will be required to meet only one technical standard compared with as many as 12 different country standards. This unification of technical standards should lead to increased trade within Europe and between Europe and its key trading partners.[36]

Sara E. Hagigh, Office of European Community Affairs, US Department of Commerce, reports:

> Harmonized European standards are being developed first for regulated products. The harmonization of technical standards is centered on health and safety aspects of product and is intended to produce minimum safety and health levels throughout the community. Estimates are that close to 50%, or $50 billion, of U.S. exports to the EU are subject to harmonization requirements.[37]

The United States is far behind Europe and the rest of the world in the adoption of international standards. A recent Office of Technology Assessment Reports indicates:

> The Europeans, however, have a schedule to meet; they are unlikely to slow the process of European harmonization for lack of international standards. To reconcile their own interests with those of countries outside the European Community, they propose to reorganize international standards bodies to hasten the development of international standards. Moreover, they call on the United States to make a greater commitment to the development and *implementation* of international standards. They point out that, whereas 85% of all CEN and CENELEC standards are identical to international standards, only 22% of U.S. national standards are identical or technically equivalent.[38]

The future of global standards
The long-term solution for global effectiveness and economies of scale will be the development of globally agreed upon technical standards for products and services. A critical determinant of the achievement of this goal will require the cooperation of the key regional trading blocs: EU (European Union), NAFTA (North American Free Trade Association) and AFTA (Asian Free Trade Association).

Reactive environmental forces

In addition to the *proactive* environmental forces encouraging globalization, there also exist threats, or *reactive* environmental forces, to which companies must respond. These reactive forces can be broken down into four (Nos. 9–12) major categories:

- Increasing competition from non-domestic competitors
- Increased risk arising from volatility in exchange rates

- Trend of customers evolving from domestic-only to global strategies
- Increased pace of global technological change

9. Competition from non-domestic competitors

Corporations that elect to remain local-only and not to engage in either exporting or establishing subsidiaries face great risks from non-domestic competitors. These new competitive threats will often appear without warning. They will appear in the form of (1) new imported products, (2) new competitive products developed as the result of an alliance between a local and foreign competitor, and/or (3) the foreign acquisition of a domestic competitor.

All three scenarios place the local-only corporation at a competitive disadvantage. The new competition for a local-only producer will have many competitive advantages, including (1) access to the newest technology available globally, (2) economies of scale, (3) global sourcing of materials and labor, (4) reduced/no trade barriers because of local content, and (5) manufacture and the transnational exchange of knowledge and innovation among subsidiaries.

Imports

Imported competitive products pose special problems for domestic-only producers. Imported products are likely to contain many or all of the five potential competitive advantages listed above. Imports and exports continue to play an ever-increasing role in commerce as consumers seek the greatest value return for their expenditure. The impact of imports versus domestically produced goods varies considerably across borders and product lines. Worldwide corporations that have excelled in the development of creating the previously cited competitive advantages can capture large market shares. In the United States, imports have been highly successful in key industries (Table 2.4).

Mergers and acquisitions

Merging with or acquiring an existing successful firm in a foreign country has been the preferred route of entry for many firms. Mergers and acquisitions provide ready access to new markets through an existing organization with a proven record of performance. Domestic-only firms can force new and severe competition from former average competitors after those firms have been acquired by worldwide corporations. The acquirer is likely to infuse significant cash, new products and global resources into the local market.

Table 2.4   Imports as a ratio of domestic US consumption: selected US industries for 1992 ($ million)

Product	Value of US manufacture	+ Imports	− Exports	= Total US domestic consumption	Imports as a % of US domestic consumption
Footwear, except rubber	3 543	+ 9 084	− 428	= 12 199	74
Semiconductors & related devices	26 839	+ 15 123	− 10 417	= 31 545	48
Computor equipment & software	60 100	+ 30 697	− 25 527	= 65 270	47
Machine tools	4 360	+ 2 335	− 1 565	= 5 130	46
Jewelry, precious metal	4 058	+ 2 700	− 585	= 6 173	44
Ceramic wall & floor tiles	628	+ 426	− 20	= 1 034	41
Crude petroleum & natural gas	74 298	+ 42 477	− 301	= 116 474	36
Motor vehicles & parts	139 800	+ 61 087	− 16 991	= 183 896	33
Power driven hand tools	2 354	+ 811	− 618	= 2 547	32
Apparel & other textile products	63 949	+ 28 176	− 4 717	= 87 408	32
Photographic equipment & supplies	17 200	+ 6 100	− 3 800	= 19 500	31
Aerospace	112 643	+ 12 718	− 42 208	= 83 153	15
Drugs*	48 292	+ 4 785	− 5 746	= 47 331	10

* 1991 figures for drugs–1992 data not available.
Source: US Industrial Outlook, 1993, US Department of Commerce, International Trade Administration, Government Printing Office, Washington, DC, 1993.

Alliances

The rate of growth of alliances has escalated significantly in recent years, and the number of new alliances is estimated to exceed the number of new companies and acquisitions.[39] The cost and availability of capital makes alliances more appealing for many companies. Alliances are less permanent in nature. For an alliance to be successful, employees are needed with flexibility and the ability to work effectively in potentially conflicting corporate cultures.

Successful alliance benefits both corporations. Satoshi Iue, president of Sanyo Electric Company, states: 'Global alliances are not only sensible for the exchange of production technology and research, but they can also play an important role in creating a healthy international business society based on the fundamental principle of mutual prosperity.'[40]

10. Increased risks arising from volatility in exchange rates

Corporations involved in non-domestic commerce face the potential for considerable financial risks. The constant fluctuation of exchange rates in multiple countries can have a significant impact on earnings. Considerable debate surrounds the variability/equality of the cost of capital in different markets and the competitive advantage that lower capital costs provide.

Exchange rates

Exchange rate-volatility in multiple markets can significantly impact a corporation's profitability. The longer the length of time between the agreement to buy/sell and the payment for same, the greater the risk for exchange gains/losses to the corporation.

Fluctuation volatility in exchange rates differs in various markets and will influence global sourcing decisions. Non-domestic sourcing continues to increase annually, making exchange-rate volatility increasingly important to purchasing departments (see Fig. 2.8 and Table 2.5). The price paid for imported goods is impacted by exchange rates when the payment is made in the supplier's currency and in the length of time between contract and payment.

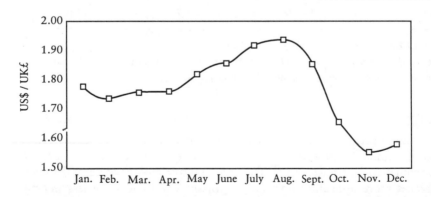

Fig. 2.8 Foreign spot exchange rates, USA/UK, 1992 (*Source*: Board of Governors of the Federal Reserve System, 'Foreign spot exchange rates: United Kingdom', *National Trade Data Bank—The Export Connection*. US Department of Commerce, Economics and Statistics Administration, Washington, DC, February 1993).

Table 2.5   Foreign spot exchange rates, UK, 1992

	US$/UK£
January	1.78
February	1.72
March	1.76
April	1.76
May	1.81
June	1.86
July	1.92
August	1.94
September	1.85
October	1.65
November	1.53
December	1.56
Annual average	1.81

Source: Board of Governors of the Federal Reserve System 'Foreign spot exchange rates, United Kingdom', *National Trade Data Bank: The Export Connection*, US Department of Commerce, Economics and Statistics Administration, Washington, DC, February 1993.

Example

Let's examine an illustration of the potential impact of exchange rates using actual exchange rates for 1992:

August 1992
$1.00 US = £0.5155 UK
$1.94 US = £1.0 UK

November 1992
$1.00 U.S. = £0.6536 UK
$1.53 US = £1.0 UK

An American firm agreed to purchase 1 000 000 units of Product X in August 1992 at £1.0 per unit. Payment, in British pounds, was due upon delivery in November 1992.

The American firm's estimated cost was:

	Units	*US$/pound*	*Cost in US$*
August 1992:	1 000 000	× 1.94	= $1 940 000

The US firm agreed to pay in British pounds upon delivery. But their total cost turned out to be only $1 530 000, because there was a significant devaluation of the pound during the three-month period:

	Units	US$/pound	Cost in US$
November 1992:	1 000 000	× 1.53	= $1 530 000

If instead the British pound had strengthened to $2.50/£, the US corporation would have incurred huge losses: it would have had to pay $2 500 000 for the units upon delivery.

Purchasing management training must include a comprehensive under-standing of the volatility potential of exchange rates. A company could source a product for the exact same price at the time of contract but actually pay a considerably different price because of exchange-rate fluctuations.

Exchange-rate forecasting also plays a critical role in the calculation of subsidiary forecasts in domestic currency. A subsidiary may experience record-breaking earnings in local currency but may not achieve its goals when earnings are finally calculated in the home-country currency. Corporations need to purchase or internally generate exchange-rate forecasts to assist in global sourcing decisions. In spite of this information, a recent survey of 150 US corporations involved in global sourcing found that only 10 per cent utilized exchange-rate information as an input to the volume-timing of purchase decisions.[41] The Eaton Corporation's iron casting sourcing provides an example:

Eaton's exchange rate forecasts indicated a downward trend, over a five-year period, in the buying power of the U.S. dollar against the European and Far Eastern currencies of interest. The result was an upward trend in forecasted price changes for these countries compared with U.S. prices for the same time horizon. Similar forecasts for other countries of interest also indicated a weakening in the buying power of the U.S. dollar.

Since exchange rate forecasts indicated a weakening of the U.S. dollar against a wide range of foreign currencies, it did not make sense for Eaton to move its iron castings to different foreign sources. Instead, Eaton brought the castings back to its domestic sources and at the same time was able to maintain a competitive price worldwide.[42]

The *volume-timing of purchases* was utilized in a key sourcing decision by Conoco for seamless tubular pipe. Conoco, one of the world's largest petroleum companies, was sourcing seamless tubular pipe from Japan in 1986. Conoco's forecasters anticipated that the value of the US dollar would continue to decline versus the Japanese yen in the coming year. They also anticipated significant price increases in seamless tubular pipe. Conoco contracted with Japanese mills for a full year's supply at a guaranteed fixed price. The savings to Conoco exceeded US$1 million.[43]

The establishment of manufacturing subsidiaries in key markets can reduce the exposure to exchange-rate fluctuations. The greater local content of materials will also positively impact the final cost of the completed product.

Exchange rates play an important role in global sourcing. Purchasing managers can minimize their exposure to losses by engaging in contracts that are quoted in the domestic currency and through risk-sharing clauses in contracts. More importantly, companies can use *exchange-rate volatility* as a competitive advantage by the careful selection of countries and suppliers and the timing of purchases.

11. Trend of customers evolving from domestic-only to global strategies

Domestic-only firms whose strategy is to remain as such need to ensure that their present and potential new customers will want only home-country products or services. If a company's major customers are themselves adopting global strategies, they may require goods and services to be manufactured or performed at the foreign subsidiary location. Foreign governments may require or provide incentives for a certain percentage of 'local content' in subsidiary produced products. Today's domestic-only firms may find themselves non-competitive in the future if their customers adopt global strategies that include global sourcing criteria.

12. Increased pace of global technological change

The rapidly accelerating pace of technological change during the 1980s has had a profound impact on corporate profitability and survival. Technological improvements in production processes have also resulted in shifts in market share between corporations. The most industrialized countries have invested the most heavily in research and development. The results clearly show that this R&D investment has yielded the largest number of new patents and that profitability is greater in firms with higher R&D investments.

Role of the subsidiary

Rapidly changing technology, in both products and processes, is expensive. These high R&D costs pressure managers to (1) spread the costs across many markets to amortize the costs as quickly as possible, and (2) globalize the innovation across many markets to capitalize on it before imitators do so.[44]

Most major investments in R&D are still centralized in the corporation's home country. Recently, however, global companies have been expanding the ratio of R&D activities in subsidiary operations. Some countries have exerted political pressure which has partly influenced this decision. The decision is also sound business logic. Robert Pearce, senior research fellow at the University of Reading (United Kingdom), notes:

> Two sets of factors contribute to the increased role for overseas R&D discerned in many leading TNC's. Firstly, the increasingly globalized basis of competition, with more strong enterprises contesting a widening rage of important markets, places even more priority on the technological scope of those TNC's. Secondly, the potential for internationally diversified inputs into the fulfillment of those research needs has also been recognized.[45]

Technological integration

In order to be successful in today's global marketplace, companies must evolve from working via segmented, step-by-step technological processes to an *integrated technological process*. This integrated process blends technological improvements from different technological fields to create products that revolutionize markets. Technological integration is essential if a firm is to remain competitive in a global arena that demands faster development, involvement from external customers and shorter product life-cycles. Philippe Montigny, special assistant to the director for science, technology and industry at the OECD, emphasizes:

> To benefit from the productivity gains that technological change can bring, corporate functions—research, design, production and marketing—must be integrated with one another. The firm will thus be able to progress from standardized mass production to customized mass production, thereby satisfying changing demand and achieving the economies of scale and scope made necessary by soaring R&D and production costs.[46]

Fumio Kodama, a professor at Saitama University, provides several examples of the integrated technological process which he terms 'technology fusion':

> Starting in the late-1960's, a number of Japanese companies, including Nippon Telephone and Telegraph, NEC, Nippon Sheet Glass, and Sumitomo Electric Industries, fused glass, cable, and electronics technologies to produce Japan's first fiber-optics. Today Japanese fiber-optics companies have established a significant share of the global fiber-optics equipment markets.
>
> In the early 1980's, Sharp developed the first commercially-viable liquid crystal display for pocket calculators from the fusion of electronic, crystal, and optics technologies—another branch of optoelectronics. Today the company controls 38 per cent of the worldwide LCD market, valued at over $2 billion; the market is expected to more than triple by 1995.
>
> In each of these cases, the companies added one technology to another and came up with a solution greater than the sum of its parts—in technology fusion, one plus one equals three. Because it combines rather than replaces technologies, fusion requires a different mind-set and new set of management practices.[47]

R&D investment versus company performance

As previously noted in a recent Conference Board study, 'outstanding' firms were twice as likely to engage in R&D activities, both inside and outside the home country.[48]

Summary

The impact of the rate and severity of change of the 12 environmental forces has resulted in an intensification of the globalization of business. Small, medium and large corporations are being impacted. Domestic-only organizations are experiencing severe foreign competition. Global firms are struggling with heightened competitive actions.

To survive and prosper in the coming decade, companies must carefully assess the impact of the recent trends and anticipate the impact of the future trends of these environmental forces. This process is one of the initial steps necessary in the formulation of the organization's global strategic vision.

Notes and references

1. Jane Szita, 'Clog makers march on', *Holland Herald*, March 1993, p. 23.
2. Charles R. Taylor, *Global presence and Competitiveness of U.S. Manufacturers*, Report no. 977 (a review of US competitiveness), The Conference Board, New York, 1991.
3. Personal communication with Alex Trotman, Ford chairman and CEO, and David Scott, vice-president of public affairs; also Alex Taylor III, 'Ford's $6 billion baby', *Fortune*, 28 June 1993, pp. 76–81.
4. Mark L. Fagan, 'A guide to global sourcing', *Journal of Business Strategy*, March/April 1991, pp. 21–5.
5. Personal communication with George A. Rabstejnek and J. William Widing, Jr; also, Harbridge House study consisting of 140 firms with membership in the Purchasing Management Association: 'How foreign is global sourcing?', *Purchasing*, 16 May 1991, p. 32.
6. A two-phase study by Robert M. Monczka and Robert J. Trent, 'Global sourcing: a development approach', *International Journal of Purchasing and Materials Management*, Spring 1991, pp. 2–8.
7. Rabstejnek and Widing, op. cit.
8. Louis Kraa, 'Asia 2000', *Fortune*, 5 October 1992, p. 138.
9. Patricia M. Carey, 'Getting ready for NAFTA', *International Business*, October 1992, p. 45.
10. Zachary Schiller and Richard Melcher, 'Marketing globally, thinking locally', *Business Week*, 31 May 1991, pp. 60–5.

11. Mark Maremont and Paula Dwyer, 'How Gillette is honing its edge', *Business Week*, 28 September 1992, pp. 60–5.
12. Julie Tilsnet, 'Duracell looks abroad for more juice', *Business Week*, 21 December 1992, pp. 52–3.
13. Robert J. Guttman, 'Coca-Cola president Donald Keough', *Europe*, May 1992, pp. 30–2.
14. Michael E. Porter , *Competitive Strategy*, Free Press, New York, 1980.
15. Clive Lewis, 'Consistency is the key to marketing across borders', *Medical Marketing & Media*, 1 September 1992, p. 46.
16. Ibid., p. 46.
17. George S. Yip, *Total Global Strategy: Managing for Worldwide Competitive Advantage*, Prentice-Hall, Englewood Cliffs, NJ, 1992.
18. Ibid., p. 90.
19. Lawrence Ingrassia, 'Gillette holds its edge by endlessly searching for a better shave', *Wall Street Journal*, 10 December 1992, pp. A1–A6.
20. An article in *Traffic World*, 16 December 1991, p. 22.
21. Stewart Pinkerton, 'A second South Korea?' *Forbes*, 21 December 1992, pp. 149–58.
22. A summary of the Cecchini Report appears in *Luxembourg: The European Financial Common Market*, Office for Official Publications for the European Communities, Federal Republic of Germany, 1989.
23. *How the Economic Transformations in Europe Will Affect the United States*, US Congressional Budget Office, Superintendent of Documents, US Government Printing Office, Washington, DC, December 1990.
24. Ronald M. Serrano, P. William Bane and W. Brooke Tunstall, 'Reshaping the global telecom industry', *Telephony*, 7 October 1991, pp. 38–40.
25. Ibid., pp. 38–9.
26. James N. Budwey, 'Competing in the global community', *Telecommunications*, November 1991, p. 55.
27. Ibid.
28. Neil Gross, 'It's the elephant against the rats for Japan's phone business', *Business Week*, 2 November 1992, pp. 112–13.
29. Anthony Ramirez, '2nd Asia link considered by AT&T', *New York Times*, 3 November 1992.
30. Ibid.
31. In an interview reported by Ronald E. Yates, 'Motorola mobilizes for wireless world', *Chicago Tribune*, 22 November 1992, sec. 7, p. 3.
32. Yip, op. cit., p. 56.
33. Ibid., p. 55.
34. Jonathan B. Levine, 'Want EC business? You have two choices', *Business Week*, 19 October 1992, pp. 58–9.
35. Ibid.
36. Sarah E. Hagigh, 'Hundreds of new product standards will apply to sales in EC after 1992', *Business America*, 13 January 1992, pp. 16–20.
37. Ibid., p. 16.

38. US Congress, Office of Technology Assessment, *Global Standards: Building Blocks for the Future*, TCT-512, US Government Printing Office, Washington DC, March 1992, p. 85.

39. In 'The marriage of true minds', *The Economist*, 19 September 1992, pp. 79–80.

40. From a Supplement on Global Alliances that appeared in *Fortune*, 24 August 1992, p. S-12.

41. Joseph R. Carter and Shawnee K. Vickery, 'Strategies for managing volatile exchange rates in international purchasing: an empirical study', *Journal of Purchasing and Materials Management*, Winter 1989, pp. 13–20.

42. Joseph R. Carter and Shawnee K. Vickery, 'Currency exchange rates: their impact on global sourcing', *Journal of Purchasing and Materials Management*, Fall 1989, pp. 19–25.

43. Ibid., p. 25.

44. Yip, op. cit., p. 51.

45. Robert D. Pearce, 'The globalization of R&D by TNCs', *CTC Reporter*, Spring 1991, p. 13.

46. Philippe Montigny, 'From technological advance to economic progress', *OECD Observer*, June/July 1991, p. 9.

47. Fumio Kodama, 'Technology fusion and the new R&D', *Harvard Business Review*, July–August 1992, p. 71.

48. Taylor, op. cit.

With our information economy at mid-life, and recession an ever present concern, the essentials of every business are being altered so fundamentally that you had better not be in the same business five to ten years from now that you are in today. You had better be the first, not the last, to know why, and the first to know what to do about it . . .

Marginal improvements won't be enough to stay competitive. You get 5, 10, 15 percent improvements in what you are doing by doing the same thing, only a bit better. But your competition will go for improvements in multiples. To attain 100, 300, 500 percent improvements, you can't do the same thing better. You have to do something fundamentally different and, in the process, your business will be fundamentally transformed.

STAN DAVIS AND BILL DAVIDSON
2020 Vision

Global strategic vision

*In the companies we know that are success-
fully making the transition to a more collaborative organization, the key to success is
developing and then living by a common
strategic vision. When you agree on an
overall direction, you can be flexible about
the means to achieve it . . .*

*Really powerful visions are simply told.
The Ten Commandments, the Declaration of
Independence, a Winston Churchill World
War II speech—all present messages that are
so simple and direct you can almost touch
them. Our corporate strategies should be
equally compelling.*

BENJAMIN TREGOE AND PETER TOBIA
Industry Week, 6 August 1990

The 'what' and 'how'

'What' does our corporation want to be in the future? 'How' will we get
there? Two simple questions. So simple that the corporate graveyard is
littered with countless examples of corporations that failed to properly
address these two questions or else failed to energize their employees to
focus all their energy on implementing them.

In this chapter we will provide examples of organizations that have
failed to properly address one or both of these crucial issues. We will also
provide a basic overview of the two processes needed to develop the
'What' (strategic thinking) and the 'How' (strategic planning). Of equal
importance is a review of 25 key pitfalls that prohibit optimal achievement
of multinational corporate goals. Moving from a domestic-only to a global
environment requires senior management to carefully craft/adjust goals to
comply with multiple cultural sensitivities. Guidance is provided in this
regard.

What is strategic vision?

Strategic vision can be defined as the ideal picture of what the company
should look like at some future point in time. This ideal picture of the
company in the future is the central rallying point for all plans, employees
and employee actions. Strategic vision is the beacon that guides the way

forward for the company. Strategic vision is designed to position the organization in the future rather than focus on how it will get there.[1,2,3]

In a recent Conference Board report, Lester B. Korn, chairman of Korn/ Ferry International, discussed the results of a recent survey developed with the Columbia Graduate School of Business. This worldwide study incorporated the views of more than 1500 senior executives from over 20 countries, representing over 12 per cent of the world's gross domestic product. Their findings placed *strategy formulation* as the number 1 challenge facing corporations both today and in the year 2000. Also, by the end of the 1990s top CEOs foresee human resource issues replacing marketing and sales as the most important area of expertise for a CEO.[4]

Strategic vision in a changing global market

The business literature contains an endless supply of examples of formerly great companies that have fallen by the wayside in the matter of a few short years. What causes a long-time market leader to suddenly find itself struggling to remain in the marketplace? There are many factors. Perhaps the single leading cause is the failure to create, communicate and implement an appropriate *global strategic vision.*

In October 1992, the 97-year-old Schwinn Bicycle Company filed for bankruptcy. Schwinn had been the leading American bicycle manufacturer and distributor for several decades. However, its market share had eroded from over 25 per cent in the 1960s to below 7 per cent in 1992. What had happened? In the 1970s Schwinn focused its energy on cutting costs by moving manufacturing to Asia. In the 1980s, when marketplace demand shifted to mountain bikes and specialty bikes made with lightweight materials, Schwinn failed to accurately assess the rapidly changing market needs and responded too late to take advantage of its competitive strengths.[5]

The Yamaha Corporation is the world leader in horns, pianos and other musical instruments. Yamaha craftsmen are experts in bending and laminating woods for piano cabinets. Some time ago Yamaha's leadership created a strategic vision focused on this core competency and expanded into less familiar business such as tennis rackets, skis and furniture. From electronic organs, it ventured into the highly competitive arena of VCRs, TVs and audio equipment. Yamaha's focus on production techniques put the company out of focus with the market's needs.

Today, Yamaha's strategic vision is focused on upscale musical instruments, combining its competitive advantages in bending and laminating woods with its leadership in computer chips that create a symphony of sounds. Yamaha's Disklavier combines pianos with a built-in computer that records and plays back performance. Disklavier sales in 1992 exceeded $100 million and accounted for 20 per cent of Yamaha's total piano sales.[6]

Impact of the 12 environmental forces

The evolutionary *rate of change* in the political and economic world in which we live is accelerating faster than previously could have been imagined. The remaining years between now and the year 2000 will prove to be the most challenging for all corporations—small and large—around the globe. As described in Chapter 2, businesses and their leaders must fully understand the implications of the changes of the 12 environmental forces on their industries and firms.

James Leontiades notes the relationship between the firm and the external environment:

> Managers thinking strategically about their business will need to identify and familiarize themselves with the firm's business environment. They will need to appraise and assess their actual and potential customers, competitors, suppliers, legal and political constraints, and so on. They will require a close knowledge of their own firm's capabilities and resources. The task of the strategist is to find a relationship or match between the firm and its environment, as well as the firm's own objectives, resources and capabilities.[7]

The strategic thinking process

The strategic thinking process can be defined as the process that is used to develop the 'strategic vision'. The terms 'strategy development process' and 'strategy formulation' can be used interchangeably with 'strategic thinking process' to define this process.

In order to create an optimal strategic vision for the company, senior management must carefully assess the business and company environment of the future. The time frame for most companies is usually 10–20 years, but it may be as long as 50 years in the oil refining business or as short as one year in the high-fashion industry.

Senior managers must carefully evaluate what they want the company to be in the future, what core competencies exist and which ones must be developed. Specific products/services and markets/users must be determined. An analysis of current and future competitors must be conducted, and an implementation plan must be developed as well as defining the appropriate corporate organizational structure to support the optimal implementation of the strategic vision (Fig. 3.1).

- Creates the global strategic vision of *what* the organization wants to be in the future
- Can be developed by the CEO and senior management
- Challenges the current direction of the company and establishes the future direction
- Is interactive among levels of management
- Determines how resources will be realigned to focus on achieving the global strategic vision
- Rallies all employees to focus activity on the global strategic vision
- Carefully assesses the impact of the 12 environmental factors on the industry and company
- Assesses internal core competencies and the competencies needed to achieve the global strategic vision

Fig 3.1 Strategic thinking process: benefits (*Source:* adapted from Michel Roberts, *The Strategist CEO*, Quorum Books, New York, 1987, pp. 33–4).

What is the strategic planning process?

The strategic planning process can be defined as the process of *how* the company will get there in the future. It consists of the long-range plans (usually three to five years but can be as long as 20 years) that provide the building blocks to make the strategic vision a reality. The goals expressed reflect such areas as growth, rates of return, market shares, new product areas, new market areas and profitability (Fig. 3.2).

- Creates the plans of *how* the organization will achieve the global strategic vision
- Is developed from the bottom up with careful review by senior management
- Changes the current direction of the company toward the global strategic vision
- Involves all employees
- Realigns human and financial resources through the planning process to focus on achieving the global strategic vision
- Rallies all employees to focus activity on the global strategic vision
- Identifies changes in the 12 environmental factors on the industry and company and allocates resources accordingly
- Enables the development of plans to build/acquire needed core competencies to achieve the global strategic vision

Fig. 3.2 Strategic planning process: benefits, when focused on a clear strategic vision (*Source:* adapted from Michel Roberts, *The Strategist CEO*, Quorum Books, New York, 1987, pp. 33–4).

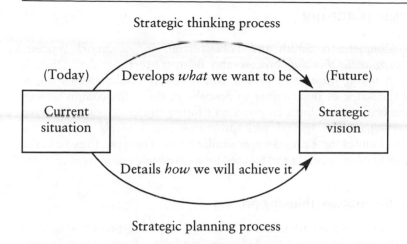

Fig. 3.3   **Strategic thinking and planning processes**

Corporations that fail to focus on both strategic thinking and strategic planning will have difficulty surviving through the remainder of this decade (Fig. 3.3). Companies that focus only on strategic planning will not pay close enough attention to the rapidly changing global environment surrounding them. Western Union's failure to assess the rapid changes in government deregulation and technological breakthroughs threatened the existence of the company in a period of only five years. Proper creation of a corporate strategic vision through the strategic thinking process would have identified the environmental forces that were changing and could have placed Western Union on a course to capitalize on those changes.

New technology and deregulation of the telecommunications industry drastically altered the competitive advantage of the Western Union Corporation during the 1980's. The rapid growth of facsimile communications is the most recent negative impact on the company's customer base. Management did not recognize this or other environmental threats that affected the market for Western Union's communications services. Incorrect assessment of the rapidly changing telecommunications market and failure to implement corrective strategies drastically weakened Western Union's financial position and performance. By 1990, the company had accumulated huge financial losses.

A key issue facing the top management of a corporation is deciding the future direction of the organization. The Western Union example illustrates how a lackof strategic vision in turbulent markets can have a negative impact on an organization.[8]

Traditionally companies have spent more time on strategic planning and less time on strategic thinking. Today, companies should be spending more time on strategic thinking and less time on strategic planning.

Strategic planning

Tregoe, Zimmerman, Smith and Tobia's *strategic framework* process, Robert's *strategic thinking* process and Below, Morrisey and Acomb's *strategic planning framework* process contain many similar elements. It is beyond the scope of this chapter to describe in detail the comprehensive steps necessary to develop a corporation's future strategic vision. We have both participated in several such programs and strongly support the adoption of one of these processes, or similar types of process, to assist in the development of an accurate and focused future strategic vision (see Fig. 3.4).

Steps in the strategic thinking process

The principle components of such a strategic thinking process (Fig. 3.5) include the development of the following modules adapted from Tregoe, Zimmerman, Smith and Tobia[9] and Robert[1]:

1. Current strategic vision

2. Evaluation of the components of global strategic vision

3. Development of a tentative new global strategic vision

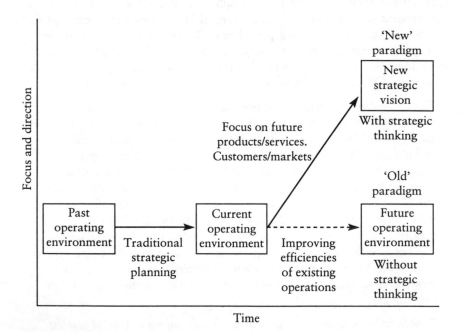

Fig. 3.4   Future direction with/without strategic thinking

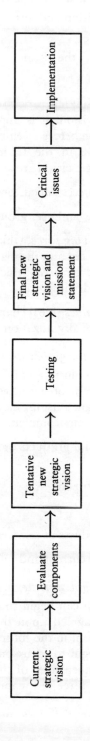

Fig. 3.5 The strategic thinking process

Current strategic vision → Evaluate components → Tentative new strategic vision → Testing → Final new strategic vision and mission statement → Critical issues → Implementation

4. Testing the tentative new global strategic vision

5. Final new global strategic vision and mission statement

6. Development of critical issues

7. Implementation plan—selling the vision

Current strategic vision

The first step in the strategic thinking process is the clarification of the corporation's current strategic vision. It is important to agree upon the company's current strategic vision before attempting to develop a vision of what the company will be like in the future (Fig. 3.6). The major components of the current strategic vision are as follows:

- List of the company's very successful current products and services

- List of current major markets and user groups served

- Determination of the key *driving force*, which has the greatest impact on the kinds of products offered and the markets serviced, and identification of the key *strategic areas* which have been the most important in support of the driving force

- Determination of the *core values* (ideal characteristics or qualities of intrinsic worth) that guide the organization.

Evaluation of the components of the global strategic vision

The CEO and management team must carefully assess which components of strategy will impact positively or negatively on the future of the company. Each member of the team must list his or her impressions on each component. A partial list of major environmental factors would include:

- Common features of successful products or services, markets and user groups

- Core competencies of the company

- Weaknesses of the company

- Characteristics of future products or services, markets or user groups

- Strengths and weaknesses of current and future competitors

Development of a tentative new global strategic vision

The CEO and management team can begin to develop the tentative new global strategy after they have agreed upon the components of strategy that will either help or hinder them in the future. This section is designed to encourage management to begin to focus on the two or three driving forces that best address the competencies of the organization. The team must then choose which driving force best capitalizes on the strengths of the organization.

- Establishment of the proper *time perspective* of the future strategy. The time perspective will vary depending on the rate of change of technology and customer preferences, lead-times required for product/service development, life-cycles of product/service, etc.

- Development of the *tentative future driving force*. This selection is made after careful analysis of the strengths and weaknesses of the company and its competitors, and external market opportunities

- Establishment of future products and services scope and future market scope

- Development of the key competitive advantage the firm will develop over its competitors and the supporting capabilities needed

- Establishment of the targets for growth, size and financial returns needed

Testing the tentative new global strategic vision

Any changes that have occurred during the strategic thinking process will impact on various organizations and personnel within the company. It is important to test the tentative new global strategic vision to insure that any issues that might hinder the ability of the strategy to work are identified.

1. In *what direction* is our industry headed?
2. *What* do we want to be in the future?
3. What *internal/external environmental factors* will enhance/impede our ability to compete?
4. What *products/services* and *markets/users* will we serve?
5. Who are/will be our *competitors*?
6. How do we create a *clear global strategic vision* and *mission* of where we will be in our industry's future?
7. What *capabilities* do we have to develop in order to expand into/ remain competitive in global competition?
8. How do we properly ensure the *optimal distribution* of capital and other resources across businesses?
9. How will we *communicate* our mission and global strategic vision to all employees and achieve their understanding and universal *implementation*?
10. What specific *tactics* must be developed to insure the success of the strategies developed?
11. How will we effectively *empower* out employees to focus their energies on achieving our global strategic vision?
12. What *reward systems* do we need to create that support the goals in our strategic vision and operations plans?

Fig. 3.6   Global strategic vision: critical questions

Testing of the future new global strategic vision should be targeted to at least the following:

- Current strategy
- Evaluation components
- Core values
- Policies and practices of the corporation
- Two or three major competitors

The management team should compare the tentative new global strategic vision with the current strategic vision (Fig. 3.6). Typical questions should include:

- How different are the strategies?
- What changes need to be made as we move to a new product scope, new services scope, new market scope and new user scope?
- Is the driving force the same or different? How will this impact on our business?
- Are the supporting capabilities the same or different? How will this impact on our business?

Management must test the tentative new global strategic vision against the evaluation component and ask:

- Are the core competencies of the company utilized properly in the tentative new strategy?
- Are the weaknesses of the company being avoided?
- Are we focused properly on the key characteristics of future products, services, markets and user groups?
- Is the tentative new global strategic vision supported by our core values?
- How does the tentative new global strategic vision compare with and support the corporation's policy and practices guidelines?
- Does our tentative new global strategic vision capitalize on our competitors' weaknesses and avoid or minimize our competitors' strengths?
- What are the driving forces of our competitors, and how can we take maximum advantage of their threat?

Final new global strategic vision
The testing of the tentative new global strategic vision should raise several

questions and critical issues that need to be addressed for the final new global strategic vision to be successful. If management is convinced that it can adequately address the questions and critical issues, it is ready to adopt the final new global strategic vision.

The key elements of the new global strategic vision of the organization or firm will contain all or most of the elements originally developed by Tregoe and Zimmerman.

The mission statement

The purpose of the organization's mission statement is to focus on the future concept of the business, the allocation of resources and the long-range and operational plans. The mission statement summarizes the intent of the global strategic vision.

The mission statement is generated as one of the last steps in the development of the global strategic vision of the organization. It attempts to summarize in one short paragraph the global strategic vision of the company based on the information developed from the organization's (1) core values, (2) driving force, (3) future product/service scope, (4) future market/user scope and (5) competitive advantage.

The terms *strategy*, *strategic vision*, *mission* and *charter* are all viewed as synonyms.

Peter Drucker views the development of a common mission statement as essential to unify the direction of various functional units within the organization:

> Because the modern organization is composed of specialists, each with his or her own narrow area of expertise, its mission must be crystal clear. The organization must be single-minded, or its members will become confused. They will follow their own specialty rather than apply it to the common task. They will each define 'results' in terms of their own specialty and impose its values on the organization. Only a focused and common mission will hold the organization together and enable it to produce. Without such a mission, the organization will soon lose credibility and, with it, its ability to attract the very people it needs to perform.[10]

The essential elements of a mission statement attempt to consolidate the strategic vision of the organization in one short paragraph. A successful mission statement will be one that all employees understand and can repeat or paraphrase when asked, one that properly embraces the core values of employees and focuses their activities on a daily basis. It is the cornerstone of the company's strategic vision.

The essential elements of a successful mission statement should include the following:

- *Purpose.*   Why does the organization exist? For whose benefit is all the effort being put in? Does the organization exist (1) to serve shareholders only, (2) to serve all its stakeholders including employees, customers, etc., or (3) for a purpose that is greater than the needs of the stakeholders?

The Ashbridge model, described in a recent *Economist* Special Report, offers several examples of this third type of purpose:

> One manager at the British retailer Marks and Spencer described the company's purpose as 'raising standards for the working man'. This rings true for many others in the company who felt, particularly in the early days of Marks and Spencer and after the Second World War, that they were improving the standard of clothing available to the average person because they were able to retail high-quality goods at affordable prices. The Japanese clothing and cosmetics company Wacoal has the purpose: 'To promote the creation of feminine beauty and to improve the culture of living'. Such companies have reached beyond the stakeholder definition of purpose and found a higher goal that can potentially be supported by all the stakeholders.[11]

■ *Products/markets/technology.*   What will be the future products/ services offered? What will be the future markets/users of these products? Will we provide any unique technological advantages?

■ *Core values.*   Core values are relatively easy to define in a domestic environment. A matter of essential concern to global organizations is to determine those values that should have the greatest priority in a multi-cultural corporation.

> A corporate philosophy developed from a singular perspective cannot be assumed to maintain its relevance in variant cultures. Corporate values and beliefs are primarily culturally defined, reflecting the general philosophical perspective of the society in which the company operates. Thus, when a company extends into another social structure it encounters a new set of accepted corporate values and preferences which must be assimilated and incorporated into its own.
>
> The critical concern for the MNC [multinational corporation] is to decide which values and philosophical priorities will be expressed, given multiple cultures. The MNC has the basic choice of adopting a company philosophy for each operating environment or of defining a supranational corporate philosophy. Although each subsidiary must verify that its philosophy is not in direct conflict with existing cultural norms, the preferable choice for the MNC is usually the latter approach—striving to define an acceptable overall corporate philosophy not contingent on specific environments.[12]

Mission statements that are found to be culturally unacceptable to employees or do not adequately reflect their values will not be embraced and implemented, as noted by Peter Drucker:

Executives in an organization—whether business or university or hospital or the Boy Scouts—must believe that its mission and task are society's most important mission and task as well as the foundation for everything else. If they do not believe this, their organization will soon lose faith in itself, self-confidence, pride, and the ability to perform.[13]

- *Competitive posture.*   The mission statement of a global organization must clearly express the company's operating philosophy in multiple external environments. Senior managers must be fully knowledgeable of their organization's strengths and weaknesses in different markets. Companies can elect to attempt proactively to change their environments, or they can choose to react to environments.

- *Public posture.*   The corporation's public image is important because many global customers attribute certain qualities to a particular organization. Purchasing decisions may be partially based on these qualities. Pearce and Roth quote from Hewlett-Packard's mission statement this excerpt that mirrors its public image:

  As a corporation operating in many different communities throughout the world, we must assure ourselves that each of these communities is better for our presence . . . Each community has its particular set of social problems. Our company must help to solve these problems.[14]

- *Economic goals.*   Mission statements also include the organization's goal of increasing its profitability and expanding its market share. In a global environment, however, not all economies share the same understanding and values concerning profit and growth. Pearce and Roth note:

  Research has shown that financial goals differ among various countries. Executives from France, Japan, and the Netherlands have displayed a clear preference for maximizing growth in after-tax earnings. Norwegian executives place a higher priority on maximizing earnings before interest and taxes. In contrast, the maximization of stockholder wealth has received little attention in any of these four countries. Thus, a mission statement which specifies a firm's ultimate responsibility as one to its stockholders may or may not be appropriate from a global perspective as the basis for the company's financial operating philosophy. This illustrates the importance of reviewing and revising the corporate mission prior to international expansion . . . A host country may view social welfare and development goals as taking precedence over free market capitalism. For example, in Third World countries, employment and income distribution goals often supersede rapid economic growth.[15]

Development of critical issues

Critical issues can be defined as key, unresolved questions that must be answered to make the successful transfer from the current strategic vision to the final new strategic vision. These critical issues are considered major and usually require significant additions, deletions or adaptations to the company's current systems, resources, competencies or organizational structure. Organizations that change driving forces will experience a greater number of more significant critical issues (Fig. 3.7).

Old paradigm	New paradigm
1. Firms were primarily 'domestic'-oriented.	1. Firms are evolving to a 'global' orientation for growth and survival.
2. Demand exceeded supply in many industries, resulting in economies of scale as a critical competitive advantage.	2. There is greater emphasis on quality, custom design, speed and small-lot size.
3. The large national concern whose origin was easily identified dominated the market.	3. Multiple, smaller entrepreneurial businesses are created within the global umbrella.
4. Companies competed through increasing the size and number of employees.	4. The complexities of global commerce are forcing companies to grow through alliances with other firms with expertise in R&D or local markets.
5. The focus was on strategic planning and continuous improvement of present processes.	5. The focus is on strategic thinking and development of a global strategic vision of future direction.
6. Concerns for the physical environment remained low with limited knowledge of potential damage.	6. Corporations are placing significant emphasis on being 'good corporate citizens' in waste management.
7. Strategy was product-driven.	7. Strategy is market-driven.
8. The need to improve efficiency was stressed.	8. The need to improve effectiveness is stressed.

Fig. 3.7   The evolving paradigm for the new economic era: strategic thinking

Implementation plan

The accelerated rate of change among the 12 environmental forces previously discussed has created significant new leadership challenges for corporate executives. Competitive threats, both domestic and non-domestic, are requiring companies simultaneously to improve quality, control costs, decrease lot size, deliver finished goods in ever shorter time-cycles, and expand into new geographic markets. Developing the optimal balance of centralization and decentralization of different activities within the firm is more complex today. Learning how to capitalize effectively on cultural diversity, both within the firm and with multinational customers, is proving to be a major challenge for management teams in the turbulent 1990s.

These factors and others are making the development of both global strategic vision and strategic and operational plans more critical than ever before. Of equal importance is the re-evaluation of the *frequency* with which these activities must be performed. For example, the global strategic vision for an oil firm may have a time horizon of 30–40 years, while that of a high-fashion clothing designing firm may only be 6–12 months. This does not imply that the oil firm should re-examine its strategic vision only every 30 years, but it is safe to say that a major clothing manufacturing firm will need to review its global strategic vision frequently.

> *The current strategic and annual operational planning cycles are no longer relevant for many companies in today's economy.*

The formal planning process varies considerably from firm to firm. Few firms have been successful over long periods without the combination of an effective leadership team and a well-designed organizational plan. Major focus by many successful firms during the era of the 1950s to mid-1970s was concentrated on developing strategic planning and operational planning systems (*how* are we going to get there—doing the same basic activities more efficiently). Reliance strictly on these systems proved sufficient in an era where demand exceeded supply and the corporate focus was on how to provide more goods in the most cost-effective manner.

In today's rapidly changing global competitive market, corporations need to place greater emphasis on developing and updating their global strategic vision.

Figure 3.8 shows 25 specific potential problems in strategic thinking and strategic planning process.

I   *Incorrect assumptions regarding purpose*
1.   Assuming that all subsidiary and corporate managers and employees understand and agree on the purpose of the strategic thinking process and strategic planning process and on what will be accomplished for the firm and for themselves.
2.   Assuming that the strategic thinking process and the strategic planning process should be developed by a corporate planning department and implemented by subsidiary line management and the corporate staff.
3.   Assuming that the strategic thinking process and the strategic planning process are not part of the regular day-to-day management process.
4.   Failing to recognize that the strategic thinking process and the strategic planning process are also part of the cultural, leadership and political processes of the global organization.
5.   Failing to understand that the strategic thinking process and the strategic planning process are learning processes with a goal of developing a unified corporate strategic vision.

II   *Potential preparation problems*
6.   Failing to fully understand the planning procedure before initiating the planning processes.
7.   Delegating the strategic thinking process and the strategic planning process to a corporate planning department.
8.   Failing to recognize the power structure and cultural norms within the global company in preparation for the development of the firm's strategic thinking process and strategic planning process.
9.   Rejecting the need for the strategic thinking process because the corporation has previously achieved acceptable results using only conventional strategic planning tools.
10.   Failing to create a corporate climate that is conducive to the development of the strategic thinking process and the strategic planning process.

III   *Potential employee involvement problems*
11.   There is a failure to obtain the necessary involvement of key employees in staff and line assignments at the subsidiary and corporate levels.
12.   The planning process is highly centralized within the corporate planning department, with insufficient input from corporate staff and subsidiary staff personnel.
13.   Too many employees are involved with the process, resulting in a strategic vision and strategic plan that are too generic and not focused.
14.   Senior management spends insufficient time in the process because of the pressing demands of focusing on current problems.
15.   Senior management spends too much time with the strategic thinking process and the strategic planning process and fails to focus on current problems.

IV   *Potential process problems*

16.   The frequency with which the processes are conducted is no longer valid, and/or insufficient time is allocated to the process of strategic thinking and strategic planning.

17.   The process is too formal; it lacks simplicity, flexibility and cultural sensitivity and stymies creativity and teamwork, frustrating subsidiary and corporate participants.

18.   Strategic vision and strategic planning are merely updated, rather than 'starting from scratch'.

19.   The strategic planning (long-range plans) process does not follow and does not fully support strategic thinking process (mission and vision of the corporation).

20.   There is too great a focus on quantitative techniques and seeking precision in numbers.

V   *Potential problems with implementation and usage*

21.   Failure of all levels of subsidiary and corporate management and employees to review the strategic vision and strategic plans and gain consensus on *what* the organization will look like and *how* it will get there.

22.   Senior management's failure to follow the strategic vision and strategic plans.

23.   Failure to use strategic and annual operating plans as standards of measure for management performance.

24.   Inadequate rewards offered for effective strategic planning by focusing financial rewards solely on short-term results.

25.   Failure to properly emphasise that strategic plans are *guidelines*, and that the company must retain the flexibility to adapt to unexpected opportunities/threats.

Fig. 3.8   **Strategic thinking and strategic planning processes: potential problems**

Potential problems in strategic thinking and strategic planning processes

George Steiner developed a survey of 50 'Pitfalls in Comprehensive Long Range Planning' which was published in 1979. The survey included responses from 215 large corporations. Many of the pitfalls identified are still common problems today and are valuable to review.[16]

In today's global economy, the challenges for both strategic planning and strategic thinking in a multi-cultural global corporation are more complex than ever. We have developed a list of potential problems in the development and implementation of these important planning activities in global organizations. They are divided into five groupings:

- Incorrect assumptions regarding purpose
- Potential preparation problems
- Potential employee involvement problems
- Potential process problems
- Potential problems with implementation and usage

The following sub-sections briefly describe these potential problems in the strategic thinking and strategic planning processes. Figure 3.8 lists the 25 specific potential problems.

Incorrect assumptions regarding purpose

It is essential that all employees within the firm have a clear understanding of and support for the strategic vision of the organization, and that their daily activities are focused on the attainment of that vision. Development of the strategic thinking process and the strategic planning process require senior management's understanding that these are learning processes and are part of the cultural, leadership and political processes of the corporation. Subsidiaries, corporate staff and the corporate planning department all play a critical role in the development of these processes and their eventual implementation.

Potential preparation problems

A proper understanding of the preparation activities required for optimal development of these two processes is essential. Senior managers and corporate planners need to have a full recognition of the cultural norms and power structure to plan for the appropriate steps needed to gain maximal input and support for the strategic thinking and strategic planning processes. It is also senior management's responsibility to ensure that all managers understand the reasons for initiating the processes, and the need to establish a corporate climate that is conducive to conducting the sessions.

Potential employee involvement problems

Employees are the essential ingredient in the development and implementation of both the strategic vision and the support plans that flow from it. Choosing the right number and the right employees are critical for senior management. In the current business environment, many companies have reduced the layers of management, and have 'empowered' employees to make a greater number of decisions. It is important that as many people as possible at the lowest levels be involved in some aspects of the development of these plans. It is even more important that proper time be allocated to educate all employees on the strategic vision and operational plans of the organization.

Employees must fully understand and embrace the strategic vision:

> Primary and secondary leaders must be able to communicate the new mindset, articulating the vision and values in ways that are not only readily understandable and acceptable to all employees but that are inspirational also. In other words, the employees must believe that it is worth giving extraordinary effort to make the vision a reality.[17]

Potential process problems

Senior management must carefully determine the degree and frequency of change in the 12 environmental forces previously described in order to determine the appropriate frequency of change necessary to develop the organization's strategic vision. Corporate executives must guard against those within the firm who are comfortable with simply 'updating' the plan rather than doing a thorough redevelopment of it from scratch. In addition, this process of evolution must be flexible, simple, culturally sensitive and informal enough to be able to respond easily to the constant changes occurring.

Potential problems with implementation and usage

Reward systems need to be tied into performance and goal achievement as defined in the strategic and annual operations plans. Implementation of the organization's plans requires employees' involvement in the creation of these plans, their full understanding of the goals and objectives contained in the plans, and their acceptance of those goals and of the reward recognition attributed to the proper execution of the goals.

Selling the strategic vision

Developing a world-class global strategic vision is only half the battle; developing a world-class plan to 'sell the vision' is just as important (Fig. 3.9).

> It is precisely during these times of chaos that leaders must possess one property: the ability to develop and share a clearly defined sense of direction—a vision of the desired future.
>
> The strength of a leader's vision, and his or her ability to articulate that vision to employees, will be the measure of leadership in the 21st century organization.[18]

Employees are most likely to accept and focus their energies on an organization's global strategic vision to the extent of their:

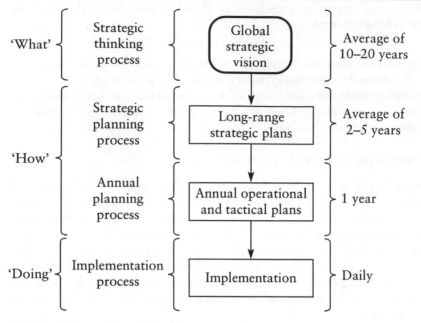

Fig. 3.9   The creation and implementation of strategic vision

- Participation in its development
- Thorough understanding of its meaning
- Acceptance that it reflects their fundamental beliefs and core values

Participation in development

Mission statements, the summary of the global strategic vision, are developed for the organization as a whole and for individual functional units. Although it is not practical for all employees to be involved personally in the development of the corporate global strategic vision, individual functional units will input environmental information that will be used to develop the strategic vision. Individual units will also develop mission statements that more finely describe their own specific roles in supporting the corporation's global strategic vision.

Role of senior management

Senior management must understand that the successful implementation of the global strategic vision is a primary accountability of theirs and requires leadership direction. They must encourage open participation by employees and open communications throughout the organization's hierarchy. Charles Fombrun describes Tichy and Devanna's transformational leader thus:

> Strategic changes therefore compel *transformational leadership*, that is, symbolic acts through which senior executives unshackle employees from the familiar constraints of bureaucracy. As some researchers argue, driven by grand passions, transformational leaders excel at articulating a new vision for their firms and mobilizing a critical mass of employees to commit to that vision. Unlike run-of-the-mill dictators, these transformational leaders both identify themselves as agents of change and act accordingly: they empower employees, insist on core values, faster learning and welcome ambiguity.[19]

Senior management must invest the personal time for discussion and interaction with middle management. Discussions concerning the vision must be viewed by all employees as a high priority of senior management. Workers should hear about the importance of the global strategic vision from their supervisors.

The role of the middle manager

Corporate failures can be attributed to improper *implementation* as often as to improper development. Middle and first-line managers frequently play a minor or even no role in the development of the global strategic vision (*what* the company will be in the future). They are, however, the keys to the successful implementation of *how* the company will achieve its global strategic vision. Organizations must fully plan for the proper role of middle managers to ensure the success of their global strategic vision.

Senior managers must ensure that they effectively communicate the global strategic vision to middle management and that middle managers link their unit mission and job responsibilities to the global strategic vision. Senior managers must also develop a system to receive critical information from middle management, which is necessary for the development of the global strategic vision.[20]

Alan Brache, director of product development for Kepner-Tregoe, suggests that middle management has four major responsibilities in strategy implementation:

- To learn about their organization's strategy by asking the top team for answers to specific questions

- To view their jobs strategically, maximizing their contribution to the strategic goals and using the standards suggested by the strategy to guide their performance

- To gather information on the implementation of the strategy (how are things progressing) and on whether the strategy itself is 'correct'

- To provide feedback in terms of both information and recommendations that enable top management to direct the implementation effort and, if necessary, adjust the strategy[21]

Teams

Successful global corporations thrive in a culturally diverse environment. Proper implementation of a global strategic vision will require input, understanding and endorsement from diverse employees around the globe. The development of the global strategic vision and its appropriate implementation will require both global and local team development to achieve consensus and a shared understanding, and to focus on the vision. It is essential that diversity be viewed as a strength and that teams be formulated with diversity as a clear goal.

> In fact, homogeneity and consensus in top teams appears to reduce corporate performance when firms are competing in turbulent environments. So, when contemplating strategic change, effective CEOs do not surround themselves with yes men. Greater diversity of opinions and lack of agreement force top managers to process more information during decision making, and so to consider more alternatives.[22]

Strategy in the global corporation

Global *and* local

Developing strategic thinking and strategic planning in a domestic organization is a challenge in today's world. Attempting to develop a global strategic vision presents unique challenges for both the CEO and the senior management of the corporation. The exponential increase in the complexity involved in developing a global strategic vision as opposed to a domestic-only strategic vision entails addressing the following issues:

- Global environmental forces
- National strategies and global strategies
- Planning processes involving subsidiary and corporate inputs

Global environmental forces

The consideration of environmental forces from a number of countries significantly complicates the strategic thinking process of firms involved in non-domestic markets. Consideration of such factors as non-domestic competitors, government intervention, exchange-rate fluctuations, global transportation costs, patent protection, tariffs, economies of scale, global sourcing, the need for local adaptability, political instability, technological standardization, etc., will also influence the global strategic vision of the global corporation.

National strategies and global strategies

Not all products are suited to global strategies. Factors that favor national strategies include overriding preferences for local adaptability and tastes, tariff regulations and high transportation costs. Examples would include food producers, cement manufacturers and beverage companies.

Global strategies are more suited to those products that can benefit from homogeneous demand, economies of scale, global sourcing of labor, energy, raw materials, etc. Computer manufacturing and electronic parts are examples of products that benefit from global strategies.

Markets and barriers

Many global corporations find that they need to develop both global and national strategies, the latter based on the environmental impact of regions and individual nations. Leontiades notes:

> Given the diversity of national and regional environments, some firms find that no strategy can be applied uniformly on a world basis. In countries where tariffs, local content programs, financial control, or other problems impede cross-border transfers, companies may find that they have little choice but to pursue a strategy that is predominantly nationally oriented. In other parts of the world, they may find that they are able to implement the cross-national coordination necessary to develop a more global competitive approach.[23]

Those countries with the largest national market size and the lowest national barriers are the most conducive to global strategies compared with those economies having the smallest national markets and highest national barriers.

Business focus and geographic focus

Global corporate strategies are further compounded by decisions to manage 2 product portfolios across both businesses and geographic borders.

George Yip categorizes the challenge for product strategy as follows:

1. *Fragmented multilocal strategy*: no organizational structure integrating either countries within a business or businesses within a country

2. *Integrated country strategies*: an approach whereby the country manager develops the strategies for all products

3. *Integrated business global strategy*: an approach whereby corporate business groups establish strategies to be implemented across countries

4. *Integrated corporate global strategy*: an approach that fully integrates both business and countries

One strategy is not necessarily correct for all businesses within a corporation.

> Last, companies need not adopt just one of the four modes depicted . . . A mixture can be best, allowing some businesses (those in industries with low globalization potential) to be managed on a country-by-country basis, some countries (those with high barriers to trade) to operate independently with extensive control over the businesses in them, and other countries and businesses to be part of an integrated global matrix.[24]

The global integrated planning process

The development of a global strategy is infinitely more complicated than a national strategy because of the need to develop a cross-country planning effort involving subsidiary and corporate managers. Input from many layers of management in multiple geographic and business functions is necessary in the complex technological and competitive environments of today. Senior managements of successful global concerns rely heavily on joint task forces, project teams and cross-functional teams to arrive at optimal global strategies. Doz, Bartlett and Prahalad provide an example:

> Bristol Myers created a pharmaceutical council within its international organization to allow geographic line managers and business development staff managers to debate new product priorities before deciding on the long-term product development strategy to be submitted to its corporate research policy committee. Proposals coming out of the pharmaceutical council incorporate the appropriate balance between the demands for global competitiveness and local responsiveness, and typically had the support and commitment of the management group involved in their development.[25]

Siemens, the large European-based electrical manufacturer, is a global corporation with 75 per cent of its sales in Europe. Klaus Dunst, vice-president for corporate development at Siemens–US, recently discussed Siemens' strategy formulation process:

> At Siemens, global strategy formulation does not mean centralized control. Developing corporate strategy includes the active involvement of senior managers of our major regional companies. Siemens Corporation in the United States acts as a management holding company supporting the group's worldwide strategies while also representing Siemens' overall U.S. interests.
>
> How we balance central and regional responsibilities for value-adding activities—product development, manufacturing, selling and service—depends on the type of business. Some businesses have the entire value chain within their home markets, from which they may also export. Others are based in a certain region but draw on value-adding activities from elsewhere. The remaining

businesses encompass the entire value chain regionally and have some worldwide responsibilities.[26]

The mission statement in the global organization

Organizations beginning their expansion into non-domestic markets may assume there is no need to re-examine their mission statements. However, when companies expand operations into foreign countries, their strategic decisions will be influenced by information that is derived from these countries, and which should be included in the planning process. These considerations will impact on the unit's mission statement and its strategic vision. The organization's mission statement transcends locations, times and strategies to reflect a consistent broadly based organizational strategic vision.[27]

Summary

The rapidly changing global competitive market requires all organizations to create an appropriate global strategic vision. The strategic thinking process assists CEOs and their staffs to clarify *what* they want their organization to be in the future and *how* they will achieve it. Senior executives must also understand and avoid the potential pitfalls that frequently impair an organization's ability to fully develop its global strategic vision. Management must understand the factors that must be considered when evolving from a domestic-only to a global strategic vision.

Optimal worldwide performance starts with a universally understood and accepted global strategic vision. All employees must focus their energies on a common mission to achieve maximal results. Formal organizational structure, the ideal flow of knowledge among workers, and appropriate centralization/decentralization of decision-making must all follow and support the development of the global strategic vision.

Notes and references

1. Michel Robert, *Strategy Pure and Simple*, McGraw-Hill, New York, 1993.
2. Patrick J. Below, George L. Morrisey and Betty L. Acomb, *The Executive Guide to Strategic Planning*, Jossey-Bass, San Francisco, 1987.
3. Burt Nanus, *Visionary Leadership*, Jossey-Bass, San Francisco, 1992.
4. Lester B. Korn, 'Identifying strategic capabilities', *Restructuring and Managing Change*, Conference Board Report no. 952, pp. 7–8.
5. Andrew Tanzer, 'Bury thy teacher', *Forbes*, 21 December 1992, pp. 90–5.

6. Brenton R. Schlender, 'The perils of losing focus', *Fortune*, 17 May 1993, p. 100.

7. James C. Leontiades, *Multinational Corporate Strategy*, Lexington Books, Lexington, Mass., 1985, p. 7.

8. David W. Cravens and Shannon H. Shipp, 'Market-driven strategies for competitive advantage', *Business Horizons*, January–February 1991, pp. 53–61.

9. Benjamin B. Tregoe, John W. Zimmerman, Ronald A. Smith, Peter M. Tobia, *Vision in Action: Putting a Winning Strategy to Work*, Fireside Books, New York, 1990.

10. Peter F. Drucker, 'The new society of organizations', *Harvard Business Review*, September–October 1992, pp. 95–104.

11. Andrew Campbell and Sally Young, *Do You Need a Mission Statement?*, Economist Publications Management Guides, Special Report no. 1208, London, July 1990.

12. John A. Pearce and Kendall Roth, 'Multinationalization of the mission statement', *SAM Advanced Management Journal*, Summer 1988, pp. 39–44.

13. Drucker, op. cit., pp. 95–104.

14. Pearce and Roth, op. cit., pp. 39–44.

15. Ibid.

16. George A. Steiner, *Strategic Planning*, Free Press, New York, 1979.

17. Richard W. Beatty and David O. Ulrich, 'Re-energizing the mature organization', *Organizational Dynamics*, Summer 1991, pp. 16–30.

18. Bob Wall, Robert S. Solum and Mark R. Sobol, *The Visionary Leader*, Prima Publishing, Rocklin, Cal., 1992.

19. Charles J. Fombrun, *Turning Points: Creating Strategic Change in Corporations*, McGraw-Hill, New York, 1992.

20. See Alan Brache, 'Strategy and the middle manager', *Training*, April 1986, pp. 31–4.

21. Ibid.

22. Fombrun, op. cit.

23. Leontiades, op. cit.

24. George S. Yip, *Total Global Strategy*, Prentice-Hall, Englewood Cliffs, NJ, 1992.

25. Yves L. Doz, Christopher A. Bartlett and C. K. Prahalad, 'Global competitive pressures and host country demands', *California Management Review*, 23 (3), 1981, pp. 63–74.

26. Klaus H. Dunst, 'Establishing a balance in the global company', Conference Board Report no. 975, *Strategic Planning for Action and Results*, 1991, pp. 33–5.

27. See Pearce and Roth, op. cit., pp. 39–44.

Why is Western industry on the decline? . . .
The cause of the decline is that management
have walked off the job of management,
striving instead for dividends and good
performance of the price of the company's
stock. A better way to serve stockholders
would be to stay in business with constant
improvement of quality of product and
service, thus to decrease costs, capture
markets, provide jobs, and increase divi-
dends.

W. EDWARDS DEMING
in *The Deming Management Method* by Mary Walton

4 Quality challenges and the globalization process

Global business success in the new millennium will require superior quality performance in both product and service provision. *Product quality* is a given in today's global arena—it is a basic requirement to compete. Those organizations that will excel will be those that truly 'delight' the customer and provide 'added' value as defined by the customer. *Service quality* may be provided by helping customers lower costs or by otherwise improving their ability to provide better service to *their* customers.

Learning to excel at both product quality and service quality is challenging even in a national environment. Attempting to excel on a global basis requires a different leadership mindset, the development of a unified global quality vision, special skill training for all employees, and the evolution of a worldwide quality culture throughout the organization. The roles of senior managers, middle managers and line workers all change dramatically in this new environment. Employees must develop a new understanding of how work processes are similar/dissimilar on a global/national basis. The importance of both vertical functional work processes and horizontal cross-functional work processes must be clearly understood and accepted. The global corporation must see itself as a learning organization, one that is in a perpetual state of change focused on continuous improvement and innovation. This organization is the *GQL* (GQL) organization.

Leadership mindset

Managers responsible for GQL understand that the complexities of mastering quality excellence in a global arena require added dimensions as compared with a national program. Stephen Rhinesmith has identified six key mindsets required of global leaders:[1]

1. People with global mindsets focus on the broader picture and are constantly looking for context. They are never content with one explanation for an event.

2. People with global mindsets understand that the world is complex and that life is constantly presented with contradictory forces and outlooks. Conflict management is a key skill needed for all global managers.

3. People with global mindsets place greater trust in organizational processes than in formal hierarchial structures. Organizational processes such as information and decision-making processes as well as norms of behavior are valued highly by global leaders.

4. People with global mindsets value multi-cultural teamwork and diversity. Global managers require flexibility and sensitivity.

5. People with global mindsets view change as an opportunity and are comfortable with ambiguity and surprises.

6. People with global mindsets continually challenge their own paradigms, experiences and assumptions. They are constantly seeking to improve themselves and those around them

GQL: evolutionary phases

The phases of evolution of GQL directly mirror the phases of evolution in the global economy described in Chapter 1. It is a basic premiss of business that industry leaders will rise to meet the expectations of the marketplace; so is it true of the evolutionary phases of GQL?

Phase One: 1945–1975

The three decades spanning the end of World War II were characterized by a newly freed world with an unquenchable thirst for goods. In the early years of this era emphasis was placed on quantity production and economies of scale. As competition increased, companies improved efficiencies through focused manufacturing planning that complemented market needs

Phase Two: 1975–1985

The economies of the world experienced a major shift in industrial focus during the mid-1970s. Surplus supply and over-capacity developed in many industries. The purchasing options for customers improved dramatically. Value rather than availability became the norm. This dramatic reversal inaugurated the birth of the quality initiative in firms around the globe. Corporations focused intensely inward to improve the quality of the products they produced. Emphasis on just-in-time (JIT) manufacturing, zero defects, meeting specifications and 'kaizen' became the norm to millions of employees.

Phase Three: 1985–2000

The 1980s saw tremendous gains in the quality of products produced. Many of those companies that failed significantly to improve their quality were forced out of business, absorbed by other firms or became marginal players in the global arena. Customers have grown to demand superior quality as a given. Organizations that will be flourishing as we enter the year 2000 will be those that embrace the catch-phrase 'Delighting the Customer'. Success in the remainder of the 1990s will be enjoyed by those firms that live by a philosophy that regards employees, customers and suppliers as equal partners in their GQL process.[2]

The essential elements of GQL

GQL requires world-class companies to be simultaneously *internally focused* (conforming to requirements) and *externally focused* (excelling in customer satisfaction). Many companies around the world are still catching up with the internal requirements of GQL. Companies will be required to develop a significant *paradigm shift* to achieve GQL. Developing the motivation and skills to focus simultaneously internally on processes and externally on 'delighting' the customer, and to create a single unified global vision with a globally diverse workforce, will be a major determinant of success in this decade.

Criteria for success

In order to prepare for these challenges, senior management must understand the criteria for success via GQL. These include:

Global environment

- Need for a 'global mindset'
- Formal and informal organizational structural dynamics
- GQL mission and vision
- Cultural change requirements with GQL
- The role of senior management, middle management and line workers
- The value of training

Internal processes

- Process improvement
- Manufacturing processes and business processes
- Benchmarking

External processes: 'delighting the customer'

- Focus on the customer

- Quality—conformance to requirements

- Speed

- Flexibility

- Service quality

- Focus on results

Needs and goals

Executives engaged in global quality initiatives need to pay careful attention to the similarities and differences of perceived needs and goals among their various subsidiaries and headquarters. A unified global strategic vision and common focus are essential if the corporation's goals are to be achieved. Throughout this chapter we will refer to various recent studies that compare the attitudes of companies from a variety of countries with the critical components of GQL.

A recent European study by Knight Wendling[3] focused on the emerging quality issues of the 1990s. The Knight Wendling report highlighted the following as key demands for change in the new Europe:

- 94% of the European companies responding to the survey said they are currently conducting quality improvement programs.

- 93% reported that the demands for quality and service have never been higher.

- 92% stated that quality problems are company issues—not just production issues.

- 89% benchmark themselves against industry rivals.

- 73% have a formal process to measure their customers' perceptions of quality.

- 73% are focusing greater emphasis on the task of controlling logistics.

- 63% have initiated customer awareness programs in their companies.

- 54% benchmark themselves against companies in other industries.

Ernst & Young and the American Quality Foundation recently conducted a survey of 102 areas of management practices related to global quality. Participation consisted of more than 500 companies from Germany, Canada, Japan and the United States within the banking, computer, automotive and health care industries.[4] The key findings of this study indicate the following:

- *Business performance.*   Virtually all corporations in the survey view quality as a critical success factor in their strategic performance. The use of quality performance as a criterion for compensating senior management has been used sparingly in the past but will rise significantly across all countries.

- *Customer focus.*   Less than 50 per cent of the surveyed companies make customer input an integral part of the strategic planning process.

- *Competitors in the strategic process.*   Benchmarking competitive activity currently occurs more frequently in Japanese and US companies and less frequently in Canadian and German companies

- *Process improvement.*   Japanese firms consistently outperform German, US and Canadian firms in their use of routine process simplification.

- *Employee involvement.*   Japanese firms maintain the highest rate of routine employee participation in scheduled meetings about quality.

A 1992 study of over 2000 US manufacturing companies was conducted by A. T. Kearney.[5] Over 200 CEOs participated in comprehensive, in-depth interviews. The findings indicate that US manufacturers see themselves as moving toward parity with their non-US competitors. These CEOs analyzed 47 determinants of competitiveness, and 15 factors were rated as critical by at least 74 per cent of them (Table 4.1). The relatively high ratings given to such a large number of factors is indicative of the CEOs' recognition of the complexity of GQL.

Core elements

Uncertainty and the rapid rate of change in today's economy require that companies develop a solid foundation in the core elements of GQL. Global corporations will not be successful in developing world-class quality products and services that 'delight' the customer without first establishing the five core elements on which GQL is founded (Fig. 4.1):

1. *Shared global vision* of the organization's strategic mission
2. *Organizational dynamics* that clearly identifies the roles of senior managers, middle managers and line workers
3. *Organizational hierarchy* that supports the strategic mission
4. *Corporate quality culture* development needed to produce world-class quality
5. *Global quality training requirements*

Fig. 4.1   Global quality leadership (GQL): core foundation elements

Table 4.1   US manufacturing competitiveness: top 15 determinants of competitiveness

Determinants of competitiveness	% of CEOs
Finished product quality	90
Focus on quality processes by total organization	89
Marketing	88
Customer service provided	85
Manufacturing production	84
Product price	82
Education/skills—white-collar workforce	82
Employee commitment and continuity	76
Process or manufacturing technology	76
Product engineering	75
Investment in R&D	74
Product technology	74
User economics	74
Manufacturing engineering/process engineering	74
Productivity of white-collar workforce	74

Source: A. T. Kearney, survey on 'US Manufacturing Competitiveness', 1992.

It is essential for corporations to master the five core elements that form the basis for GQL before becoming too involved with implementation programs such as JIT, quality circles, total quality control, process improvement projects, *kaizen* and inventory reduction. All of us can cite examples of failure or of only modest success with 'quality' programs that focused extensively on implementation programs and paid inadequate preparation and attention to the core elements of GQL.

Shared vision of the organization's strategic mission

A successful GQL program requires all personnel of the organization to develop a shared 'global strategic vision' of the company and of its quality initiative. This is a monumental task when one considers the problems of communicating and gaining acceptance of such a concept across multiple cultures and geographic locations.

A well-designed shared global strategic vision of the organization clearly defines the businesses the organization will be concerned with in the future. A *quality vision statement* will clearly explain how the organization will work after quality improvement thinking has occurred. It will describe how things will get done and who will be responsible for what. Most importantly, it will embrace the values and beliefs that will motivate all employees to pursue quality excellence in a united, focused manner.[6,7]

The quality vision statement must be developed with a clear view to the future and must be based on a set of quality principles that are understood and embraced by all employees. It is important that the senior managers who develop the quality vision statement focus on the end-results desired without allowing themselves to be limited by current perceived obstacles to their success.[8,9]

Organizational dynamics

The roles of senior management, middle management and line workers require new focus and skills for companies pursuing GQL (Fig. 4.2). Many problem-solving decisions and responsibilities will be driven downward. The organization will begin to see that the previous number of layers of management are no longer needed to successfully accomplish unit goals.

Role of senior management.   The focus of senior management's activity is to create a clear, unified strategic vision of the future direction of the company. Senior management must also develop an appropriate strategy to achieve the unified vision while balancing both short-term and long-term company needs. Some of senior management's decision-making responsibilities will be transferred to lower levels of management.

Role of middle management.   Middle management's role evolves from one focused primarily on directing to one with an emphasis on coaching. This evolutionary change requires special training and is a difficult transition for many first-line supervisors. A major responsibility of middle management is to assimilate and transfer the corporation's quality vision statement and strategies into everyday tactical activities. Middle managers must develop an atmosphere that encourages work-teams and group problem-solving. They must assist line workers in identifying key problem areas, and they must empower workers to develop and initiate solutions.

Role of line workers.   Those closest to the work have always been the most knowledgeable concerning what actions are needed to improve efficiency. Under a GQL program, empowered line workers are encouraged to work closely with cross-functional teams to develop process improvement and product innovation.

Restructuring the organizational hierarchy

Organizational restructuring is a powerful tool of the GQL organization. Corporations can develop strategic competitive advantage by continuously adapting the organization's hierarchy when the changes are focused on achieving its 'quality vision'. Unfortunately, very few restructuring decisions are based on a clear vision of the long-term goals of the

Old paradigm	New paradigm
1. Quality is the responsibility of line workers and first line supervisors	1. Senior management is responsible for quality and must establish a unified 'quality vision' complementary to cultural and geographic differences
2. Quality is the responsibility of the quality control department	2. Quality is everyone's responsibility
3. Line workers follow directions from management on quality initiatives	3. Line workers are empowered to initiate quality improvements and to improve work processes
4. Training is formalized, generic and focused on line workers	4. Training starts with senior management; training programs are developed locally and focus on local needs while supporting the 'quality vision'
5. Vertical work processes and hierarchial control dominate; unit goals take precedence over customer needs	5. Cross-functional work processes are viewed as the critical focus of how work is done and focused on the customer's needs
6. The degree of emphasis on quality varies by department and subsidiary	6. Emphasis on a corporate 'quality culture' with all employees focused on the needs of the customer

Fig. 4.2 The evolving paradigm for the new economic era: organizational hierarchy and dynamics

organization. Few corporations carefully access their global strategic vision and modify their organizational structures to best align themselves with the long-term needs of the organization. Many companies restructure as a *reactive* mechanism to short-term pressures and tend to organize to achieve short-term objectives.

The classic example is those corporations that reduce head count and expenses equally among units and divisions. Although many managers may view this as 'fair', the better decision would be to carefully examine the future global strategic vision of the company, and reorganize human and financial assets in a way that will maximize the long-term goals of the organization.

Quality culture change

Successful corporations of the future will demonstrate the ability to develop and embrace changes in senior management accountabilities, middle management focus and line worker acceptance of responsibility and empowerment. The evolution of these new roles is difficult to develop in a national environment; developing these changes in a global environment is even more challenging. Corporations practicing GQL will need to be successful in developing a global attitude and a global culture focused on superior quality and customer service.

Companies engaged in quality initiatives should carefully scrutinize educational and training programs to ensure that they actively account for national cultural differences. One program rarely fits all.

Several excellent recent studies have documented cultural differences towards quality and customer service. A recent study by Knight Wendling focused on Dutch, German and British attitudes toward quality.[10] It found that:

- 82% of UK customers were perceived to be more influenced by price compared with 65% of Germany customers.

- 82% of UK customers were seen to be influenced by quality compared with 65% of Dutch customers.

- 63% of Germany and UK companies planned to change the way they organized customer service activity compared with only 30% of Dutch companies.

A clear and unified culture among all workers in all geographic locations is needed to meet the competitive pressures of the 1990s. This common culture, spearheaded by a shared global strategic vision, will be a basic requirement to compete successfully in the remaining years of this decade. Peter Drucker has noted:

> Because the modern organization is composed of specialists, each with his or her own narrow area of expertise, its mission must be crystal clear. The organization must be single-minded, or its members will become confused. They will follow their own specialty rather than apply it to the common task. They will each define results in terms of their own specialty and impose its values on the organization. Only a focused and common mission will hold the organization together and enable it to produce. Without such a mission, the organization will soon lose credibility and, with it, its ability to attract the very people it needs to perform.[11]

The cultural change required in GQL focuses on *common, shared values*. Implementing a change in quality culture requires a program of well-designed education and coaching. All employees must share in the same experience and develop a common business language and a common focus based upon shared values with a common mission.[12]

Global quality training

Appropriate training measures are necessary to ensure a smooth transition in culture and to enable the quality revolution to develop in a predictable fashion.

According to Juran,[13] quality training should include the entire hierarchy of the company and should begin with senior management. Juran recommends a training program that is designed by broadly based task forces rather than prefabricated, commercially available courses. The basic purpose of quality training should be to change behavior, and line managers should participate in the planning of the training program.

Programs that will be rolled out to subsidiaries require early input from senior subsidiary management. These training programs should be written at the subsidiary level while using the corporate program as a prototype. This will allow for proper cultural adaptation and proper language translation.

World-class training programs will enable workers to:

1. Understand the need for quality improvement and not rebel against it

2. Develop a sense of unified global vision and mission which will be reflected in increased productivity

3. Utilize new tools to solve problems

4. Identify customers' true needs

5. Show how each employee fits into the organizational structure

6. Help create a culture devoted to problem-solving and to continuous improvement

7. Develop new organizational models based on employee initiative, teamwork and multi-skills[14]

Process innovation: adding value to products

The majority of today's global corporations continue to struggle with outdated functional hierarchies that organize work around traditional approaches to managing people, processes and information. Our corporate structures are often bureaucratic and lack sufficient flexibility to allow cross-functional processes to adequately meet customer demands. Information tends to be centralized in traditional corporate hierarchies, and unit objectives often supersede customer needs.[15]

Cross-functional process teams

Cross-functional processes (Fig. 4.3) provide a basic solution to meeting customer needs by providing empowered employees with the ability to develop process improvements, increase speed of delivery, allow greater flexibility, improve cross-divisional communication and information-sharing, allow for more concurrent (as opposed to sequential) production flows and eliminate duplicative or unnecessary steps.

It is important that senior managers, middle managers and line workers *view all work as a process*. If all employees focus their energies on meeting and exceeding customer demands, the organization's fundamental approach to work will result in a recognition of the value of vertical, functional needs and horizontal, cross-functional needs. This new approach will allow employees to see the firm as a flexible, changing organism.

In autumn 1992, Compaq Computer Corporation introduced its Pro-Lineas line of computers to Japan and undercut market-leader NEC's prices by 50 per cent . In October 1992 Compaq cut prices by as much as 32 per cent across all product lines in the United States. Compaq executives said the move was in line with their new high-volume strategy and the economies of scale they had achieved. A critical component of this new strategy had been changes in the manufacturing process initiated in Compaq's global plants:

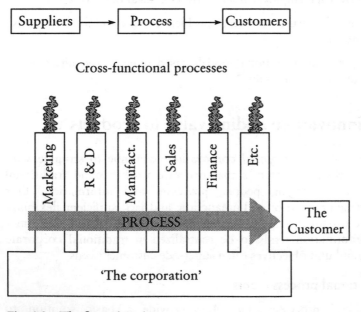

Fig. 4.3   The flow of work

To get manufacturing costs down at the plants in Houston, Singapore, and Scotland, Compaq had to rethink its processes. It started building an entire system on a single assembly line instead of making the motherboard in one building and the chassis in another. It stopped testing every subassembly and now tests a sample. All finished systems are still fully tested.[16]

Work process flow: vertical and horizontal work processes

Global work processes

Work processes that transcend functional, business and geographic activities between subsidiaries and corporate headquarters significantly compound the flow of work (Figs 4.4 and 4.5). Many corporations are still

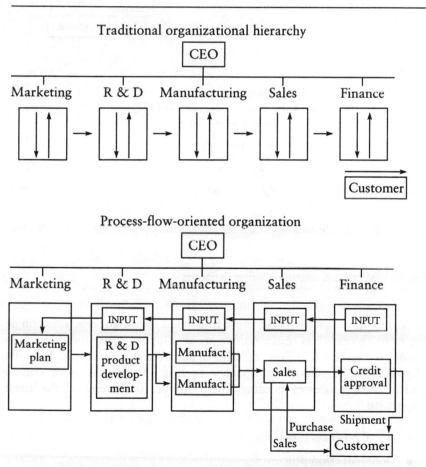

Fig. 4.4 Work process flow and vertical and horizontal work processes

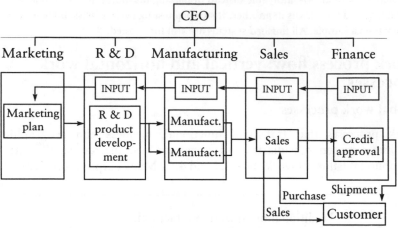

Micro work-flow processes
(*within* subsidiaries or division HQ)

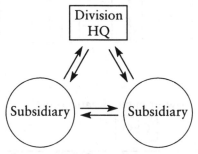

Macro work-flow processes
(*between* subsidiaries and division HQ)

Fig. 4.5   Micro and macro work-flow processes

struggling to improve basic cross-functional work processes in single locations. World-class organizations are developing transnational process teams to examine the flow of critical global work processes. It is the responsibility of senior management to help identify the most critical global work processes needing attention, i.e. to determine the most important:

- Global business processes

- Global function processes

- Global geographic processes

Success in the coming decade will depend on the corporation's ability to develop process teams on a global basis to improve products in a timely and cost-effective manner. The importance of developing a unified global quality vision and a united corporate quality culture cannot be too strongly emphasized.

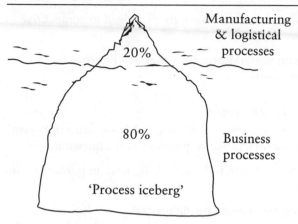

Fig. 4.6   Corporate processes: the 'hidden iceberg'

Focus on business processes

Most corporations have traditionally started quality programs and process improvement projects in the areas of manufacturing and logistics.

In the remainder of the 1900s, successful enterprises will make process improvement a company-wide activity. If we carefully examine all company processes, it is likely that we will find that *at least 80 per cent of work processes are non-manufacturing businesses processes* (Fig. 4.6). This would include all those work processes associated with:

- Office administration
- Corporate finance
- Corporate accounting
- Engineering
- Marketing
- Sales
- Human resources
- Information systems

Corporations need to refocus their efforts to improve their business processes during the remainder of the 1990s. Focusing on improving business processes will result in:

- Improving market share by improving the key business processes
- Reducing costs by identifying and eliminating waste
- Allowing the corporation to focus on the customer to meet/exceed customer expectations
- Developing cross-functional teamwork that can lead to competitive advantage
- Establishing/adapting business processes that will improve both efficiency and effectiveness

Recent studies on process improvement

In the 1992 Grant Thornton 'Survey of American Manufacturers Report', of the 504 medium-size manufacturers responding to the question,

Thinking about innovation generally, which is most important to the health of the US economy?

- 47% said improving the manufacturing process
- 30% said developing new products
- 18% said improving existing products

Ernst & Young's 'International Quality Study' revealed major differences among countries on their views concerning process simplification. When asked whether businesses always or almost always use process simplification,

- 47% of Japanese firms said that they did, and
- 19% of Canadian firms
- 12% of US firms
- 6% of German firms

Global competition will force business to make every effort to improve the quality of their products at lower cost. Process simplification is a basic tool to achieve this goal.

Global benchmarking

Global benchmarking is an essential tool for corporations in the development of the strategic planning process. Global benchmarking helps companies gain the knowledge of their relative strengths and weaknesses in essential business processes and core competencies. Benchmarking consumes considerable human resource time and budget funds. It is essential that senior management focuses global benchmarking activities on those areas that indicate the need to improve performance in core business competencies and on those areas that truly distinguish the company's performance compared with its competitors.[17]

True global benchmarking will require a company to compare its key business processes with other units within the firm, other firms in the industry, other unrelated industries and the 'best' firms globally. The study by Ernst & Young and the American Quality Foundation reported that only high-performing companies derive strong benefits from benchmarking.[18]

It is important that information about competitors be carefully considered during the development of the global strategic vision. One must carefully consider the future direction that competitors and potential competitors may take (Fig. 4.7). With regard to the 580 companies participating in the 'International Quality Study' by Ernst & Young, when asked whether they regarded the importance of competitors' comparisons as primary in the development of their global strategic vision,

- 32% of Japanese firms replied that they did, and

- 29% of US firms

- 25% of Canadian firms

- 5% of German firms

Of the 504 US firms participating in the 1992 Grant Thornton 'Survey of American Manufacturers', a staggering 65 per cent reported that they had never practiced competitive benchmarking. Of the 35 per cent that had practiced it, the companies benchmarked themselves as follows:

- 81% against a competitor

- 72% against the industry as a whole

Xerox is highly recognized as one of the original firms that developed benchmarking. In the later 1970s Canon introduced a mid-size copier that sold for less than the unit cost price of the Xerox copier. Xerox adapted its manufacturing practices between 1980 and 1985 and was successful in cutting its manufacturing costs in half and its inventory by two-thirds. Since that time, Xerox's share of the US market has grown nearly 50 per cent to roughly 15 per cent.[19]

Old paradigm	New paradigm
1. Quality is defined as conformance to standards or specifications	1. Quality is defined as 'delighting' the customer by surpassing expectations for production quality and customer service
2. Focus on meeting 'minimum-quality standards', permitting some defects to be passed on	2. Focus on defect-free products through appropriate process improvement techniques
3. Short-term view of suppliers; cost-centered; frequent switching and little loyalty	3. Suppliers are highly valued and viewed as 'partners'; fewer suppliers are selected, with an intense focus on quality and long-term relationship
4. Emphasis on quality decreases productivity and increases cost	4. Quality is a requirement to compete; higher quality and perceived value generate greater profits
5. Quality initiatives are 'inner-directed' and focused on manufacturing and logistics	5. Quality initiatives are 'inner-directed' and 'outer-directed', involving significant input from suppliers and customers
6. Improvement efforts are focused on manufacturing and logistics	6. Business process improvements account for 80% of GQL activity, with manufacturing and logistic accounting for only 20%

Fig. 4.7 The evolving paradigm for the new economic era: characteristics of quality

Quality and profitability

Perceived quality and profitability are directly related. The landmark work conducted by the Profit Impact of Market Strategy (PIMS) program clearly documents that superior quality is the single most important factor in a business unit's performance over time. The PIMS database consists of over 450 companies and 3000 business units. Research by Buzzell and Gale indicates that relative costs are equivalent for both low- and high-quality products.[20] They emphasize that the benefits to high-quality producers include:

- Stronger customer loyalty
- More repeat purchases
- Less vulnerability to price wars
- Ability to command higher relative price without affecting share
- Lower marketing costs
- Improvements in market share

The Ernst & Young 'International Quality Study'[21] showed that more than half of all businesses in the four countries studied frequently evaluated the impact of quality on financial performance. The results showed that senior management does *not* review the consequences of quality performance at least annually in:

- 18% of US companies
- 14% of Canadian companies
- 9% of German companies
- 2% of Japanese companies

Quality performance and executive compensation

Senior management compensation (Fig. 4.8) is tied to some degree to quality results in less than 20 per cent of all companies in all countries surveyed by Ernst & Young. Their report indicates that this trend will change dramatically in all countries surveyed during the next three years: the importance of quality improvement as an assessment criterion for executive compensation in 1995 will be primary in:

- 31% of Japanese companies
- 35% of Canadian companies
- 39% of German companies
- 51% of US companies[22]

Old paradigm	New paradigm
1. Measurement systems focused on unit objectives	1. Measurement systems focused on degree of customer satisfaction
2. Focus on inspection	2. Focus on designing work processes that eliminate defects and the need for inspection
3. Rewards rarely linked to quality	3. Compensation systems designed to base rewards partially on quality performance
4. Emphasis on production quantity, not quality; not individual oriented goals	4. Emphasis on improving quality and productivity with compensation and stock ownership as rewards for excellence in group performance

Fig. 4.8 **The evolving paradigm for the new economic era: measurement and rewards**

Results-driven versus activity-centered quality programs

It is well documented that many company quality programs have met with minimal financial impact on corporate earnings. Schaffer and Thomson have noted that 'activity-centered' quality programs confuse ends with means, processes with outcomes. Activity-centered programs focus on benchmarking, assessing customers' expectations, and training employees in problem-solving. Consultants frequently tell management not to focus on improving results because results will eventually occur as an end-product of the quality improvement activities mentioned.[23]

Results-driven quality programs are focused on achieving measurable gains quickly. Schaffer and Thomson emphasize that results-driven programs prioritize process innovations based upon the targeted goals they wish to achieve. Modifications to work style, leadership style and customer relationships are introduced as they appear to be able to accelerate change in speeding progress toward achieving measurable goals. This is in contrast to traditional activity-centered programs, which send all employees to generic quality training programs and to initiating dozens of activity-centered projects. Results-driven programs introduce each process and managerial innovation in an organized and sequential fashion focused on short-term goals. This method enables them quickly to discover to what degree each change yields results.[24]

Focus on the customer

Customer demands will continue to escalate throughout the remainder of this decade. Suppliers will experience ever-increasing requirements for improved quality, flexibility to produce small lot sizes at ever reducing costs, and turnaround times of hours instead of days and weeks. All of this will be further compounded by the fact that both customers and competitors will be located throughout the world.

Focusing on the customer will become paramount. Suppliers and customers will grow closer together and will come to behave more as partners. Mutual dependence will escalate as customers rely on fewer suppliers. Suppliers will demand greater loyalty and exclusive sourcing privileges in exchange for meeting the growing demands of customers.

Suppliers and manufacturers will be required to develop 'real-time' market knowledge of what is happening in the marketplace. Information transferability among workers will reach unimagined heights.

All workers will need to be operating in a synonymous mode with a unified global vision of the direction of the organization. Cross-functional work-teams and processes focused on 'delighting' the customer will rule. Although organizational hierarchies will remain in place, they will exist with fewer layers of management, and their focus will evolve from control-oriented to coordination-oriented activities. Cultural diversity will be viewed as a strength, and successful organizations will invest heavily in appropriate skill training for all employees. The most successful senior management teams will focus on strategic thinking and planning functions and will empower middle management to make key tactical decisions and to provide coaching to line workers. Line workers will be empowered, to the appropriate level, to foster continuous improvement in customer-focused manufacturing and businesses processes. Financial rewards will reflect the achievement of quality and financial targets.

The customer, then, will be king. Successful global companies of the 1990s understand that the bellwether test of quality is understanding, meeting and exceeding customers' requirements—'delighting' the customer. All quality initiatives and utilization of quality tools must be singularly focused on wildly exceeding the customers' desires. It will be the role of senior management to create a global corporate quality culture that focuses its energy on customer needs. The global corporations that emerge as the most successful in the remainder of this decade will not have lost sight of this one simple, basic truth: the customer is supreme. Customers will show their allegiance to those suppliers that provide the greatest perceived added value.

Most corporations understand this basic concept, but is easy to see how quickly sub-units within the corporation can become misfocused. Vertical organizations tend to focus on quality improvements within their functional areas—with little understanding of how these initiatives are perceived by the customer. Cross-functional teams can easily become engulfed in improving work processes without fully appreciating their degree of importance to the customer. Many organizations have improved the quality of a product that customers don't want!

Senior management must re-engineer many business processes in order to truly 'delight' customers. Customers must be allowed to become active partners in the company's strategic planning sessions, and senior managers must learn to listen to customers. They must let customers define what exceptional service levels should be, instead of establishing these levels on their own. Senior management must focus on providing exceptional perceived value to customers those key areas where the company has established core competencies and competitive advantages.

Have all firms around the globe fully grasped the urgency of this basic truth and adopted it as their guiding beacon? The answer is an astounding NO! Ernst & Young's recent 'International Quality Study' revealed that, of those businesses whose departments always or almost always (>90% of the time) translate customer expectations into the design of new products/services,

- 58% of Japanese firms said they did this
- 40% of German firms
- 22% of US firms
- 14% of Canadian firms

Incorporating customer expectations into the design of new products/services will clearly provide a competitive advantage. Global competition means that the winning companies will be those that meet and exceed customer expectations. Harry G. Hohn, chairman and CEO of New York Life Insurance Company, fully embraces the importance of this fundamental concept:

> In the nineties, the key differentiator between successful companies and their competitors will be quality—not price. And the key to quality is strong customer focus.[25]

Nordstrom, Inc., the Seattle-based fashion specialty retailer, is known by its customers for providing the best possible service, selection, quality and value. Nordstrom achieved sales in excess of $3.42 billion in 1992 in its 72 store locations. It has planned five new locations for 1994 and another five for 1995. Sales growth during the past five years has exceeded 32 per cent.

Why do customers flock to Nordstrom's? One of the authors recently purchased a suit from an out-of-state Nordstrom location. The sales representative, assured him of proper tailoring and prompt delivery via United Parcel Service. The suit arrived in perfect condition and ready to wear because Nordstrom's took extra care to package it in the same type of cardboard box used by airlines to pack carry-on luggage. Several months later the suit was returned by the author's dry cleaner with several crushed buttons. Replacement buttons could not be found locally. The author called the sales representative on a Saturday, and he scoured the store to find replacements. Several hours later he called and vowed to mail the buttons at the local post office before 5:00 pm to ensure receipt by Monday. On Monday evening he called to check that the buttons had arrived in good condition! It's easy to see why the author is eager to return to Nordstrom's and to place additional business with his personal salesman and new friend.

Product quality

Enhancement in product quality provided many firms with a competitive advantage in the 1970s and 1980s. Today, exceptional product quality is a requirement for entry into the marketplace, and it is expected by customers—so much so that it no longer serves as a competitive advantage in most industries.

Speed

Global corporations that can produce world-class products and deliver those products much more quickly than their competitors will have a competitive edge in the coming decade. The rate of global technological innovation is increasing, resulting in shorter product life-cycles. Speed to market high-quality products developed to meet customer needs is essential if a firm is to recoup R&D investments and to achieve acceptable financial returns.

Flexibility and small lot size

In addition to speed, the successful companies of the late 1990s will be those that have mastered the art of flexible manufacturing and production in small lot sizes.

Global corporations that learn how to read the market quickly, to make many products on the same production line, to devise highly profitable short production runs and to switch product production quickly and cheaply will emerge as the leaders in the year 2000.

'Delighting' the customer in the coming decade will mean being able to make a production run of one, in record time, at the lowest cost, with exceptional quality and delivered in record time.

A recent study of 900 Japanese and US companies by Deloitte and Touche consultants focused on manufacturing strategies. They found that American manufacturers stressed product quality (conformance to specifications, durability, on-time delivery). To the Japanese, these were all assumed to be given. The Japanese focus centered on highly flexible factories, improved product features, increased customer service and an outpouring of new products.[26] Toshiba is a firm focused on flexibility as a competitive advantage:

> Flexibility is an explicit goal at Toshiba, whose $35.5 billion in sales last year came from products as diverse as appliances and computers, light bulbs and power plants. Okay, so the slogan 'synchronize production in proportion to customer demand' probably made few hearts leap when Toshiba workers first heard it in 1985. The idea, explains Toshiba President Fumio Sato, is to push Toshiba's two dozen factories to adapt faster to markets. Says Sato: 'Customers wanted choices. They wanted a washing machine or a TV set that was precisely right for their needs. We needed variety, not mass production.'
>
> Sato hammered home his theme in an almost non-stop series of factory visits. The key to variety: finding ways to make money from ever shorter production runs. Sato urged managers to reduce setup times, shrink lead times, and learn to make more products with the same equipment and people. He says: 'Every time I go to a plant I tell the people, "Smaller lot!"'
>
> If that's your creed, says Lester Thurow, dean of the Sloan School of Management at MIT, a visit to Toshiba's computer factory in Ome, 30 miles from downtown Tokyo, 'is like being in heaven.' Toshiba calls Ome an 'intelligent works' because a snazzy computer network links office, engineering, and factory operations, providing just-in-time information as well as just-in-time parts. Ome workers assemble nine different word processors on the same line and, on an adjacent one, 20 varieties of lap top computers. Usually they make a batch of 20 before changing models, but Toshiba can afford lot sizes as small as ten.[27]

Dell Computers changed the retail computer business in 1992 with their direct-to-consumer telephone sales concept. This new program allowed consumers to order directly from the factory. Customized orders were manufactured on the line the same day

> Moreover, if a customer wanted a customized version, he often had to wait for the retailer to send in an order and for the factory to get around to filling it and shipping it. With Dell, it was different. The retailers were stunned when they saw how quickly the Texas upstart could deliver customized products—in substantially less time than it would take them to place the order and wait for the manufacturer to ship it.
>
> Says Torresi: 'Dell could respond to the small custom orders—the onesies and twosies that we wouldn't attempt to deal with. Suddenly, everyone realized what he had wasn't just a product, it was a process.'[28]

Global service quality

Global service quality can be defined as the quality, freedom from defects and speed with which goods or services are delivered to the customer. As mentioned earlier, quality and freedom from defects are basic requirements for competing in the marketplace today and are assumed as given by leading customers and manufacturers.

L.L. Bean Inc., the mail order retailer of outdoor clothing and gear, mailed 500 000 packages in the Spring of 1992 with zero errors. Its 1992 average was 99.9 per cent even shipping up to 134 000 packages per day during the Christmas season. Manchester Stamping Corporation makes automotive parts for Honda of America. In 1989 it shipped 540 000 parts of which seven were defective. The employees and management of Manchester are dissatisfied with their performance and are feverishly working on improving the process to achieve perfection.[29]

Product innovation

Product innovation is a natural outflow of any quality initiative. Product innovation takes quality improvement one step further, which is to design and build new products that meet unmet customer needs. The challenge is trying to marry what customers say they need with the technology that can be developed.

A recent survey of over 550 US electronics companies showed that the most critical considerations for developing new products were:

- 80% : definition of customer needs

- 73% : product quality

- 48% : time-to-market

- 44% : enhance product features/functionality[30]

Summary

Corporations involved in worldwide commerce must excel at GQL. Companies must develop both the internal and external global quality processes needed for success. These must be linked with a single, unified quality vision and be implemented by a globally diverse workforce dedicated to making globalization work.

Notes and references

1. Stephen H. Rhinesmith, 'Global mindsets for global managers', *Training and Development*, October 1992, pp. 63–8.
2. See Patrick M. Byrne, 'Global leaders take a broad view', *Transportation and Distribution*, February 1992, pp. 61–2.
3. A summary of a recent European Quality Study conducted by Knight

Wendling, 'Logistics/quality and service', is reported by John Macdonald and John Piggott, *Global Quality*, Mercury Books, London, 1990, pp. 20–1.

4. Ernst & Young and the American Quality Foundation, Cleveland, Ohio 'International Quality Study', 1991.

5. A. T. Kearney, 'US manufacturing competitiveness', Chicago, Ill., 1992.

6. Described by Ernst C. Huge in a book developed by the Ernst & Young Quality Improvement Consulting Group, *Total Quality: An Executive's Guide for the 1990's*, Business One Irwin, Homewood, Ill., 1990, p. 59.

7. David L. Calfee, 'Get your mission statement working', *Management Review*, January 1993, pp. 54–7.

8. Huge, op. cit., pp. 59–60.

9. Alexander Hiam, *Closing the Quality Gap: Lessons from America's Leading Companies*, Prentice-Hall, Englewood Cliffs, NJ, 1992, pp. 44–5.

10. Knight Wendling, op. cit., pp. 22–3.

11. Peter Drucker, 'The new society of organizations', *Harvard Business Review*, September–October 1992, p. 100.

12. Macdonald and Piggott, op. cit., p. 36.

13. Joseph M. Juran, *Juran on Leadership for Quality*, Free Press, New York, 1989.

14. Huge, op. cit., pp. 104–5.

15. Monograph published by the international consulting firm A. T. Kearney, *Transforming the Enterprise*, Monograph no. 38, December 1992.

16. Catherine Arnst, Stephanie Anderson Forest, Kathy Robello and Jonathan Levine, 'Compaq—how it made its impressive move out of the doldrums', *Business Week*, 2 November 1992, p. 149.

17. Gregory H. Watson, 'How process benchmarking supports corporate strategy', *Planning Review*, January–February 1993, pp. 12–15.

18. H. Kevin Vaziri, 'Questions to answer before benchmarking', *Planning Review*, January–February 1993, p. 37.

19. Otis Port and Geoffrey Smith, 'Beg, borrow—and benchmark', *Business Week*, 30 November 1992, pp. 74–5.

20. Robert D. Buzzell and Bradley T. Gale, *The PIMS Principles*, Free Press, New York, pp. 103–8.

21. Ernst & Young study, op. cit., p. 17.

22. Ibid., p. 15.

23. Robert H. Schaffer and Harvey A. Thomson, 'Successful change programs begin with results', *Harvard Business Review*, January–February 1992, pp. 80–9.

24. Ibid., p. 86.

25. 'Quality 1992 leading the world class company', *Fortune*, 21 September 1992, supplement.

26. Thomas A. Stewart, 'Brace for Japan's hot new strategy', *Fortune*, 21 September 1992, pp. 62–74.

27. Ibid., p. 64.

28. Julia Pitta, 'Why Dell is a survivor', *Forbes*, 12 October 1992, p. 86.

29. Ibid., p. 72.
30. In an Ernst & Young study of 550 US electronics manufacturers, as reported in an Ernst & Young publication, *Electronics 91: Framework for the Future*, San Francisco, Calif., 1991.

WE TRAINED HARD . . . but it seemed
that every time we were beginning to form
up into teams we would be reorganized. . . .
I was to learn later in life that we tend to
meet any new situation by reorganizing; and
a wonderful method it can be for creating
the illusion of progress while producing
confusion, inefficiency, and demoralization.

PETRONIUS ARBITER
210 B.C.

Part II

This part explains the need for senior management to concentrate on the global strategic vision of their organizations in order to capitalize fully on these rapidly changing external forces.

The following five chapters examine 'traditional' organizational structures and their strengths and weaknesses in dealing with today's global business environment. Attention is focused on the complexities of global learning and decision-making. The 13 core characteristics of the 'optimal worldwide organization' are identified. This should enable readers to examine the strengths and weaknesses of their own organizations and determine what areas need improvement in order to achieve global excellence.

Portions of this part may be a little longer and more detailed than may be required by many experienced senior global managers. However, many questions persist concerning optimal organizational structures. For this reason, a thorough examination of the subject is presented, which will serve as the foundation for new paradigm thinking.

Global learning and decision-making

The development of global corporate organizational structures and work-flow processes is critical for the achievement of maximal results. Global organizations are faced with a growing variety and complexity of challenges, as identified by Bartlett and Ghoshal:[1]

- Need for the economies of central control

- Need for local adaptation and flexibility

- Need for worldwide knowledge transfer and learning

All of these needs must be achieved in the face of flattening hierarchical structures, empowerment of employees, understanding and integration of cultural differences, the quest for quality, superior cost-effectiveness, speed of development and delivery, diminishing production lot sizes and a need to 'delight' the customer.

Centralized versus decentralized decision-making

Should critical business decisions be made centrally for global economies of scale, or should they be made locally to meet local market needs? The answer is, *it depends*. Certain key decisions are best made centrally, others locally, and still others require a shared process. In this chapter we will help to clarify how optimal decision-making can be achieved in a changing global environment. Chapters 7–9 will explore organizational structures that inherently favor differing approaches to decision-making.

The need for centralization and control

As discussed in Chapter 2, the evolution of certain environmental forces has encouraged the need for global centralization and control. Organizations need to be able to manage the global integration of their activities.[2] Figure 5.1 lists some of the advantages and disadvantages of centralization and strategic control.

Advantages
- Direct line of authority
- Centralization of key resources, decisions, tight financial controls and information flows
- Economies of scale for R&D and manufacturing
- Central control of global strategic vision and strategy
- Clear performance accountabilities for corporate headquarters management
- More unified subsidiary follow-through of plans

Disadvantages
- Reduced ability for subsidiary management to respond to local market changes
- Inability to modify products for local demand
- Minimal cross-subsidiary exchange of ideas, products or cooperation
- Reduced accountability at the subsidiary level
- Centralized decision-making by corporate executives who have minimal local market knowledge
- Strained relationships between corporate and subsidiary staffs and management

Fig. 5.1   Centralization and strategic control: advantages and disadvantages

Economies of scale

Certain industries profit from manufacturing in a few selected locations where they can profit from the economies of mass production. Selected technological patent advantages also play a critical role in the location and size of plants.

Some economies of scale can be achieved by centralizing research and development activities in one or a few locations. Financial resources are usually limited for R&D, and certain synergies and coordination can often be achieved by locating such activities in one or only a few locations. The smaller the number of manufacturing and R&D locations, the easier it is to control quality, speed, and cost—essential elements for success. Furthermore, the high costs of research and development mean that local market sales are usually not sufficient to cover R&D costs. These costs must be spread out among several subsidiaries. For example, large pharmaceutical firms typically spend approximately 15 per cent of total worldwide sales on R&D; these costs must be spread over many markets to justify the investment.[3]

It is estimated that the scale and complexity of large telephone exchanges mean that they can cost approximately \$2 billion to develop. So high a cost requires the scale of these exchanges in many countries in order to spread the cost of development over a much larger sales base.[4]

Trends toward homogeneous demand

Centralization of decision-making and control are especially suited to products that have a more homogeneous appeal to customers. Many such products that are in the mature stage of the product life-cycle. Customer demands for these products usually focus on uniformity of quality and cost effectiveness; examples include computer chips and some electronic parts.

Societies are developing more homogeneous consumer tastes through the impact of regional TV advertising and the resultant movement toward more homogeneous lifestyles. In Europe, as governments deregulate, advertising is zinging across airwaves once off-limits to commercials. By 1997 Europe will outspend the United States on TV advertising.

Lifestyles are also moving somewhat closer. Throughout the industrialized world, more women are working outside the home and households are becoming smaller. This means that the convenience of packaged goods will continue to grow in appeal. Global consumers are more frequently buying their groceries and everyday items in large supermarkets, often shopping just once a week and snapping up discounts. Some Japanese, for example, are beginning to spurn quaint neighborhood shops for new '7-Eleven' stores and supermarkets with plenty of shelf space.[5]

Global sourcing of raw materials, components, energy and labor

The demand to produce high-quality products in a cost-effective manner is increasing steadily. Key industries such as mining, petrochemicals and paper are located at the sites of raw materials because of prohibitive transportation costs. In industries that are labor-intensive, factories are being relocated to optimize the cost of labor. Low energy costs can provide a competitive advantage for certain industries and play a key role in plant location.

The Xerox Corporation initiated a focused plan on global integration of sourcing and manufacturing in the early 1980s:

> Senior managers at Xerox realized the potential for cutting costs if the company consolidated raw material sources. They created a central purchasing group that included representatives from over a dozen of Xerox's multinational operating companies. This group of commodity managers identified and cultivated suppliers that could provide Xerox with high-quality, low-cost components on a worldwide basis.
>
> In the process, Xerox trimmed its global supply base from about 5,000 suppliers to just over 400, which now accounts for more than 90% of raw material purchases. For instance, Xerox now buys many of the lamps for its copiers from a single supplier with plants in Asia, Europe, and the United States. Because the consolidation of raw materials simplified purchasing, overhead rates have fallen from 9% of total costs for materials in 1982 to about 3% today. Result: Xerox now saves over $100 million annually on raw materials.[6]

Coulter Electronics also found that global sourcing could yield significant savings:

> Coulter Electronics, which produces medical electronics equipment, created commodity management teams that included representatives from all five of its plants. Early on, the semiconductor commodity team found that the company could consolidate half of all semiconductors it purchased into a few large contracts, saving more than $1 million a year. In another instance, the team discovered that the same three-way solenoid valve cost $20.87 in France, $17.50 in the United Kingdom, and $10.54 in the United States. By consolidating the purchasing of this valve, Coulter saved over $100,000 annually.[7]

Decreasing transportation and communication costs

Reduced transportation costs have opened up new markets for many firms. The revolution in telecommunications breakthroughs has 'reduced' the size of the world and has opened many markets for firms.

Many major motor carriers have formed global alliances to improve their speed of delivery and reduce prices to customers. Consolidated Freightways, Sea-Land, United Parcel Service, Federal Express, TNT, Roberts Express and P-I-E Nationwide are examples of firms that have formed global alliances. The purchase of Flying Tigers by Federal Express gained the carrier much needed overseas landing rights and a ready-made business in heavy freight.[8]

Global customers

Many domestic firms are finding that they are being challenged to provide products in multiple countries as their previously domestic-only customers begin to evolve into multinationals. These customers not only require an availability of parts in non-domestic locations, but also are beginning to look at non-domestic sourcing of these parts. This can threaten both the non-domestic and domestic operations of local manufacturers who have ignored the evolutionary global warning signs.

Global competitors

Competitors operating in multiple markets pose real threats to firms that are domestic-only. Global coordination is necessary to prepare for competitive threats to both subsidiaries and domestic markets. It is important to assess the degree to which competitors have taken advantage of the benefits of global sourcing, access to raw materials, global labor supply, economies of scale, decreasing transportation and telecommunication costs and new global customers.

The need for decentralization and local autonomy

Protectionism and trade barriers

A country may find that its basic industries are being threatened by a large increase in imports of selected products. If more than one non-domestic firm is simultaneously competing with local firms, further weakening the domestic producers' competitive position, there is even greater cause for concern.[9] The initiation of selected trade barriers can slow, halt or reverse the competitive threat by non-domestic firms. However, this action is best conceived as a short-term 'solution', providing time for local manufacturers to reassess their strategies and begin to react in a more competitive fashion.

Host-government protective activities include restricting imports, requiring that imports and exports to countries are equalized, providing tax incentives for locally manufactured goods, raising tariffs for imported goods, requiring a certain amount of 'local content' in products and initiating price control policies. Host governments are increasingly requiring significant ownership and management by local nations, and employees are demanding positions on subsidiary company boards.[10]

Host-government protectionism favors national manufacturers; but at the same time, of course, it adversely affects its country's consumers by denying them the opportunity to purchase lower-priced imports.

Local competitors

If the non-domestic firm faces many local competitors, or if the local competitors maintain a large market share, then the need to respond locally increases significantly. Companies that are centrally controlled will have difficulty in gaining market share with a generic product that cannot be adapted to local needs. Local competitors will also maintain the advantages of cultural similarity.

Local customer needs

Locally responsive strategies are needed in businesses that require significant local adaptation to customer desires. Without the ability to meet local tastes, centrally focused firms will meet with only marginal success.

Examples of industries that require significant adaptability because of local differences in taste include food products, cosmetics, beverages, automobiles and pharmaceuticals.

Laundry detergent is an excellent example of a 'global product' that requires local modification to meet country and region preferences based on differing washing conditions. In 1987 the Kao Corporation, a leading Japanese household products manufacturer, introduced in Japan a new super-concentrated detergent called Attack. This highly successful product was quickly copied and modified by Proctor and Gamble (P&G) and Unilever who market it under such names as Tide, Wisk and Ariel. For example, P&G has varied the density of the formula to national preferences and has added a special dosing device to help the detergent clean better in Europe's markets; this adaptation was necessary to meet the demands of Europe's hard water and heavy clay soil.[11]

Ore-Ida, an American frozen food producer, has successfully adapted its products to local customer preferences:

> In contrast, Ore-Ida showed interest in overseas markets and the willingness to make necessary product adaptations. It downsized its frozen potato packages, pre-cooked the product for easy use in toaster ovens (a common kitchen appliance in Japan), and repositioned it as a breakfast food. Sales took off, and the company was rewarded with a 30% market share.[12]

Distribution needs

Distribution needs can vary considerably from market to market and increase the need for local responsiveness. Changes in distribution channels can also impact on product positioning, advertising, pricing and promotion.[13]

The uniqueness of the multi-layered distribution systems in Japan has proven to be a significant barrier to entry for many non-Japanese firms. The relationship between Japanese firms, banks and distribution systems has resulted in a greater number of partnerships between non-Japanese and Japanese firms compared with the preferred route of independent subsidiaries.

Privatization

The privatization of many publicly-owned corporations in the United Kingdom has resulted in strong decentralization pressures on management. The need is for flexible, dynamic management as water, telephone and electricity companies face the demands of the marketplace for innovation, economies of cost, local market adaptation and evolving business environments. This represents a radical change from the 'public service culture' of inflexibility and centralized control, whereby management decisions were developed by consensus and committee and industrial relations were highly centralized. Centralization discouraged risk-taking and emphasized the comfort of conformity.

The focus on the 'profit center' concept has met with some difficulties because of the inability of local management to gain control over the key element of the bottom line: pay rates and other worker demands remain under central control. Where regulations of prices, quality and competition continue to exert a strong central influence, this has created confusing messages for line managers and has resulted in some recentralization of power and authority.[14]

British Telecom is a case-in-point:

> But in BT, faced with the conflicting pressures of its rapidly evolving, technologically complex market, the tensions between decentralizing and centralizing forces were particularly noticeable. On the one hand, the need to be innovative, flexible, to 'get close to the customer,' implied devolution of authority and the minimizing of central constraints. But on the other hand, the

context of regulation and the political sensitivity of privatization meant that localized quality-of-service problems could have wider consequences. This, together with the requirements of big corporate customers, encouraged greater central control. In other words, BT was caught between different competitive strategies of 'quality enhancement' and 'innovation,' to use Schuler's terms . . ., with conflicting implications for organizational structure. As this suggests, there were also differences between the companies according to their political sensitivity.[15]

Global changes in decentralization

The growing shift in power from the industrial age to the information age is resulting in a mustering of global forces for decentralization in government, business structure and geographical locale (Fig. 5.2).

The revolution of democracy that is sweeping the communist world is resulting in the dissolution of centrally controlled bureaucracies. The migration of many corporations to smaller communities is another indication of a more equitable diffusion of concentration.

Political power is moving in the direction of local government as people

---

Advantages
- Subsidiary management maintains high degree of local autonomy.
- Subsidiary management has significant ability to respond quickly to local needs.
- Local managers will be more 'entrepreneurial'.
- Cultural similarity provides advantages.
- Local focus provides the basis for strong subsidiary morale.
- Local managers are held accountable for performance.

Disadvantages
- Subsidiary 'independence' will result in diversified strategic implementation of plans, losing the united, focused approach.
- There will be difficulty in developing and adopting a 'global strategic vision' by all employees.
- Global competitors can launch a united, global action against a fragmented, multinational approach.
- There will be a minimal cross-subsidiary exchange of ideas, products or cooperation.
- Local management will need to have many competencies that are usually provided centrally.
- Local adaptability requires the drain of subsidiary resources for R&D and manufacturing modifications.

Fig. 5.2   Decentralization and local autonomy: advantages and disadvantages

around the world sense that social, economic and political problems are too difficult to solve from a large, bureaucratic hub.[16]

The evolution of technological change has opened up the world to allow the establishment of factories and offices anywhere on earth. The island of Mauritius provides an excellent example. Mauritius is located 500 miles from Madagascar. It has attracted over 200 firms to invest in businesses there. The impact of tax advantages and foreign technology has made this small island the world's third largest exporter of knitwear.[17]

Achieving a balance between centralization and local autonomy

The need for successful companies to effectively balance the benefits of centralization and local autonomy (Fig. 5.3) have been effectively described by Prahalad and Doz[18] and by Bartlett and Ghoshal.[19] The challenge is for companies to achieve these goals *simultaneously*.

Conflicting views

Local managers frequently favor greater subsidiary autonomy because of their understanding and sensitivity to local needs. Corporate managers, who are concerned with global competitive strategies, focus their efforts

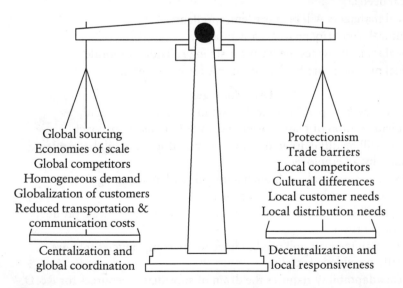

Global sourcing
Economies of scale
Global competitors
Homogeneous demand
Globalization of customers
Reduced transportation &
    communication costs

Protectionism
Trade barriers
Local competitors
Cultural differences
Local customer needs
Local distribution needs

Centralization and
global coordination

Decentralization and
local responsiveness

The global corporation

Fig. 5.3   The need for centralization and decentralization in the global corporation

on increasing cross-border coordination and centralization of strategy. Each set of managers presents different facts, analyzes them differently and proposes different strategic solutions.[20]

The development of an appropriate global strategic vision is the first step in developing cooperation and teamwork between corporate and subsidiary perspectives.

Doz, Bartlett and Prahalad point out:

> To preserve both national and global views, increasing agreement should *not* be sought. Top management wants both perspectives to be strong, and must develop a way to selectively favor the views of one or the other side for any particular decision. Some projects need to be approved even though they do not draw consensus from the various subunits in the organization . . . Multidimensionality and flexibility are the key requirements of the desired strategic decision process.[21]

A fundamental role of senior management is to develop a *decision-making process* that allows for the proper consideration of the needs of local nationals and the needs of central coordination that support the corporation's global strategic vision.

Decision-making: businesses, functions and activities

Successful global corporations must create appropriate global strategic visions, form optimal organization structures and develop work-flow processes that achieve excellence and surpass customer expectations.

Within each organization, different businesses, functions and activities will require different degrees of centralization and decentralization. The result will be a need for different formal reporting structures and different work-flow designs.[22]

Businesses

Senior executives should carefully examine the factors relating to centralization and decentralization for each business in order to determine the most appropriate structure and work-flow processes needed (Fig. 5.4).

Functions

Functions within each business will also require differing degrees of centralized and decentralized decision-making (Fig. 5.5). For many businesses, functions such as R&D and strategy formulation will require greater centralization and worldwide coordination, whereas functions such as sales will usually be better served on a local basis. Manufacturing is frequently a function that is best met through a mixture of global, regional and local needs.

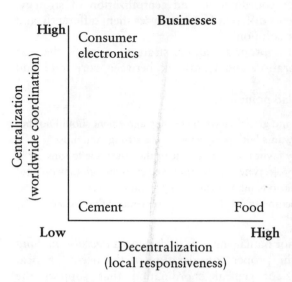

Fig. 5.4   Degrees of centralization/decentralization: businesses.

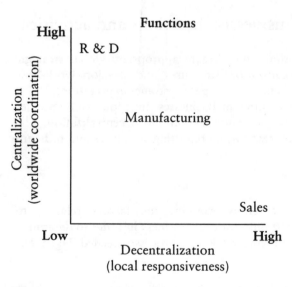

Fig. 5.5   Degrees of centralization/decentralization: functions.

Activities

Each of the various functions of the company contains specific activities which should be carefully analyzed regarding centralization or decentralization of decision-making (Fig. 5.6). For example, within an R&D

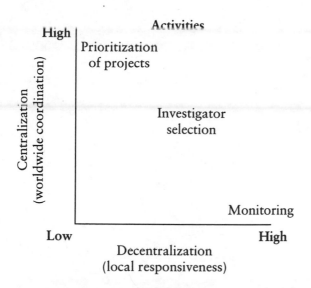

Fig. 5.6   Degrees of centralization/decentralization: activities

function the prioritization of research projects would normally be a highly centralized decision; selection of clinical investigators might be a mixed centralized/decentralized decision; and monitoring of study compliance would usually be highly local and decentralized.

Act appropriately

The old phrase, 'Think Globally, Act Locally', is an oversimplification of the true complexities of today's global competition; 'Think Globally and Locally, Act Appropriately' better describes the real marketplace (Fig. 5.7).

Communication: the need for worldwide knowledge transfer and learning

The exponential rate of change in the 12 environmental forces discussed in Chapter 2 has caused many domestic-only firms to redefine their strategic visions to encompass global activities in the future. Global organizations need to develop business processes that maximize knowledge and learning transfer between subsidiaries and corporate staffs. Certain formal organizational structures are more conducive to knowledge transfer and learning than others. Chapters 6–9 will explore these differences and look at ways to optimize worldwide learning.

Old paradigm

New paradigm

THINK
globally
and locally

ACT
appropriately

Fig. 5.7   Old and new paradigms

Informal networks

Many corporations are focusing considerable time and energy on reorganizing their formal organizational structures in an effort to increase communication and speed decision-making. Yet, few executives pay adequate attention to the *informal networks* within their organizations; and it is these informal networks, which slice across functional and divisional obstacles, that can enable world-class corporations to achieve goals in record time with superior quality.

Formal organizational structures play an important role in vertical, functional decision-making and learning; *informal* networks play an equally important role in horizontal, cross-functional learning and decision-making. Formal organizational structures can be thought of as the anatomy or skeleton of an organization; informal, cross-functional networks serve as the physiology or central nervous system through which decision-making and learning take place.[23,24]

The learning organization

Leading companies around the globe have initiated *continuous improvement programs*. As many fail as are successful. Why? Because so many executives have lost sight of the fact that continuous improvement requires a sincere *commitment to learning*. David Garvin states:

> A learning organization is an organization skilled at creating, acquiring and transferring knowledge, and at modifying its behavior to reflect new knowledge and insights.[25]

Successful learning organizations utilize effective tools to measure assumptions and diagnose problems. Effective learning organizations *change the way work is done*.

The new technology

The new technology of computers and telecommunications equipment has had a profound impact on the transfer of corporate knowledge. The demands of customers and the pressure of competitors are key driving forces for globalization. Core competencies are enhanced by the utilization of these new technologies.

The pace of innovation in the integration of computer and telecommunications technologies continues and is expected to heighten throughout this decade. These new technologies have provided breakthroughs in the ability of worldwide organizations to improve both macro and micro work-flow processes. Chapters 7–9 discuss specific competencies/deficiencies and how to correct them for each 'traditional' organizational structure. When used properly, these new technologies can radically improve the worldwide transfer of knowledge and learning throughout a company with multi-country subsidiaries.

Summary

Global corporations need to develop the ability to simultaneously achieve the economies of central control, the flexibility to meet local customer demands and the ability to provide for maximal worldwide knowledge transfer and learning.

Organizations must assess the degree of centralization/decentralization and shared decision-making needed for each of their businesses, functions and activities. Chapters 7–9 examine the strengths and weaknesses of 'traditional' formal organizational structures and propose the core characteristics needed for an 'optimal, worldwide organization'.

Notes and references

1. Christopher A. Bartlett and Sumantra Ghoshal, *Managing across Borders: The Transnational Solution*, Harvard Business School Press, Boston, Mass., 1989.
2. C. K. Prahalad and Yves L. Doz, *The Multinational Mission*, Free Press, New York, 1987.
3. Stephen J. Kobrin, 'An empirical analysis of the determinants of global integration', *Strategic Management Journal*, 12, Summer 1991, pp. 17–31.
4. Ibid.
5. Zachary Schiller and Richard Melcher, 'Marketing globally, thinking locally', *Business Week*, 31 May 1991.
6. Michael E. McGrath and Richard W. Hoole, 'Manufacturing's new economies of scale', *Harvard Business Review*, May–June 1992.
7. Ibid.
8. Perry A. Trunick, 'The world is your market', *Transportation and Distribution*, September 1990.
9. Prahalad and Doz, op. cit.
10. Yves L. Doz, Christopher A. Bartlett and C. K. Prahalad, 'Global competitive pressures and host country demands', in Jadish N. Sheth and Golpira S. Eshghi (eds), *Global Strategic Management Perspective*, South-Western Publishing Company, Cincinnati, Ohio, 1989.
11. Schiller and Melcher, op. cit.
12. Sak Onkvisit and John J. Shaw, 'Myopic management: the hollow strength of American competitiveness', *Business Horizons*, January–February 1991, p. 18.
13. Prahalad and Doz, op. cit.
14. Trevor Colling and Anthony Ferner, 'The limits of autonomy: devolution line managers and industrial relations in privatized companies', *Journal of Management Studies*, 2 March 1992, p. 29.
15. Ibid.
16. David A. Heenan, 'The end of centralized power', *Journal of Business Strategy*, March–April 1991.
17. Ibid.
18. Prahalad and Doz, op. cit.
19. Bartlett and Ghoshal, op. cit.
20. Doz, Bartlett and Prahalad, op. cit.
21. Ibid.
22. Bartlett and Ghoshal, op. cit.
23. See Christopher A. Bartlett and Sumantra Ghoshal, 'Matrix of management: not a structure, a frame of mind', *Harvard Business Review*, July–August 1990, pp. 138–45.
24. See David Krackhardt and Jeffrey R. Hanson, 'Informal networks: the company behind the chart', *Harvard Business Review*, July–August 1993, pp. 104–11.
25. David A. Garvin, 'Building a learning organization', *Harvard Business Review*, July–August 1993, p. 80.

Formal organizational structure

Business organizations involved in non-domestic operations must choose a formal organizational structure through which they can implement their global strategic vision. Each traditional formal structure contains inherent strengths and weaknesses. The global demands of the marketplace require that business leaders fully understand each of these structures, pick the structure that best complements their competitive advantages, and develop innovative methods to minimize its limitations.

A new management approach in a complex world

The rate of change and the complexities of the 12 environmental forces confronting businesses today have strained the capabilities of traditional formal organizational structures. Attempting to achieve a global strategic vision in an environment of complex implementation problems has resulted in less-than-optimal results by many worldwide organizations. Research by Bartlett and Ghoshal[1] indicates that key factors of success in worldwide markets lie with corporations that can achieve, simultaneously,

1. Local, national responsiveness

2. Centralized control and coordination

3. The ability to transfer knowledge and learning, leading to global innovation[2]

By the mid-1980s global competition for non-domestic markets had become as fierce and challenging as it had been for domestic markets in the 1950s and 1960s. Corporations began to understand that success required a firm not just to master one of the three competencies mentioned, but to attain simultaneous excellence in global integration, local differentiation and worldwide innovation.[3]

Developing the strategic core competencies of global integration, local differentiation and worldwide innovation have become *organizational* challenges and have necessitated corporations developing new organizational solutions (Fig. 6.1).

Old paradigm	New paradigm
1. Organizations exercised control through their hierarchical structures	1. Market demands for speed, flexibility and local responsiveness will result in flatter organizations
2. Corporations internalized many support functions to exercise control	2. 'Outsourcing' of non-essential support activities will escalate
3. Companies attempted to develop a more homogeneous style	3. 'Cultural diversity' is viewed as a strength
4. Function-driven	4. Process-driven
5. Competitive strength through functional expertise and top down control	5. Competitive strength through 'cross-silo' teamwork and networking
6. Upward mobility	6. Lateral mobility
7. Information technology advances assisted in economies of scale	7. Information technology to provide a key component to facilitate networking
8. Need for mass labor at the lowest cost possible	8. Rewards for companies that develop and retain 'knowledge workers'

Fig. 6.1 The evolving paradigm for the new economic era: organizational hierarchy and dynamics

The complexities of managing in the turbulent 1990s have led to the need for *operating in new ways that overcome the limitations of each of the three traditional structures in use today.*

Structure follows strategy

The organizational structure that a company chooses to pursue should change as its corporate global strategic vision changes. It is essential that senior corporate management understand that corporate structure is a *tool* that facilitates the implementation of the global strategic vision. Global strategic vision dictates *where* the company is headed; corporate strategic plans dictate *how* we will achieve our strategic vision; and corporate structure dictates the reporting relationship *through which* the vision and plans will be implemented.

Alfred Chandler observed three decades ago that:

> The thesis that different organizational forms result for different types of growth can be stated more precisely if the planning and carrying out of such growth is

considered a *strategy*, and the organization devised to administer these enlarged activities and resources, a *structure* . . .

As the adoption of a new strategy may add new types of personnel and facilities, and alter the business horizons of the men responsible for the enterprise, it can have a profound effect on the form of its organization . . .

The thesis deduced from these several propositions is then that structure follows strategy.[4]

Processing systems

Organizational structures are designed as processing systems that are charged with collecting and pooling information, implementing goals, making decisions, monitoring performance, adapting goals and achieving corporate expectations.

Domestic-only corporations focus their energies on the structurally conflicting demands of the day-to-day activities between line management and corporate functions (e.g. marketing, manufacturing, research and development). In addition, companies that enter the global arena are also challenged with the complexities that geographical and cultural diversity interject.

Historical development

International trade and commerce have taken place for many centuries. The development of modern worldwide corporate structures has been directly influenced by the centuries of experience acquired through such exchanges. The 'know-how' of process development has also directly influenced the philosophy of management culture and the reporting relationships within organizations.

Significant factors

The three traditional organizational structures of modern times can trace their core characteristics to the following four influences occurring at the time of the structure's establishment:

1. Geographic continent of origin

2. Decade in which initial development occurred

3. Trend of influence of the 12 environmental forces

4. Impact of local cultural forces of the home country

The advent of the modern business organization

Prior to the middle of the nineteenth century, virtually all commerce was carried out by small companies that specialized in either production or distribution. The Industrial Revolution initiated the transformation from small independent firms to large multi-task corporations. Economies of scale and volume output created the need, for the first time, for organizations in which salaried managers handled the processes of manufacturing and distribution. The development of the modern steamship, railroad and telegraph services created the demand for large department stores and mail order houses. Corporations prospered as demand increased. Success bred the formalized organizational structure. Each company's final structure was a result of the developmental pattern of management philosophy and external environmental factors.[5]

The mass production of newly invented machines through the assembling of interchangeable parts required significant investments in personnel. Distribution of such products as adding machines, sewing machines, typewriters, harvesters, gasoline pumps, etc., required additional such services. Those firms most successful at improving the economies of scale prospered for decades.

Traditional organizational structures

All three of the following traditional structure models created, for the firms that utilized them during the relevant era, competitive advantages which *matched the strength of the structural model with the appropriate environmental forces.*

Multinational (decentralized, European) model

In the post World War I era, the demand for goods and services was significantly changed by the influence of evolving environmental forces. The worldwide business community witnessed the escalation of higher import tariffs, communication barriers and logistical problems between countries. Significant national differences in consumer preferences and legal requirements emerged to a degree that mandated local manufacturing and decentralization. Companies expanding beyond their borders during this era focused on establishing highly independent, self-sustaining subsidiaries.

International (bipolar, American) model

In the three decades following World War II, we again witnessed significant changes in key environmental forces. War had ravaged the manufacturing capabilities of Europe and Japan. America possessed technology and know-how, a large and homogeneous demand for goods, and intact factories which were able to produce large quantities of goods at competitive prices.

A gradual reduction of tariff barriers, communication costs and transportation costs occurred. Demand from the non-American market-place resulted in the establishment of subsidiaries with partial autonomy and a partial flow of knowledge and learning between these subsidiaries and the domestic division. These organizations were characterized as having strong domestic divisions and international divisions.

Global (centralized, Japanese) model

The last 25 years have seen a continuation of change in several environmental forces favoring the benefits of centralization. These include a continued decrease in tariffs, a decrease in transportation costs, and the emergence of highly efficient manufacturing capabilities. Global economies of scale have led to centralized strategy development and manufacturing. This has resulted in the development of subsidiaries whose primary responsibilities are focused on selling and distributing goods and carrying out the orders from the global headquarters.

The implementation dilemma

The formal structure of the organization (multinational, international or global) creates the basic architecture through which all key business processes must flow. This formal structure should serve as a framework for success rather than as a straitjacket that binds, hinders and eventually strangles the flow of information and decision-making. It must become the vehicle through which the company develops its core competencies, competitive advantages and global strategic vision.

Today's market environment

Today's market environment is different from any of the environments under which the three traditional organizational structures were developed. None of the traditional models meets all of today's market demands for the *simultaneous* needs of global integration, local differentiation and worldwide innovation.[6]

Each of the traditional organization structures—multinational, international and global—possesses some strengths and some weaknesses in meeting the challenges of today's economic environment. Those companies that operate in one of the traditional formats will be conducting business at a distinct disadvantage (Fig. 6.2). Those companies that *create a paradigm shift*, and focus on achieving their global strategic vision by adapting the limitations of their formal structure's decision and knowledge flow processes, will be successful in the future.

To compete successfully in the coming decade, management must properly address the following questions:

1. What direction is my industry heading? (Environmental factors)
2. Where does my company want to go? (Global strategic vision/mission)
3. How will we get there? (Strategic planning—long- and short-term operations plans)
4. What formal structure (multinational, international, global) will best support my global strategic vision and strategic plans?
5. What are the operational advantages and disadvantages of the formal structure we will use?
6. What disadvantages need to be addressed to allow my corporation to provide simultaneously for the benefits of coordination and control, local adaptability and inter-organizational learning and sharing?

Fig 6.2   The critical questions

> *Critical need: A decision-making and knowledge transfer process that addresses the major needs of worldwide implementation through the corporation's current formal organization structure.*

Senior and middle management will be most actively involved in addressing the first four questions set out in Fig. 6.2. It is essential that both managers and employees fully understand the answers to questions 5 and 6. It is the unfortunate truth that in many corporations it is the line employees and first-line supervisors who have the greatest knowledge of the issues involved in these two questions. It is one of senior management's greatest challenges to address these questions and focus sufficient time and energy in solving them.

The need for a significant change in structure

Corporations need to possess simultaneously the conflicting abilities of (1) developing world-class coordination and control, (2) responding to local needs and (3) maximizing inter-organizational learning. Bartlett and Ghoshal termed this type of organization the *transnational solution.*[7] Each of the traditional organizational structures provides for only partial achievement of these three goals. The successful firms of the future will fully understand the advantages and limitations of each of these structures, will pick the structure that best meets their global strategic vision and will develop *implementation solutions* to overcome the limitations of that structure.

We have further refined Bartlett and Ghoshal's three critical needs into *13 core characteristics* essential for success in today's global economy.

These are summarized in Fig. 6.3, and also discussed in some detail here.

Core characteristics	Worldwide organizational solution
Strategy	
1. *Strategic focus* Competitive advantage of this type of organization	Growth through simultaneous and coordinated centralization and local adaptability
2. *Global strategic vision* Where the corporation intends to go; emphasis here is acceptance of vision among units	Unified, understood and accepted by all employees
Structure	
3. *Control* Flow of direction and degree of centralized control from headquarters	High
4. *Local autonomy* Degree of freedom allocated to the subsidiary to change/ modify products and direction	High
5. *Coordination* The degree of teamwork subsidiary–subsidiary, headquarters–subsidiary	High
6. *Corporate–subsidiary relationships* The flow of decision-making and information-sharing	High, shared and interdependent
7. *Subsidiary–subsidiary relationships* The flow of decision-making and information-sharing	High, shared and interdependent
8. *Domestic–subsidiary relationships* The flow of information-sharing	High, shared and interdependent
Culture and processing	
9. *Corporate culture* Characteristics that unite people in an organization	Central and unified
10. *Management selection* Predominant leadership trait needed and country of origin for general managers	Flexibility; best candidate available from any country
11. *Employee selection* Country of origin for subsidiary management and corporate management staff	Best available candidate from any country
12. *Decision processes* Control and flow of decision-making	Shared and complex; emphasis on the customer and 'empowering' employees
13. *Information processes* Control and flow of information and knowledge	Shared and complex; high flow of information and knowledge

Fig. 6.3 The worldwide organizational solution (the New Paradigm)

Success in each of these core characteristics will be necessary to achieve the *'worldwide organizational solution'*.

Note: Recently we asked three different groups of graduate students to define what is meant by 'multinational', 'international' and 'global'. No two answers were the same. Many people use the terms interchangeably. The definitions we have chosen to use are those developed by Bartlett and Ghoshal and are described later in this chapter.

The worldwide organizational solution: core characteristics

Those companies that excel today and in the future will be those that develop the following 13 core characteristics within the *confines* of one of the traditional organizational structures.

1. Strategic focus

Growth will require companies to develop the skills of working in a fully integrated organization, which achieves optimal central coordination and at the same time takes full advantage of local adaptability.

Each of the three traditional structures contains natural impediments to a simultaneous achievement of optimal control, coordination and local adaptability. Senior management must clearly identify the current situation and needs, and develop action plans to attain the appropriate levels of central coordination and control and local adaptability.

2. Global strategic vision

Those companies that develop a clear global strategic vision of the future direction of their firms will be more successful than those that focus on updating their strategic plans and doing the same work more efficiently. Development of an appropriate global strategic vision will require a comprehensive analysis of the current and future environmental trends examined in Chapter 2. A careful review of the long-range plans of both company and industry will help senior management set the best course for successful positioning in the marketplace in the year 2000. Senior managers must clearly communicate with all employees. Employees must review, discuss, understand, accept and fully support the global strategic vision if the company is to meet the competitive challenges ahead.[8]

3, 5. Coordination and control

Successful companies of the future will need to develop methods to provide the optimal benefits of global coordination and centralized control, including:

- Economies of scale in production
- Speed of development
- Speed of delivery
- Centralized 'critical mass' for research and development
- More uniform product for a more homogeneous demand
- Global sourcing of raw materials and components
- Reduced tariff barriers
- Trends toward homogeneous technical standards
- Lowered global transportation costs
- Increased telecommunications options at reduced costs

4. Local autonomy

The most successful companies will need to empower their subsidiaries to make critical decisions on the local level. Local adaptability, combined with the authority to move quickly with little to no corporate approval, will prove to be a critical competitive advantage. Local autonomy is essential to fully capitalize on:

- Local tastes and needs
- Protectionism and trade barriers from local governments
- Threats from local, in-country competitors
- Local regulations
- Specialized distribution requirements
- Differing national standards

6, 7, 8. Corporate–subsidiary, subsidiary–subsidiary and domestic–subsidiary relationships

Under ideal circumstances, the working relationships between all of these organizations should be high, shared and interdependent. Traditional multinational, international and global structures do not facilitate all of these needs.

Again, corporate and subsidiary management teams must assess the degree of openness and sharing of ideas that occurs at subsidiary–subsidiary, corporate–subsidiary and domestic–subsidiary levels. Specific strategic initiatives that will achieve these goals must be designed and implemented. Suggestions for achieving this follow in subsequent chapters.

9. Corporate culture

The development of a unified corporate culture will depend upon the degree to which a company's global strategic vision is accepted among all employees. It is also influenced by the diversity and cultural experiences of the management and workforce.

10. Management selection

The complexity of global business will require a highly skilled, culturally diverse leadership team that has benefited from personal working experience in the domestic subsidiary, foreign subsidiary and corporate headquarters. It will be essential for senior managers to have a high tolerance for ambiguity and the flexibility in order to deal with unfamiliar business and cultural challenges.

The *cross-pollination* of a truly effective global leadership team takes many years to develop. Business managers must rotate promising executives at earlier ages in positions that are closer to the customer and have greater interaction with local employees and customers. The utilization of third-country nationals (TCNs) in other subsidiaries and in home-office headquarters assignments will further add to the diversity of the leadership team.

11. Employee selection

Great care must be exercised in selecting promising employees who will be most likely to be receptive to a corporate philosophy that embraces change, cultural diversity, flexibility and empowerment. Common communication and language skills are important considerations as companies evolve to become more fully integrated.

The development of a company's 'corporate business language' will become increasingly important for global coordination efforts. For example, if English is chosen as the company's standard language, senior management must develop a strategic initiative to ensure English-language competency with all appropriate global personnel. Allocation of resources for language instruction and a human resource plan for implementation must be developed.

12. Decision processes

The control and flow of decision-making will continue to become more complex. Emphasis will focus on 'empowering' employees at the lowest possible levels. Those employees who are closest to the customers will need to be able to make more responsible decisions. However, appropriate decision-making will require a high degree of knowledge, information and a thorough understanding of the organization's global strategic vision. Specialized training will therefore be required, and this will be different for each of the traditional structural designs. Cross-functional teams will be required in all organizations to improve decision-making. Later chapters will offer specific suggestions for optimal performance.

13. Information processes

The control and flow of information and knowledge between organizations must also be carefully assessed by corporate and subsidiary management teams. The best firms will design and implement solutions that will enhance the integrated flow of information and knowledge among all organizational units. Different solutions are required depending upon the company's principal formal structure. We shall offer suggestions for addressing these issues later in this book.

Corporate–subsidiary management accountabilities

Developing the proper balance of centralization and localization of decision-making will vary among companies depending upon product mix, formal structure, and chosen and environmental forces. Key accountabilities for corporate headquarters and subsidiary management are highlighted in Fig. 6.4.

The evolutionary process

Firms competing in the global marketplace traditionally evolve through several organizational structural designs (Fig. 6.5 on page 135). Unfortunately, today many organizations first 'reorganize' their structure, placing key personnel in important positions, and then begin to focus on their global strategic direction and work processes.

Successful firms achieving the core characteristics of the worldwide organizational solution will:

1. *Develop a global strategic vision* of the future through the strategic thinking process.

2. *Re-engineer work-flow processes* that focus on 'delighting' the customer.

3. *Design an organizational structure* that best aligns itself with the re-engineered work-flow processes and global strategic vision.

4. *Assign the best personnel available* to key positions, regardless of country of origin.

5. *Evaluate and understand the inherent strengths and weaknesses* of each traditional organizational structure.

Corporate management accountabilities

- Analyzes the 12 environmental force groupings of the industry and company

- Establishes global strategic vision and mission

- Develops strategic plans

- Creates a corporate culture

- Distributes capital resources

- Facilitates activities that capitalize on centralization and coordination

- Provides a global 'nationality-less' corporate staff that treats all subsidiaries equally

Subsidiary management accountabilities

- Ensures that all members of the subsidiary understand, agree with and 'live' the global strategic vision

- Implements the corporation's strategic plan and adapts the plan to meet local market needs

- Provides a conduit to share information and knowledge between subsidiaries, domestic and corporate headquarters

- Makes maximum utilization of the benefits of economies of scale, etc., when they meet local market demands

- Develops personnel, facilities and core competencies to maximize market potential

Fig. 6.4 The worldwide organizational solution: corporate and subsidiary management accountabilities

6. *Develop appropriate training programs and networks* to achieve optimal centralized/decentralized decision-making and transfer of knowledge.

Export structure

Corporations typically initiate non-domestic activity by means of exporting. The export structure that is developed is typically a modification of the domestic structural design.

Definition of an export structure

An export structure is established in the early stages of non-domestic activity. It relates to the means of selling and shipping of domestically

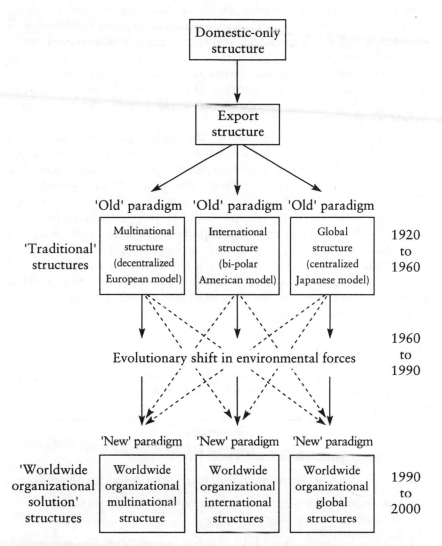

Fig. 6.5   The evolutionary process and formal organization structure

produced goods and usually comes under the jurisdiction of the marketing department or the CEO.

In many corporations, the export function will be attached to one of the existing functional departments—usually the marketing and sales organization. In companies with large diversified product lines, the export function is developed to handle several product lines and typically reports directly to the CEO.

The export department's primary accountability is the coordination of activities with key foreign customers or with trading companies. Trading companies provide local market expertise. Working through a trading company, an organization will derive the advantages of local customer knowledge, cultural negotiation skills, decreased transportation costs, and a knowledge of local governmental tax and regulatory issues. On the other hand, strategy and management will be delegated to the trading company, whereas utilization of the company's own sales force in foreign countries may ensure better implementation of the corporation's strategy.

The advantages of consolidating the export functions of several product divisions under one export organization such as a trading company include reduced travel expenses, reduced head count and consolidation of shipping expenses. The disadvantages include the distancing of the reporting relationship, lack of comprehensive product knowledge with a large, diverse product line and the reduced focus for exports by the marketing and sales department because of the change in accountability (Fig. 6.6). Use of trading companies has an additional disadvantage in that management is focusing on local domestic issues and 'delegating' the global issues to the trading company; the strategic focus of the producer remains 'local' while that of the trading company remains 'non-local.'

Historical perspective

Companies pursuing export strategies rely on the domestic company, and its geographic base, for manufacturing, R&D, finance, marketing, human resources, etc.

Advantages

- Export activities unified under one department

- Usually one sales representative to foreign customers for all products

- Efficiencies in shipping, tariffs exchange rates, etc., under one department

- Trading companies provide local marketing and distribution economies

Disadvantages

- Domestic divisions stay focused on home market

- Trading companies:
  - Lack focus on your products
  - Sell their strategic vision, not yours
  - Prevent company from gaining knowledge of non-domestic markets

Fig. 6.6   Export structure: advantages and disadvantages

All companies are influenced by their cultural and historic heritage. Many Japanese companies utilized Japanese trading companies during their early years of entry into markets outside of Japan. A close examination of Japanese culture and the post-World War II environment are keys to understanding this route of global expansion.

Formal matrix structure

Formal matrix structures, popular in the early 1970s, were an attempt to capture the benefits of at least two of the formal structural designs of worldwide organizations. Figure 6.7 shows how some corporations attempted to develop a dual reporting structure to glean the benefits of at least two of the formal structural designs. For example, in the formal matrix structure subsidiary marketing managers report on an equal basis to two bosses: the local subsidiary general manager and the corporate product division manager. The formal matrix structure attempts to align the coordination of the company on both: an area focus and a product focus.

The critical challenge to companies adopting this structure is the abandonment of unity-of-control. Coordination of personnel, and the conflicting directions received from two different managers, located

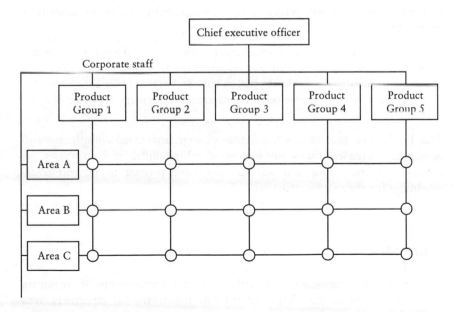

Fig. 6.7   Formal matrix structure

thousands of miles apart, with radically different cultural backgrounds and business experiences, make the formal matrix structure impossible to administer for most companies.

A balance of power between the two managerial forces is critical to achieving success with this structure. Obtaining the cooperation and focus of personnel becomes ever so much more complicated as the matrix's structure evolves to larger subunits within the firm. When conflict develops between two facing managers, the decision must be forwarded up the line to senior management for resolution. A number of similar situations can quickly tax the available time of senior executives who should be focused on more pressing corporate issues.

The reality of the market of the 1990s has shown that the complexities of a formal, dual reporting relationship have presented an overwhelming challenge for corporations. Today's growing need for a more flexible, leaner organization that uses speed as a competitive advantage has dampened the enthusiasm for the formal matrix structure. As noted by James W. Dudley:

> The matrix structure has very little to say for itself in a business setting and its proneness to conflict and the creation of organizational impotence makes it a poor structure for coping with the threats of global competition. The matrix structure is difficult to direct and, except where energies are focused on a limited range of problems, is too unwieldy to provide the basis for the structure of global organization.[9]

Corporate strategies will evolve at an ever-increasing rate in the latter part of the 1990s:

> The complexities of society, and the human systems required to meet continuing and new needs, requires a pooling of resources and talents. Inflation, resource scarcity, reduced personnel levels, budget cuts, and similar constraints have underscored the demands for better coordination and synergy in the use of brainpower.[10]

This heightened rate of environmental change, increased complexity and demands, increased focus on new leadership skills, and emphasis on cultural understanding and adaptability have proved to be too overwhelming for the matrix structure.

Summary

This chapter has focused on the early historical development of corporate structures. Each of the three traditional organizational structures was successful in the early years after its development because it fitted the demands of the economic forces of the time.

Today's market environment is different. The conflicting demands of centralization and localization of decision-making and the need for global learning and knowledge transfer require new work-flow processes and leadership competencies. The successful application of these 13 core characteristics is known as the '*worldwide organizational solution*'. The application of its principles to any of the three traditional structures will be necessary for success in today's market.

Notes and references

1. Christopher A. Bartlett and Sumantra Ghoshal, *Managing across Borders: The Transnational Solution*, Harvard Business School Press, Boston, Mass., 1989.
2. Ibid., pp. 13–17.
3. Ibid.
4. See Alfred Chandler, *Strategy and Structure*, MIT Press, Cambridge, Mass., 1962.
5. See Alfred Chandler, 'The evolution of modern global competition', in Michael E. Porter (ed)., *Competition in Global Industries*, Harvard Business School Press, Boston, Mass., 1986.
6. See Christopher A. Bartlett, 'Building and managing the transnational: the new organizational challenge', in Michael E. Porter (ed.), *Competition in Global Industries*, Harvard Business School Press, Boston, Mass., 1986, p. 377.
7. Bartlett and Goshal, op. cit.
8. See David W. Cravens and Shannon H. Shipp, 'Market-driven strategies for competitive advantage', *Business Horizons*, January–February 1991, p. 5.
9. James W. Dudley, *1992: Strategies for the Single Market*, Kogan Page, London, 1989, p. 345.
10. Philip R. Harris and Robert T. Moran, *Managing Cultural Differences* (3rd ed.), Gulf Publishing Company, Houston, Tex., 1991.

Multinational structure (decentralized, European model)

The advantages of utilizing the services of a trading company or exporting from home are offset by the extent to which non-domestic sales in the home country are increasing at the same time. Governments are eager for their own industries to expand, prosper and engage in production and exportation. As the sales volume of the imported product continues to escalate, many governments will encourage local production by imposing tariffs and other restrictions on the imports. Local firms will hasten to develop similar products.

Locally produced products frequently offer the advantages of lower transportation costs, easier access to raw materials, cheaper labor rates, reduced taxes/tariffs, greater knowledge of local market needs and reduced time required to adapt to a changing environment.

Description

A *multinational structure* consists of a domestic division and multiple non-domestic subsidiaries that operate with a high degree of autonomy and a low level of central control (Fig. 7.1). The subsidiaries frequently report directly to the CEO. This decentralized structure can trace its origins to a European heritage of structural design.

The decision to manufacture in a foreign country and to establish subsidiaries has a great impact on the way a company does business. It is essential that this structural change is the result of a well-designed *refocusing of the global strategic vision*.

Management process

In the early stages of expansion, the subsidiaries of the traditional multinational structure are usually headed up by a senior management official of the parent company or a family relative. Subsidiary general managers usually maintain an informal relationship with the CEO and often report directly to him or her. They are generally given significant autonomy to develop their companies because of the central office's limited knowledge of the local marketplace. This frequently results in the

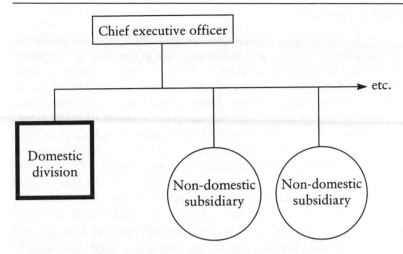

Fig. 7.1 Multinational structure (decentralized, European model)

development of subsidiaries with different *strategic visions*, cultures, processes and leadership styles from those of the home country.

Among the advantages of the traditional multinational structure (see Fig. 7.2), subsidiaries have direct contact with the CEO, and the home office support staff remains small. The independence of control provides subsidiaries with the flexibility to respond to local market needs.

Advantages
- Locally produced goods, offering:
  - Lower transportation costs
  - Access to raw materials
  - Reduced taxes/tariffs
  - Greater knowledge of local market
  - Reduced time need to adapt designs
- General manager usually responsible directly to CEO
- Usually 'informal' reporting relationship
- High degree of local autonomy
- Lean corporate staff

Disadvantages
- Usually little coordination between subsidiaries
- Lack of focus on a global strategic vision
- Competition between subsidiaries for resources
- Low level of sharing of information between subsidiaries
- Low level of interaction and exchange with the domestic organization

Fig. 7.2 Traditional multinational structure (decentralized, European model): advantages and disadvantages

Historical perspective

The traditional multinational structure is frequently referred to as the 'mother–daughter' structure, and it has its roots in the early development of multinational corporations in Europe. Early European firms frequently entered surrounding markets by establishing subsidiaries that were staffed primarily by the owner's relatives. These general managers maintained strong, personal relationships with the company's owner (the CEO) and usually reported to him or her directly. The presence of high tariff barriers encouraged subsidiaries to focus inward, and little coordination or transfer of knowledge occurred between such subsidiaries. What control existed was derived from direct communication with the owner and focused primarily on expected sales and earnings forecasts (Fig. 7.3).

Many European companies have grown up with small domestic markets. European executives are comfortable with cultural diversity, and most have frequently traveled to other countries. Their tradition in international trade dates back to colonial times. This offers them a competitive advantage when compared with the local-only market knowledge and cultural experiences of many Japanese and US organizations.

In a recent published interview, Glaxo Pharmaceutical's former deputy chairman Dr Ernest Mario emphasized Glaxo's delight with a multinational structure. Dr Mario acknowledged that Glaxo's intimate knowledge of how to work effectively with 12 different regulatory agencies in Europe provided it with a competitive advantage over Japanese and some American companies. Dr Mario further described Glaxo's corporate policy as being firmly based on decentralization.

Glaxo's manufacturing is customer-oriented, with 42 sites in 31 countries. Its R&D operations are likewise diversified. This philosophy, Mario claims, portrays the company as a good corporate citizen. Glaxo places much emphasis on its policy of subsidiaries being manned by local nationals and views corporate headquarters as responsible for providing guidance, establishing structure and policies and supplying investment funds. Dr Mario also emphasizes that Glaxo deliberately avoids building European-wide manufacturing and marketing organizations, unlike many US pharmaceutical companies that tend to 'love to centralize'.[1]

'Old' and 'new' paradigm core characteristics

Most companies that develop a multinational structure do so to take advantage of local manufacturing and sales in the non-domestic marketplace. To achieve optimal results today, the multinational firm must develop the 'new paradigm' core characteristics of the *worldwide organizational solution* (Figs 7.4 and 7.5 on pages 144 and 146–147).

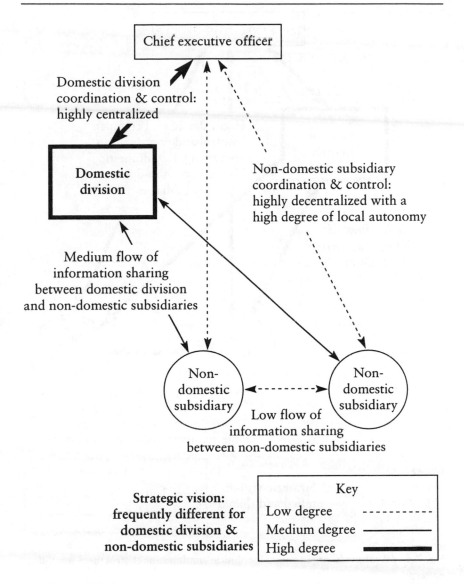

Fig. 7.3 **Traditional multinational structure (decentralized, European model): work-flow patterns**

1. Strategic focus

- *Old paradigm.* In the traditional, 'old' paradigm, decentralized multinational structure, the major strategic focus is on growth through the establishment of free-standing subsidiaries. The competitive advantage that this structure provides, compared with

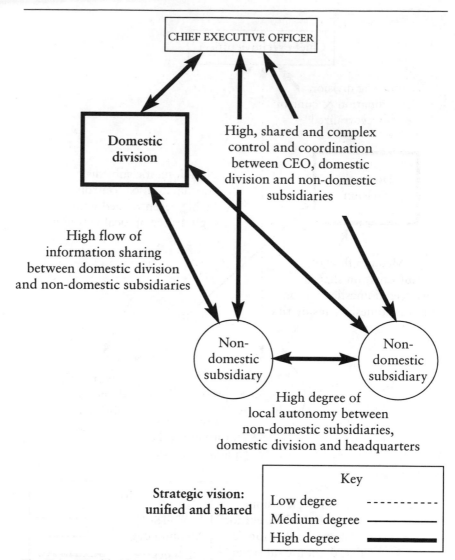

Fig. 7.4 'Worldwide organizational solution' multinational structure: work-flow patterns

an export structure, is the ability to allow for local adaptability and closeness to the customer. The company grows externally by establishing multiple subsidiaries and having little direct control over their activities.

- *New paradigm.* The organization must develop micro- and macro-work processes that capture, simultaneously, growth through local responsiveness, and the economies of scale, control and coordination of centralization.

2. Global strategic vision

- *Old paradigm.* Although the global strategic vision is developed centrally, it frequently differs in non-domestic subsidiaries. This difference develops as a result of the high degree of independence of subsidiaries and their lack of centralized control and coordination.

- *New paradigm.* Successful multinationals need to develop work processes that result in a *unified, understood and accepted global strategic vision.* Senior non-domestic subsidiary managers will participate in the development of the global strategic vision, which will ensure greater acceptance at the subsidiary level.

3, 5. Coordination and control

- *Old paradigm.* Coordination and control in a traditional multinational structure is the lowest of the three formal structures. Coordination between subsidiaries is often at a minimum. Subsidiaries frequently compete with each other for the limited resources available from the parent company.

- *New paradigm.* The corporation must capitalize on the advantages of increased coordination and global effectiveness without sacrificing its traditional strengths in local responsiveness. This change will require the development of new management skills and work-flow processes, to be discussed in later chapters.

4. Local autonomy

- *Old paradigm.* The multinational structure allows for the highest degree of local adaptability. General managers have significant freedom to use their own judgment in modifying products to local needs.

- *New paradigm.* Local autonomy will remain unchanged as multinationals move to this new paradigm structure.

6. Corporate–subsidiary relationships

- *Old paradigm.* The CEO communicates freely and informally with the subsidiary general manager. High local autonomy is coupled with a low level of knowledge and information exchange.

- *New paradigm.* Corporate–subsidiary relationships evolve to a high degree of interdependence and a sharing of knowledge and information.

Core characteristics	Traditional 'old' paradigm multinational structure			Worldwide organizational solution
	Weaknesses	Neutral	Strengths	
Strategy				
1. *Strategic focus.* Competitive advantage of this type of organization		Growth through free-standing subsidiaries		Growth through simultaneous and coordinated centralization and local adaptability
2. *Global strategic vision.* Where the corporation intends to go; emphasis here is acceptance of vision among units		Developed centrally, adapted significantly by subsidiaries		Unified, understood and accepted by all employees
Structure				
3. *Control.* Flow of direction and degree of centralized control from headquarters	Low			High
4. *Local autonomy.* Degree of freedom allocated to the subsidiary to change/modify products and direction			High	High
5. *Coordination.* The degree of teamwork subsidiary–subsidiary, headquarters–subsidiary	Low			High
6. *Corporate–subsidiary relationships.* The flow of decision-making and information-sharing	Informal and low			High, shared and interdependent

Fig. 7.5 Multinational structure: required paradigm shifts (*Continues*).

Core characteristics	Traditional 'old' paradigm multinational structure			Worldwide organizational solution
	Weaknesses	Neutral	Strengths	
7. *Subsidiary–subsidiary relationships.* The flow of decision-making and information-sharing	Low			High, shared and interdependent
8. *Domestic–subsidiary relationships.* The flow of information-sharing		Medium and direct		High, shared and interdependent
Culture and processing				
9. *Corporate culture.* Characteristics that unite people in an organization		Variable from subsidiary to subsidiary		Central and unified
10. *Management selection.* Predominant leadership trait needed and country of origin for general managers		Entrepreneurial Initially general managers from domestic country		Flexibility Best candidate available from any country
11. *Employee selection.* Country of origin for subsidiary management and corporate management staff		Sub.: local nationals HQ: domestic and non-domestic		Best available candidate from any country
12. *Decision processes.* Control and flow of decision-making		Decentralized; made within subsidiary		Shared and complex Emphasis on 'empowering' employees
13. *Information processes.* Control and flow of information and knowledge		Decentralized; made within subsidiary		Shared and complex High flow of information and knowledge

Fig. 7.5 Multinational structure: required paradigm shifts (*Concluded*)

7. Subsidiary–subsidiary relationships

- *Old paradigm.*   In the traditional multinational structure, a low degree of coordination takes place between subsidiaries because of the uniqueness of business problems, language and cultural differences and the competition between them for corporate resource allocations.

- *New paradigm.*   Subsidiary–subsidiary exchange of knowledge and information increases dramatically.

8. Domestic–subsidiary relationships

- *Old paradigm.*   Exchanges between the domestic division and the subsidiaries are generally open and are dependent upon the subsidiary's general manager's relationship with the domestic organization.

- *New paradigm.*   Domestic–subsidiary exchange of knowledge and information and decision-making will become highly interdependent and shared.

9. Corporate culture

- *Old paradigm.*   In the traditional multinational, each subsidiary develops its own unique culture because of the high degree of local autonomy and the lack of exchange of people, information and knowledge.

- *New paradigm.*   The corporate culture will evolve to become more unified throughout the whole organization.

10. Management selection

- *Old paradigm.*   In the early stages of forming a multinational firm, general managers are frequently expatriates from the home country and are usually chosen from family relations, or are long-term managers previously involved in the company's export operations. These general managers report directly to the CEO, and communication is informal and open. As time evolves and the number of subsidiaries increases, expatriates from other home-country firms may be integrated into the corporation. The use of local nationals (LNs) is initially low to non-existent.

- *New paradigm.*   Management selection will shift to the best available candidate, regardless of country of origin. Management personnel will frequently assume assignments in various subsidiaries and corporate home office locations throughout their career.

11. Employee selection

■ *Old paradigm.* Almost all corporate headquarters personnel are chosen from the domestic-country location. Subsidiary personnel are likewise chosen almost exclusively from the local country.

■ *New paradigm.* Employee selection will continue to rely heavily on the local country, but key positions and 'trainee' positions will be filled by employees on specific career tracks from various countries. This *cross-pollination* of lower-level personnel with potential for key management positions is a critical step in the globalization process.

12. Decision processes

■ *Old paradigm.* Decision-making is highly decentralized with a great degree of independence afforded to the local general manager.

■ *New paradigm.* Decision processes will evolve to carefully consider the impact of decisions on both corporate strategy and other subsidiaries. Decision processes will become shared and complex, and will reach the best-case scenarios for the local subsidiary, other subsidiaries and the domestic division.

13. Information processes

■ *Old paradigm.* Since subsidiaries often compete for resources and are often rewarded for their performance in relation to other subsidiaries, limited inter-subsidiary exchange of information usually occurs.

■ *New paradigm.* The exchange of information and knowledge among major units within the multinational firm will become interdependent, high and shared.

Summary

The traditional multinational structure traces its roots to post-World War I Europe. The high degree of nationalism and the high barriers to trade existing at that time resulted in subsidiaries with a very large degree of independence and little central control or coordination.

In today's global economy, firms with multinational organizational structures must develop work processes and training programs that move their firms closer to achieving the core characteristics of the world organizational solution.

Notes

1. A summary article that appeared in *SCRIP*, no. 1756, 25 September 1992, p. 10. This summary was derived from an interview with Dr Mario that appeared in British Airway's *Business Life Magazine*.

International structure (bipolar, American model)

Organizations evolve to form an international structure as a natural progression from either an export structure or a multinational structure. As non-domestic subsidiaries increase in number, size and financial importance, the complexities involved in supporting these units frequently call for the establishment of an international headquarters. This form of organizational structure occurs most frequently with organizations that have very large domestic operations (usually 40 per cent or more of sales). This is more typical of American-based corporations because of the large, homogeneous nature of the US market. The result is the creation of a bipolar organization consisting of a domestic division and an international division. The international division headquarters provides the necessary vehicle to initiate increased control and coordination within the non-domestic marketplace.

Description

An *international structure* is an organizational design that is characterized by a large, domestic division and a corresponding international division (Fig. 8.1). Both divisions of this bipolar structure report to the CEO. This structure increases the control and the transfer of knowledge between non-domestic subsidiaries. Its heritage has evolved from American corporations with very large domestic operations and a need for better coordination and control of non-domestic subsidiaries.

Historical perspective

The traditional international structure traces its roots to the non-domestic expansion of large US firms following World War II. Most large US corporations during this era were organized by either functional divisions or product divisions. As these firms began to expand and form subsidiaries, it was a natural extension for these subsidiaries to be grouped under a division for international operations.

Change in strategy

The decision of a corporation to establish an international structure from an export structure, or to evolve from a multinational structure to an

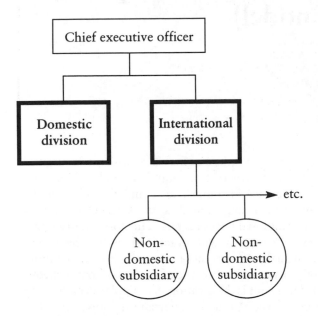

Fig. 8.1   International structure (bi-polar, American model)

international structure, is, again, one that must be based upon the corporation's refocusing of its global strategic vision.

An international structure offers several advantages to the corporation (Fig. 8.2). The appointment of an international vice-president and the setting up of international headquarters provides for a unified voice to address non-domestic needs with the corporate staff. This increased central focus allows for better coordination and control of subsidiary activities, enabling the global strategic vision to be more easily disseminated and implemented. Considerable local autonomy continues in this structure, and subsidiary general managers maintain a medium degree of autonomy and flexibility. The development of international line and staff managers is accomplished via this new international structure.

The *strategic* change to an international structure is a major turning point in the life-cycle of the corporation. It is usually accompanied by a significant shift in resource allocation and an increased awareness of and focus on the non-domestic marketplace. The formation and growth of the international division has the potential to cause friction with the domestic organization as the two divisions begin to compete for limited financial and human resources.

Adequately preparing all employees for this strategic shift in corporate strategy and focus is one of the greatest challenges of the CEO and senior staff. Failure to involve key employees early in the decision-making

Advantages

- Central focus on non-domestic strategy
- Combined international focus offers greater impact within the corporate framework
- Increased centralization and coordination while maintaining significant local autonomy
- Framework for the development of international managers
- International staff can focus on the development of new subsidiaries and offer unified assistance, i.e. training
- International staff can provide better decisions on regional manufacturing, raw materials, capital, etc.

Disadvantages

- Potential for domestic versus international power struggles
- Cultural evolution (conflicts between domestic and international)
- Development of subsidiary personnel tends to be from country to country—little training in cross-national coordination
- Separation of domestic managers from subsidiary managers
- Two 'semi-autonomous' organizations with different leadership and different corporate cultures
- R&D usually remains domestic oriented

Fig. 8.2   Traditional international structure (bipolar, American model): advantages and disadvantages

process, and to gain support from all employees before the transformation begins, will lead to a slow and difficult evolution.

Management process

The role of the general manager changes as a company moves to a traditional international structure design (Fig. 8.3). The general manager no longer reports directly to the CEO on an informal basis; he or she now reports to an international vice-president, who represents a united position for the combined interests of all subsidiaries. The implications for this change are significant. The vice-president and the international staff will initiate the development of formal reporting procedures, and a certain degree of autonomy will be removed from the general manager.

It is highly likely that the initial international staff will be composed of a large percentage of domestic employees who previously served on the domestic corporate staff. Their familiarity with corporate procedures and the high cost of transferring subsidiary personnel to the home office will be key determinants in the staffing decision. Cultural differences, a limited knowledge of the non-domestic market and the formulation of new

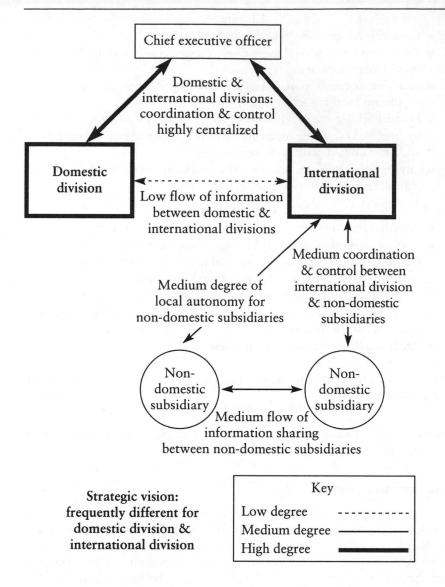

Fig. 8.3 Traditional international structure (bipolar, American model): work-flow patterns

policies and procedures for the international division can all lead to a difficult transitional period.

In the early stages of the formation of the traditional international division, many firms maintain their R&D organizations in the home country. This means that products will continue to be oriented to the domestic marketplace, with international needs being considered only after the greater and more profitable domestic needs have been satisfactorily addressed.

Another drawback of the traditional international structure is that its design can formally sever the interaction between subsidiary personnel and their domestic colleagues. Most information and decision-making must now find its way through the maze at the international staff headquarters.

The organization of subsidiaries reporting to the international vice-president does not lend itself to the unbridled flow of information between subsidiaries. Subsidiaries are frequently competing against one another for resources and the financial rewards of better comparative performance.

'Old' and 'new' paradigm core characteristics

The traditional international structure developed as a more effective means to administer non-domestic operations. Companies that adopt this structure do so to increase coordination, control and information transfer among their non-domestic subsidiaries. To achieve optimal success in today's marketplace, firms with international structures must excel at the 'new' paradigm core characteristics of the worldwide organizational solution (Fig. 8.4 on page 156 and Fig. 8.5 on page 160-161).

1. Strategic focus

- *Old paradigm.* The creation of an international division headquarters offers the advantages of centralizing certain common non-domestic functions. It is a significant structural change that follows a basic change in global strategic vision. Subsidiaries receive specific directions from an international vice-president and staff. Less autonomy is available to the general manager and subsidiary staff. The competitive advantage of centralizing some activities (e.g. certain marketing, finance, training) contributes to the growth of the corporation. Senior managers now relate to two core organizations—the domestic division and the international division.

- *New paradigm.* Organizations with an international structure must develop a paradigm shift within both the large domestic division and the international division. Senior management must change the predominant attitude of these divisions from one of operating in separate silos or as competitors to one focusing on mutual shared learning and teamwork.

2. Global strategic vision

- *Old paradigm.* Traditional international structured organizations frequently developed two different strategic visions with justification that their divisions' needs and marketplaces are unique and different.

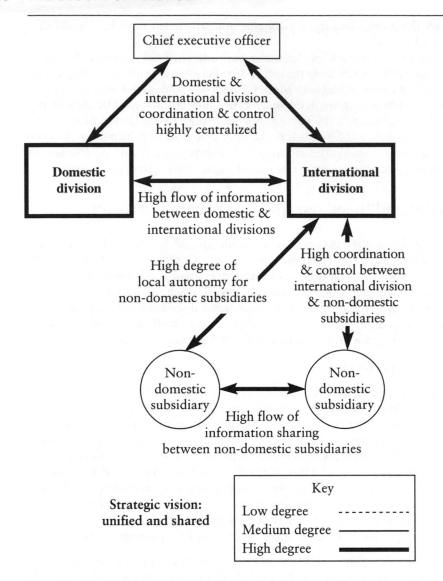

Fig. 8.4 'Worldwide organizational solution' international structure (bi-polar, American model): work-flow patterns.

- *New paradigm.*   In today's marketplace, both the domestic and the international division require a shared, common and unified global strategic vision. Both organizations must focus their strategies and tactics on achieving this common goal and must frequently interact to exchange knowledge and improve cross-divisional learning.

3, 5. Coordination and control

- *Old paradigm.* Coordination and control are both moderate in the traditional international structure. Coordination, control and the transfer of knowledge between the domestic and international divisions remain traditionally low. At times the relationship may even be described as confrontational.

- *New paradigm.* Under a united and shared global strategic vision, the domestic and international divisions move to form an organization that becomes highly dependent upon increased coordination and transfer of knowledge between the two divisions. Success requires a high degree of interdivisional learning and teamwork.

4. Local autonomy

- *Old paradigm.* Local autonomy remains but is deemed less important as a strategic competitive advantage than in the previous multinational structure. The corporation's management changes its strategy to reflect a more important focus on coordination and control within the international division.

- *New paradigm.* Local autonomy and adaptability increase in importance but are properly balanced with those decisions that need to be made at higher levels.

6. Corporate–subsidiary relationships

- *Old paradigm.* Communication between the CEO and the subsidiaries must flow through the international division. This middle step can delay communication and can result in alteration of meaning or intent.

- *New paradigm.* Work-flow processes are improved to ensure a high degree of coordination, focus and knowledge transfer between corporate headquarters, international division headquarters and subsidiaries.

7. Subsidiary–subsidiary relationships

- *Old paradigm.* A medium degree of subsidiary–subsidiary communication and coordination occurs as a result of the development of certain 'standard practices' and joint training and marketing efforts resulting from the development of the international staff.

- *New paradigm.* Subsidiary–subsidiary knowledge transfer and learning increase significantly to meet competitive threats and to improve speed and economies of scale.

8. Domestic–subsidiary relationships

- *Old paradigm.*   Little to no direct communication and coordination exist between the domestic division and the subsidiaries in the traditional international structure. What limited activity occurs will usually flow first through the international headquarters staff.

- *New paradigm.*   Domestic–subsidiary coordination and learning improve to a high degree through the development of cross-functional and cross-divisional networks and teams. New product introductions and competitive activity vary among countries. A high degree of cross-organizational communication is essential.

9. Corporate culture

- *Old paradigm.*   Companies frequently see the development of two distinct corporate cultures—the domestic culture and the international culture. While some components of these two cultures may be similar, it is likely that there will be considerable areas of dissimilarity. Reasons for this invariably are the result of different historical backgrounds, unique and different business problems, cultural background differences of employees and the small number of employees rotating between the domestic and international divisions.

- *New paradigm.*   The corporate culture of the organization evolves to become shared and unified. Key employees are 'cross-pollinated' between the two divisions and serve to establish the development of cross-divisional networks and teams.

10. Management selection

- *Old paradigm.*   The role of the general manager changes significantly as the company adopts a traditional international structure. General managers need to possess the ability to deal effectively with the home-office international staff. This international staff usually maintains a high percentage of employees from the corporate headquarters country in the early stages of development. General managers and subsidiary employees must properly balance the demand of both the international staff and the local marketplace. General managers are frequently selected, over time, from the subsidiary management team. In mature international structures, a significant number of general managers and key staff members are selected from the subsidiary country.

- *New paradigm.* Corporate culture evolves to become shared and unified. This change is accomplished through joint global strategic vision development, 'cross-pollination' of key employees, global training programs, cross-divisional process teams and global networks of key decision-makers.

11. Employee selection

- *Old paradigm.* Local nationals (LNs) predominate the subsidiary companies and their staffs. Exceptional candidates for senior subsidiary management positions are given rotational opportunities on the international staff. Some become permanent members of staff of the international organization's headquarters.

- *New paradigm.* Employee selection for subsidiary and international staff management positions evolves to the point where the best qualified candidates from any country are selected.

12. Decision processes

- *Old paradigm.* General managers have less autonomy in decision-making under the international structure than with the multinational structure. A considerable number of decisions are made at the international headquarters.

- *New paradigm.* Decision processes come to be shared, between the domestic and international divisions.

13. Information processes

- *Old paradigm.* A greater degree of information is communicated between subsidiaries and from subsidiary to international headquarters because of the redirected focus on the need for coordination and control by headquarters. There is limited access to domestic divisions except through the international headquarters.

- *New paradigm.* Information processes develop to high degree among both subsidiary, international and domestic divisions.

Core characteristics	Traditional 'old' paradigm international structure			Worldwide organizational solution
	Weaknesses	Neutral	Strengths	
Strategy				
1. *Strategic focus.* Competitive advantage of this type of organization		Growth through partial centralization of decisions and practices		Growth through simultaneous and coordinated centralization and local adaptability
2. *Global strategic vision.* Where the corporation intends to go; emphasis here is acceptance of vision among units		May be different between domestic and international divisions		Unified, understood and accepted by all employees.
Structure				
3. *Control.* Flow of direction and degree of centralized control from headquarters		Medium		High
4. *Local autonomy.* Degree of freedom allocated to the subsidiary to change/modify products and direction		Medium		High
5. *Coordination.* The degree of teamwork subsidiary–subsidiary, headquarters–subsidiary		Medium		High
6. *Corporate–subsidiary relationships.* The flow of decision-making and information-sharing		Formal and through international HQ: some decisions central, others at subsidiary level		High, shared and interdependent

Fig. 8.5 International structure: required paradigm shifts (*Continues*)

| | Traditional 'old' paradigm international structure | | | Worldwide organizational solution |
Core characteristics	Weaknesses	Neutral	Strengths	
7. *Subsidiary–subsidiary relationships.* The flow of decision-making and information-sharing		Medium		High, shared and interdependent
8. *Domestic–subsidiary relationships.* The flow of information-sharing	Low and through international HQ			High, shared and interdependent>
Culture and processing				
9. *Corporate culture.* Characteristics that unite people in an organization	Domestic and international highly variable			Central and unified
10. *Management selection.* Predominant leadership trait needed and country of origin for general managers		Coordinator Usually domestic country and local nationals		Flexibility; best candidate available from any country
11. *Employee selection.* Country of origin for subsidiary management and corporate management staff		Sub.: local nationals HQ: domestic and non-domestic		Best available candidate from any country
12. *Decision processes.* Control and flow of decision-making	Domestic and international separate; some decisions by international HQ, others by subsidiary			Shared and complex; emphasis on 'empowering' employees
13. *Information processes.* Control and flow of information and knowledge	Domestic and international separate; some flow between international HQ and subsidiary			Shared and complex; high flow of information and knowledge

Fig. 8.5 International structure: required paradigm shifts (*Concluded*).

Summary

The bipolar, American model traditional international structure originated in the decade following World War II. Companies using this structure typically maintain a large domestic division and a correspondingly large international division. It is common for these two divisions to compete for limited financial and strategic resources.

Firms with international structure need to develop the core characteristics of the worldwide organizational solution to achieve optimal success in today's global economy.

Global structure (centralized, Japanese model)

As worldwide corporate activity continues to increase, and as competition with foreign imports heightens, firms are being forced to allocate resources and acquire raw materials, finished goods, etc., from the best global source, without regard to the country or corporate division of origin.

Companies that adopt a global structure undergo a significant change in their strategic vision. These firms develop a highly centralized decision-making philosophy. All geographical locations are treated exactly the same as the home market. The company becomes 'nationality-less'.

Herbert Meffert and Brian Bloch have identified three major factors that are critical to gaining competitive advantage through a centralized, global structure:

1. Reaping *economies of scale*, that is global cost reduction through the exploitation of volume effects or the advantages of specialization (e.g. Philips, Benetton);

2. Exploitation of *economies of scope*, that is raising innovative potential through learning effects, pooling of resources, and know-how; such strategies can lead to worldwide quality leadership as in the cases of IBM and Kodak;

3. Coping with risk through *structural hedging*, that is locating production facilities in high sales areas in order to maximize foreign exchange earnings (e.g. Honda in the USA).[1]

Description

A global structure is an organizational design characterized by a centralized world headquarters that exerts tight overall control (Fig. 9.1). Domestic and international divisions are usually not consulted, as most decisions are made from headquarters. All geographical field units, including the domestic unit, are treated equally. The corporation becomes 'nationality-less' in its pursuit of optimal economies of scale and speed of decision-making.

Global structures may be organized by product division, area division or functional division.

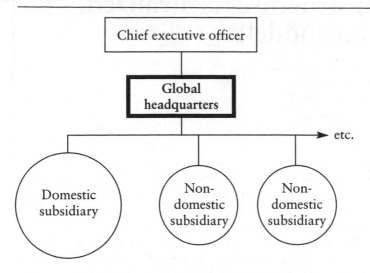

Fig. 9.1   Global structure (centralized, Japanese model)

Historical perspective

Japanese firms began their major worldwide expansion in the post-World War II era. The external environment they faced was very different from that of European and American firms, which had started their worldwide expansions earlier. The cultural perspective and values made them ideally suited to select a corporate strategy and structure that favored a centralized, coordinated approach. The Japanese focused on building highly efficient factories that produced premium-quality, cost-effective products. Distribution was initially achieved through trading houses. The Japanese cultural emphasis on coordination, consensus and control made the adoption of a centrally controlled structure natural. Many features of the global structure are similar to those of Japanese cultural perspectives.[2]

The global structure originated from Japanese corporations' early experiences in worldwide activities. These experiences predominantly related to centralized decision-making and manufacturing. Subsidiaries served primarily as implementers of corporate strategy.

Matsushita Electric Company has developed into a global leader through such brands as Panasonic and National. This company has successfully controlled the global strategy from the center and has shown flexibility and responsiveness at the customer level. Its success with video cassette recorders (VCRs) is directly attributed to tight central control of research and development and production:

> The research project that began Matsushita's development of its enormously successful VCR product was launched in the late 1950s under the leadership of Dr. Hiroshi Sugaya, a young physicist in the company's Central Research

Laboratory. As the product evolved into its development stage, the core members of Dr. Sugaya's team were kept together as they transferred from CRL to the product development and applications laboratory located in the product division. After a long and difficult development process, the product was finally ready for commercial production in 1977.

In other companies we surveyed, it was not uncommon for research engineers to move to development, but not with their projects, thereby depriving the companies of one of the most important and immediate benefits of such moves. We also saw no other examples of engineers routinely taking the next step of actually moving to the production function. This last step, however, is perhaps the most critical in integrating research and production, both in terms of building a network that connects managers across these two functions, and also for transferring a set of common values that facilitates implementation of central innovations.[3]

Change in strategy

The global strategic vision in a global corporation requires that strategic decisions be centralized and made for the best interests of the corporation as a whole, without consideration for the domestic or non-domestic location. All decisions are refocused toward the best solution for the company's overall mission.

Companies adopting the global structure treat the domestic market without favoritism—as an equal with all other markets. Arvind Phatak has noted:

> But most importantly, it is the structural conflict between the geographic orientation of the international division and the product orientation of the domestic divisions that motivates the top management to reorganize the company in a fashion that merges the domestic and international sides of the business into one integrated global structure.[4]

Management process

Chief executive officers who are considering adopting a global structure should spend considerable time and energy assessing the impact of this change on employees. Attempting to 'blend' the leadership teams of domestic and international divisions will present a challenge. At best, these two semi-autonomous organizations will have grown up and existed side-by-side in a non-competitive fashion. At worst, the domestic and international divisions will have been competing for many years for limited resources.

The decision of who will head the combined domestic/non-domestic global groups will send a clear but alarming message to all employees concerning which division's 'policy' will rule the new structure. This new 'hybrid' organization will experience many challenges in its early days as two groups of employees with significantly different leadership and cultural experiences attempt to forge a partnership.

Many members of staff will now be faced with 'global responsibilities'. These dedicated employees will have spent the majority, if not the entirety, of their careers climbing the corporate ladder in either the domestic or the international division. All will be stressed by their lack of knowledge of dealing in geographic and product areas that are unfamiliar to them. Each will be working with 'new' employees from the other division.

The critical question that faces the CEO and senior staff is how to develop a new corporate culture—a hybrid that capitalizes on the best that the former domestic and international divisions have to offer. How will senior management avoid imposing one of the former two cultures on the new amalgamated work-groups? Those organizations that will excel will be those that successfully forge global hybrid work-teams and cultures that utilize the best features of each division and work together to achieve a common global strategic vision.

CEOs that do not take an active role in achieving this new team-oriented hybrid culture will risk the potential struggle for power and dominance by managers of the former structure's two divisions.

CEOs and other senior executives who have not had previous line management experience in both domestic and international divisions and in subsidiary management will be ill-prepared for the leadership challenges that await them.

Types of global structure

Global structures of firms are organized into one of three configurations:

- Global area structures
- Global product structures
- Global functional structures

In deciding which of these structural designs is the most appropriate, many factors must be taken into consideration, including maturity and depth of product lines, degree of national-level coordination required, importance of economies of scale, need for unique technologies, degree of local product adaptation needed and the degree of centralized control desired.

Global area structures

In global area structures, the head of the area division has both the authority and the responsibility for all operations in that geographical area (see Fig. 9.2). All geographical locations within the corporation are treated as equals, and corporate strategy dictates that all areas work in union

Advantages

- Regionalization helps to blend economies of scale with the need for local adaptation
- Authority to make modifications lies with area division leadership
- Provides for a unified, focused global strategic vision
- Equal treatment of all geographic areas
- Improved communication and coordination between subsidiaries within the area

Disadvantages

- Communication and coordination with other area divisions and corporate headquarters difficult
- Difficulty in obtaining proper product focus with a geographic-oriented management team
- Global product planning problems
- Less-than-optimal central control
- R&D coordination, focus and transfer difficult

Fig. 9.2   Global area structures: advantages and disadvantages

toward a common global strategic vision. Assets, including capital, are distributed with the intent of optimal return on corporate goals—not area goals. In this structure the domestic market is treated the same as all other area divisions.

Global area divisions attempt to manufacture within their own areas. They focus on producing the highest-quality and most cost-effective products to compete effectively in their areas. Companies that frequently use global area division structures are those in mature businesses with narrow product lines. These products offer few technological advances. For companies that are successful using this structure, their marketing skills constitute their competitive advantage. Economies of scale and pricing are essential tools to their success. Companies competing in the pharmaceutical, food, automotive, cosmetics and beverage industries, among others, tend to utilize the global area structure.

Food and beverages are examples of products that require significant global adaptation to appeal to local tastes. Although most types of coffee can be found in specialty shops around the world, local markets have individual preferences. Americans tend to favor lighter, less bitter coffees than many European countries; and decaffeinated coffee is more widely demanded in the American market.

The global area structure encourages improved communication and transfer of knowledge between subsidiaries within the area worldwide. This represents significant progress over other structural designs. This shift to greater central coordination and control decreases the autonomy at the subsidiary level.

Global product areas

Corporations that evolve from an international structure to a global product structure create global product divisions. These divisions have the worldwide responsibility for all product promotional activities (e.g. marketing, finance, production).

The executives who run the global product divisions assume the authority that used to reside with the subsidiary managers. Each of the various global product divisions operates as a profit center and does so with a great degree of autonomy. Companies that tend to adopt this structural style are those with many products in the early stages of growth. Their principle goal is to achieve a greater degree of worldwide coordination. This increased coordination encourages greater economies of scale and an improved flow of product knowledge and technology across borders. The global product structure provides for a united, focused worldwide plan which should improve the uniformity of introduction in all subsidiaries (see Fig. 9.3). It also facilitates adaptation of the product(s) to meet local needs. Global product divisions are also used for products that have reached the maturity stage in the home market but are considered to be in the earlier growth stages in other markets.

Other critical benefits (and different ones from the multinational and international structural models) are the improvements in centralization and the coordination of manufacturing and research and development. The global product division attempts to maximize economies of scale with a quality product of world-class stature by choosing the best manufacturing locations for labor, raw materials, transportation, tariffs and taxes.

The focus of research and development, which was centered on the domestic market in the multinational and international models, now shifts in an attempt to satisfy the needs of the global marketplace. Many firms

---

Advantages

- All support functions focused on product, not area
- Easier to tailor products to needs of buyers
- R&D and manufacturing focus on global needs of customers
- Increased global focus and cross-border coordination
- A unified, focused global strategic vision provided for

Disadvantages

- Duplication of corporate support functions for each product division
- Product division executives usually chosen from the domestic marketing organization
- Tendency to focus efforts on subsidiaries with the greatest potential for quick returns

Fig. 9.3   Global product areas: advantages and disadvantages

---

report that this benefit alone is sufficient to change the corporation's strategy and structure.

Companies shifting to the global product division structures have experienced certain drawbacks as well as the advantages mentioned. It has been observed that the executives chosen to head the newly created global product divisions tend to be predominantly from the marketing division of the domestic company. This focus of control and direction from domestic-only experienced executives may lead to (1) too great a focus on domestic concerns, (2) lack of adequate understanding of the cultural differences between foreign and domestic workers and customers, and (3) difficulty in retaining and attracting non-domestic executives for corporate assignments.

The global product structure design requires the formation of duplicate staff functions within each division. This can create considerable additional overhead for the corporation and must be carefully evaluated by senior management.

Another criticism of this structure is the tendency for global product division heads to desire to concentrate on those subsidiaries that have the greatest potential for a quick financial return. Senior management must provide guidance to ensure that those subsidiaries that would be considered longer-term investments are given adequate home-office support.

Global functional structures

The global functional structure is adopted by corporations that are organized globally primarily on the basis of function and secondarily on the basis of area or product. Each function is coordinated from corporate headquarters. This type of structure is used infrequently, but is most often seen in the extractive industries—mining, metals, oil, etc. Firms that employ this structure view product knowledge as a key competitive advantage.

Among the advantages of the global functional division (see Fig. 9.4) are (1) small central staff, (2) increased central control and (3) a major focus on expertise within the function. The major disadvantages structure include: (1) lack of accountability for sales and earnings except at the senior management position, (2) multiple product lines presenting significant management problems because of the separation of functions (e.g. production and marketing in different divisions) and (3) the problem of coordinating marketing and manufacturing in different geographical locales.

It is because of the above complexities that few organizations utilize the global function structure. Those organizations that do are concerned with moving raw materials globally and with operations requiring a high degree of centralized control and coordination in a globally integrated manufacturing process.

Advantages

- Small central staff
- Strong central control and coordination
- Provides for a unified, focused global strategy and vision
- High degree of functional expertise

Disadvantages

- Coordination of manufacturing and marketing in different geographic areas
- Lack of accountability for sales and earnings except with the CEO
- Significant management problems presented by multiple product lines

Fig. 9.4 Global functional structure: advantages and disadvantages

'Old' and 'new' paradigm core characteristics

Companies that evolve to a global structure have determined that one of their greatest competitive advantages lies in achieving economies of scale through global sourcing of raw materials, labor, capital, etc. To achieve optimal results in today's economic environment, firms with global structures must strive to achieve excellence in the 13 core competencies of the 'new' paradigm worldwide organizational solution (Fig. 9.5 on page 171, Fig. 9.6 on page 172 and Fig. 9.7 on page 174-175).

1. Strategic focus

- *Old paradigm.* In a traditional global structure, the corporation's headquarters focuses all activity on achieving the global strategic vision. The domestic and international headquarters staffs are dismantled; in their place is created a new global headquarters staff. All geographic areas are treated equally, without preference for the home market.

- *New paradigm.* The global structure continues to utilize the strengths of centralizing key decisions but also provides for local autonomy under appropriate situations.

2. Corporate vision

- *Old paradigm.* Global strategic vision is centralized and unified. A high degree of emphasis is placed on the development and implementation of a singular global strategic vision. Although unified at the top, however, understanding and implementation may vary at the employee level.

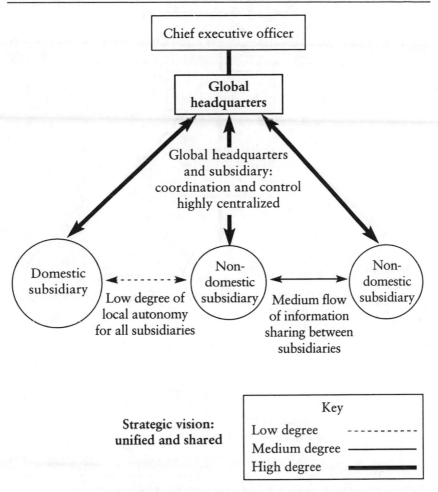

Fig. 9.5 'Traditional' global structure (centralized, Japanese model): work-flow patterns

- *New paradigm.* The global strategic vision in the global structure continues to evolve and is carefully communicated, understood and accepted by all levels of management and employees. Care is taken to ensure that the global strategic vision is culturally acceptable in key markets. All employees focus their efforts on doing their part to achieve the global strategic vision.

3, 5. Coordination and control

- *Old paradigm.* The strategic focus in the traditional global structure emphasizes a high degree of centralized coordination and control as a key competitive advantage. The elimination of the domestic and

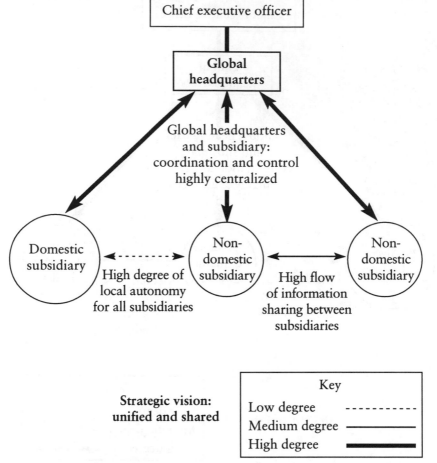

Fig. 9.6   'Worldwide organizational solution': global structure

international headquarters and their replacement with a centralized corporate headquarters makes this competitive advantage possible.

■ *New paradigm.*   Control remains high, but cooperation improves still further as all employees come to understand and accept the global strategic vision.

4. Local autonomy

■ *Old paradigm.*   Local adaptability and autonomy are not seen as of major importance to companies that assume a traditional global structure; economies of scale and the ability to access raw materials, parts, labor, capital, etc., on a worldwide basis are viewed as greater competitive advantages.

- *New paradigm.* Local adaptability *combined with* a high degree of centralized control and coordination become the norm.

6. Corporate–subsidiary relationships

- *Old paradigm.* Corporate headquarters communicates directly and frequently with subsidiary management. Since most key decisions are developed centrally, the flow of decisions is primarily from the top down.

- *New paradigm.* Corporate–subsidiary relationships improve as headquarters allows greater input from subsidiaries.

7. Subsidiary–subsidiary relationships

- *Old paradigm.* In a global area structure the coordination between subsidiaries will be adequate under the area head. Interactions between subsidiaries with different area heads will be few.

- *New paradigm.* Subsidiary–subsidiary coordination and knowledge transfer increase dramatically through cross-functional and cross-divisional teams.

8. Domestic–subsidiary relationships

- *Old paradigm.* The domestic organization is treated as just another subsidiary, without special or separate treatment.

- *New paradigm.* The domestic subsidiary continues to be treated like all other subsidiaries, but communication, knowledge transfer and learning improve significantly.

9. Corporate culture

- *Old paradigm.* The development of a unified corporate culture focused on a common global strategic vision and guided by senior management may take several years to develop fully and become effective.

- *New paradigm.* Corporate culture will remain unified. The scope of this unification will expand beyond the center to encompass appropriate subsidiary cultural needs.

10. Management selection

- *Old paradigm.* The senior managers selected to head the new 'nationality-less' global headquarters are charged with establishing a new global strategic vision for the company and with discarding their previous preferences for either a domestic or an international

| | Traditional 'old' paradigm global structure | | | Worldwide organizational solution |
Core characteristics	Weaknesses	Neutral	Strengths	
Strategy				
1. *Strategic focus.* Competitive advantage of this type of organization		Growth through centralization and economies of scale; 'Nationality-less'		Growth through simultaneous and coordinated centralization and local adaptability
2. *Global strategic vision.* Where the corporation intends to go; emphasis here is acceptance of vision among units		Centralized and unified		Unified, understood and accepted by all employee
Structure				
3. *Control.* Flow of direction and degree of centralized control from headquarters			High	High
4. *Local autonomy.* Degree of freedom allocated to the subsidiary to change/modify products and direction	Low			High
5. *Coordination.* The degree of teamwork subsidiary–subsidiary, headquarters–subsidiary		Medium		High
6. *Corporate–subsidiary relationships.* The flow of decision-making and information-sharing		Formal; most key decisions made at HQ		High, shared and interdependent

Fig. 9.7 Global structure: required paradigm shifts (*Continues*)

Core characteristics	Traditional 'old' paradigm global structure			Worldwide organizational solution
	Weaknesses	Neutral	Strengths	
7. *Subsidiary–subsidiary relationships.* The flow of decision-making and information-sharing		Medium		High, shared and interdependent
8. *Domestic–subsidiary relationships.* The flow of information-sharing				High, shared and interdependent
Culture and processing				
9. *Corporate culture.* Characteristics that unite people in an organization			Central and unified	Central and unified
10. *Management selection.* Predominant leadership traits needed and country of origin for general managers			Implementer; best candidates regardless of country of origin	Flexibility Best candidate available from any country
11. *Employee selection.* Country of origin for subsidiary management and corporate management staff			Best available candidate from any country	Best available candidate from any country
12. *Decision process.* Control and flow of decision-making		Centralized		Shared and complex Emphasis on 'empowering' employees
13. *Information process.* Control and flow of information and knowledge		Centralized; retained at HQ		Shared and complex High flow of information and knowledge

Fig. 9.7 Global structure: required paradigm shifts (*Concluded*).

orientation. A careful blend of the most effective leaders of the old organization are needed. General managers and their staff, many of whom will have limited knowledge outside their previous domestic or international experience, will need to adjust to a new set of corporate headquarters personnel. A greater number of decisions will be centralized in the global structure, and the role of general manager will change to become one of greater accountability for implementation of the corporate plan. A greater number of management positions are filled in both headquarters and subsidiaries by third-country nationals (TCNs).

- *New paradigm.*   Senior management personnel will be given greater autonomy to run their subsidiaries while still maintaining a high degree of centralized decision-making and coordination.

11. Employee selection

- *Old paradigm.*   Employees have greater mobility in relocating between subsidiaries and also in relocating to the corporate headquarters. Criteria for selection are shifted to the best qualified person, without regard to country of origin.

- *New paradigm.*   Employee selection continues to focus on the best available candidate from any country.

12. Decision processes

- *Old paradigm.*   Decision-making is highly centralized in the global structure. The advantages of this approach include a more uniform product across different geographies and greater speed of introduction.

- *New paradigm.*   The control and flow of decision-making evolves from highly centralized decision-making to one that is more shared and complex. This effort maintains the ability to make centralized decisions in those areas that require it and to make joint corporate–subsidiary decisions where they are appropriate.

13. Information processes

- *Old paradigm.*   Information is also highly centralized and flows most heavily from corporate headquarters to the subsidiaries.

- *New paradigm.*   Information flow and knowledge improve dramatically between subsidiaries and between corporate headquarters and subsidiaries. This is accomplished through re-engineering work-flow processes, cross-divisional informal networks and the 'cross-pollination' of key employees.

The Ford 'Mondeo' experience

The Ford Motor Company has traditionally maintained an organizational structure that most closely resembles that of the international (bipolar) structure (Chapter 8). It is characterized by a large North American division and a European division (and smaller Asia-Pacific and Latin American divisions) which have operated fairly independently of each other in all aspects including engineering, sourcing, manufacturing and distribution. Limited cross-pollination of personnel and limited knowledge transfer between divisions have occurred in the past.

Ford can be recognized as the first global car company. In fact, more than half the cars in the world in 1920 were identical Model T Fords. The Model T achieved exceptional economies of large-scale production and was an ideal solution for the marketplace based upon the environmental forces of its era. In the 1960s the Volkswagen Beetle became the second international car, providing simple transportation in an uncomplicated global marketplace.

Tomorrow's world car must be different. It must be designed to the *highest uncommon denominator* to achieve global acceptance. Ford of Europe's new Mondeo ('Contour'—Ford in the USA—and Mercury 'Mystique') is such a car.

Mondeo's 'uncommon denominators' include meeting the world's toughest noise requirements, using no CFCs, no asbestos or cadmium, and the most recyclable car ever produced by Ford—more than 85 per cent recyclable. Mondeo exceeds the most demanding crash test requirements in the world, incorporates dual air bags and has a new generation seatbelt configuration. Its engineers have developed truly superior suspension and braking systems combined with a new family of fuel-efficient engines.

The Mondeo/Contour/Mystique is both a *global* car and a *local* car. All major systems, including transmissions, engines, suspension and body-structures, are universal in design. But it is also localized—North American versions of the car have unique interior and exterior appearances that address differing tastes from those of European consumers.

The organizational structure used to design this vehicle represents a *major paradigm shift*. Typically, basic car designs are developed locally for local markets and are 'modified' for other markets. Ford took an entirely different approach with the Mondeo. Ford developed a unique structural team to capitalize on its global resources, which resulted in a unique worldwide development process.

Ford developed a worldwide team of experts from all locations to develop the Mondeo. Engineers representing 'centers of excellence' were assembled in Genk, Belgium. America contributed its superior expertise in higher-powered modular engines, automatic transmissions, power steering and air conditioning. Europeans' expertise in smaller car design, manual transmissions and four-cylinder engines were employed. Worldwide suppliers were chosen at the start of the project and were integrated into the team. Alex Trotman, Ford chairman and chief executive officer, remarked:

'The organizational structure chosen for the development of the Mondeo represents a major new direction for Ford. We assembled a team of 140 top engineers from around the world representing different areas of Ford expertise. Team members were empowered to make key decisions without exhaustive review by corporate headquarters. Special attention was focused on meeting customers' desires which ultimately led to our decision to tailor certain interior and exterior components to local consumer preferences.

We believe we have captured global engineering excellence, economies of scale and adaptability to meet local demand.'[5]

Ford's structural solution represents a 'new' paradigm shift in worldwide excellence. Their success in developing cross-functional teams has resulted in an infrastructure for the continuous interchange of views and new work-flow processes designed for worldwide excellence.

Your organization today

Where is your organization today? What basic traditional structural design does your firm use? Does your company successfully meet all of the 13 core characteristics of the worldwide organizational solution?

The chart reproduced as Fig. 9.8 on page 180-181 has been designed to allow you to self-examine the strengths and weaknesses of your basic structural design, work processes and selection of key employees. It can serve as a valuable tool with which to begin to develop a world-class organization.

Summary

The traditional global structure features a highly centralized organization in which all geographical locations are treated equally. It is said that the organization becomes 'nationality-less'. At the same time, the demands of the 12 environmental forces in today's economy require firms with global structures to develop local responsiveness. To achieve this, globally structured companies must develop the core characteristics of the worldwide organizational solution.

Notes and references

1. Herbert Meffert and Brian Bloch, 'Globalization strategies: their implementation', *Industrial Management*, vol. 91, no. 5 (1991), pp. 3–9.
2. Arvind V. Phatak, *International Dimensions of Management*, 2nd edn, PWS-KENT, Boston, Mass., 1989, p. 88.
3. See Christopher A. Bartlett, 'Building and managing the transnational: the new organizational challenge', in Michael E. Porter (ed.), *Competition in Global Industries*, Harvard Business School Press, Boston, Mass., p. 375.
4. Christopher A. Bartlett and Sumantra Ghoshal, 'Organizing for worldwide effectiveness: the transnational solution', *California Management Review*, vol. 31 (Fall 1988), p. 60.
5. Remarks made during a personal interview with Alex Trotman, Ford chairman and CEO. Additional material provided by David Scott, vice-president for public affairs.

| Core characteristics | Company name: | | | Worldwide organizational solution |
	Weaknesses	Neutral	Strength	
Strategy				
1. *Strategic focus.* Competitive advantage of this type of organization				Growth through simultaneous and coordinated centralization and local adaptability
2. *Global strategic vision.* Where the corporation intends to go; emphasis here is acceptance of vision among units				Unified, understood and accepted by all employees
Structure				
3. *Control.* Flow of direction and degree of centralized control from headquarters				High
4. *Local autonomy.* Degree of freedom allocated to the subsidiary to change/modify products and direction				High
5. *Coordination.* The degree of teamwork subsidiary–subsidiary, headquarters–subsidiary				High
6. *Corporate–subsidiary relationships.* The flow of decision-making and information-sharing				High, shared and interdependent
7. *Subsidiary–subsidiary relationships.* The flow of decision-making and information-sharing				High, shared and interdependent

Fig. 9.8 Global structure: corporate profile evaluation (*Continues*).

| Core characteristics | Company name: | | | Worldwide organizational solution |
	Weaknesses	Neutral	Strength	
8. *Domestic–subsidiary relationships.* The flow of information-sharing				High, shared and interdependent
Culture and processing				
9. *Corporate culture.* Characteristics that unite people in an organization				Central and unified
10. *Management selection.* Predominant leadership trait needed and country of origin for general managers				Flexibility Best candidate available from any country
11. *Employee selection.* Country of origin for subsidiary management and corporate management staff				Best available candidate from any country
12. *Decision processes.* Control and flow of decision-making				Shared and complex Emphasis on 'empowering' employees
13. *Information processes.* Control and flow of information and knowledge				Shared and complex High flow of information and knowledge

Fig. 9.8 Global structure: corporate profile evaluation (*Concluded*).

Summary, Part II

Successful companies competing in today's marketplace will need to have a clear understanding of the environmental forces affecting their industries and themselves. They will need to be able to predict the future trends of these environmental forces with a high degree of accuracy.

The global strategic vision of such companies will complement and take advantage of the rapidly evolving marketplace. Their strategic plans and annual operating plans will be designed with maximal input from all appropriate staff and field organizations. Managers and employees will develop, understand, gain consensus and enthusiastically implement the corporation's global strategic vision.

Management will fully understand that the 'achilles heel' of success may be the limitations imposed by the formal reporting structure selected. Selection and training of managers and key employees will remain a cornerstone of success. Senior management will thoroughly understand the core characteristics of the worldwide organizational solution. They will carefully design training programs and develop work processes that will maximize the strengths of the structure chosen and overcome the limitations with which each of the traditional structures described in this part is burdened.

Part III

Chapters 1–9 have focused on the historical reasons for the evolution toward globalization, the necessity of adjusting corporate strategy to this new reality, the new paradigm shifts and the resulting corporate structure modifications required to facilitate the newly articulated strategic vision.

Chapters 10–13 will discuss 'global managers'—the individuals who are responsible for making globalization work. It is our belief that organizations will not achieve their globalization objectives without highly skilled managers. Simply stated, the skills that made individuals and organizations successful in multinational, international and global structures will not necessarily be the skills that will help them be successful in the future. To remain competitive, corporations will have to employ and train managers with global capabilities and competencies and to achieve the worldwide organizational solution.

In this part we will describe the 12 competencies and what must be done to prepare the organization to be successful in the new economic environment.

Amanda Bennett states: 'Recognizing a need for change, many companies are focusing on different skills in their training,'* In the same article she states that Dow Chemical 'asked 300 senior managers what skills their successors should have. Among the most common answers: an ability to lead effectively in ambiguous, complicated and dynamic situations.' Specific competencies are required to make globalization work, and these are identified and discussed in the ensuing chapters.

---

* Amanda Bennett, 'Path to top job now twist and turns,' *Wall Street Journal*, 15 March 1993, pp. B1, B3.

The global manager and global attitudes

> *The multinational of the 1970s is obsolete. Global companies must be more than just a bunch of overseas subsidiaries with executive decisions made at headquarters. Instead, a new type of company is evolving. It does research wherever necessary, develops products in several countries, and promotes key executives regardless of nationality.*
> Business Week, 14 May 1990[1]

> *. . . there's a lot that's going on in the world that's changing the nature of business, and therefore the management task. The question is: Are we preparing managers adequately for the new competitive dynamic, the world of the 21st century?*
> *CHRISTOPHER BARTLETT*[2]

Changing environmental circumstances are demanding new global strategic visions and new organizational structures in which these visions are conceptualized, articulated and implemented by managers. Who are these managers? What skills, attitudes, education and experiences can they contribute to establishing and/or maintaining their company's global competitiveness? We believe that the excellence of an organization will be a reflection of the competencies of its employees. Without these competencies, we believe it will be impossible for individuals in organizations to think both globally *and* locally, and to act appropriately in the global economic environment.

Significant societal changes like the discovery of electricity and the Industrial Revolution were initiated by just a few individuals; the resulting changes and necessary adjustments were implemented by many. So it is with globalization.

For the successful implementation of global strategies, the global strategic vision must be clearly articulated. Those persons in an organization who are responsible for implementing globalization must understand, support and develop the required competencies to make it work.

The root of the problem regarding competencies

Normally, the individuals who run a country's businesses are graduates of that country's educational system, and the essence of global competition is the skills, training, experience, and education of the business people involved.

Improved state education is critical if a country is to remain globally competitive, but the transformation will take many years. In the meantime, as graduates of their imperfect educational systems enter the workforce, massive entry-level training will be required. In addition, significant retraining of the current workforce will also be necessary.

A new kind of manager

In the 29 September 1986 issue of *Fortune*, Richard Kirkland wrote, 'A new breed of manager is taking charge in Western Europe.'[3] He described this new manager as 'aggressive and well-educated'. Such managers see their country as say France or Germany, but their business world is Europe and beyond. Asia's managers are also changing, as job mobility and greater individuality become more the norm than the exception.

It is difficult and risky to make generalizations about groups of people, but the following subsections sketch the background, education and experience base from which this 'new breed' of individual we call the 'global manager', may be emerging. The profiles are based on interviews of managers from various countries.

The British global manager

Most British global managers have a level of education comparable to that of American global managers working in international business. The majority have a graduate degree in business, engineering or law.

While study of a foreign language is required in British secondary schools, British managers do not have a reputation for linguistic skills. They tend to rely upon the fact that English is the most common language of international business.

Typically, the British manager has traveled extensively in Europe, and also to the United States. Many have lived, studied, or worked somewhere in Europe or the United States.

Their outlook is European; they tend to keep up with political and economic developments with an emphasis and priority on Britain. Many appear to convey an aura of cultural superiority, which perhaps stems from the days when Britain was a hegemonic power.

The Japanese global manager

Although the Japanese global manager is not required to have a degree, most have completed four years of university study concentrating on economics, political science, engineering or business. Graduate degrees are relatively rare, and a specific academic background is not as important as the manager's age and history within the company.

Reflecting the Japanese respect for age and experience, corporate structure is arranged according to an 'age–grade pay system'; that is, management position and promotion decisions are based first on seniority, then on age, the employee's record within the company and skill, in that order.

Most managers are able to read and speak English at a basic level but few are proficient or fluent. English is becoming more important for those who wish to attain management status, however. In recent years, a growing number of managers have also been exposed to an overseas living experience of approximately three years.

The typical characteristics expected of a Japanese manager are the ability to think long-term, to consider the welfare of subordinates, and to be objective and unemotional in their decision-making.

The Swedish global manager

Swedish managers have a high degree of education and many have at least one graduate degree in business, law or engineering. Many are fluent in English, and they usually have proficiency in other Scandinavian and European languages such as French and German.

As a general rule, they have traveled extensively in Europe and many have studied and/or worked there. It is also common for them to have traveled to the United States. For this reason, it is not surprising that they have a thorough knowledge of domestic, European and international current events, politics and economics. Their outlook is international, with particular emphasis on Europe and Sweden's future involvement with Europe.

The Mexican global manager

In Mexico the education of global managers varies according to the size of the company—the larger the corporation, the more education its managers tend to have. Specifically, they will have graduate degrees in technical fields, business or law. It is very common for them to have studied in the United States, and such educatiion/training is highly valued by Mexican professionals.

English is spoken proficiently by most managers in Mexico. Knowledge of French, German or Japanese is rare. Most Mexican managers have traveled extensively in the United States and in other Latin American countries, but travel elsewhere is usually limited. Their knowledge of domestic, US, and Latin American politics and current events is vast. Much of their knowledge regarding the United States comes from the media.

Their outlook extends beyond their country's borders, particularly to the United States, also to the rest of Latin America. Mexicans have an immense national pride and many desire to study abroad, then return to Mexico and use their knowledge for the betterment of their country.

The German global manager

German managers are highly educated, usually attaining at least a master's degree and often possessing a PhD. They tend to come to management from diverse fields such as engineering, chemistry or law. People with a background in sales or marketing are not as likely to achieve top management levels, although this is slowly changing as German business becomes less product-oriented.

German managers have a tendency to manage 'behind the scenes', trying not to attach too much importance to a charismatic personality. They would rather be heard and not seen.

German managers are likely to possess good English skills and to have traveled extensively in Europe and the United States, although most will have spent little time actually living abroad. They carry with them a very international outlook, and are very knowledgeable about domestic as well as European and American politics.

The Indian global manager

The employees of smaller, family-owned trading companies usually do not have graduate degrees; most have bachelor's degrees, in science, commerce or engineering. The larger corporation managers, on the other hand, tend to have master's degrees. These managers speak both Hindi and English proficiently. They also have some knowledge of French or German.

Their travel exposure is generally limited, and they have most likely never lived abroad. Indian managers keep up with their domestic politics, and their knowledge of international politics is good, but often is concentrated on Britain as a result of their colonial past. Their long history as a trading nation has given Indian managers an outward, international perspective of commerce and events.

The Korean global manager

The Korean manager tends to take a long-term view of business, and decisions are arrived at after much thought. Loyalty to the company is expected and managers are accustomed to the idea of 'life-time employment'. Working long hours is common, with many managers routinely putting in 60 or more hours a week.

Korean managers usually have at least an undergraduate degree. Degrees are typically completed in either business or economics, and graduates of the top schools such as Seoul National University, Yonsei University or Korea University are highly sought after. Once the company deems a manager to be a suitable candidate, it will sponsor his or her graduate degree, most often in the United States or Japan, since much of Korea's business is conducted with those two countries.

Conversational English is required of Korean managers. In recent years, increasing numbers of managers are also able to speak Japanese or Chinese well.

The competencies required for globalization

> *For the times, they are a'changing.*
> BOB DYLAN

Nowhere is this more apparent than in today's business world. Change was the overwhelming theme in a survey conducted with executives from 88 global companies around the world.

Executives' responses

In January 1993, 88 surveys were mailed to members of Thunderbird's World Business Advisory Group (from the American Graduate School of International Management, Glendale, Arizona). The Advisory Group represents a cross-section of large global firms, many from Fortune 500 companies, with 10 000 or more employees. Only senior-level personnel completed the surveys, including CEOs, presidents, vice-presidents and directors; 49 questionnaires were returned, giving a cooperation rate of 56 per cent.

The survey was divided into several parts. The first asked executives to respond to eight quotations. The results are given in Table 10.1. (The Appendix to this book reproduces the questionnaire in full.)

Whether asked about strategic change, globalization, training issues or future concerns, executives indicated that the ability to adapt to ever-changing conditions is a prerequisite for survival in the increasingly international business environment.

Executives also identified some of the competencies they believed to be crucial to globalize successfully. In the cross-cultural literature, too, there has been considerable research in the area of identifying cross-cultural competencies. Brent Ruben of Rutgers University has been in the forefront of many of these studies.[4] He correctly states that the impetus for much of the research comes from an attempt to understand the phenomena of culture shock, adaptation and adjustment, and other problems experienced by those working in another culture.

In the management literature, C. K. Prahalad of the University of Michigan, an influential teacher of corporate strategy, among others, has urged organizations to focus on 'core competencies'.[5] The impetus from a

Table 10.1   Replies to Globalization Questionnaire*

	Does not apply				Applies
	0%	25%	50%	75%	100%
1. 'We decided to globalize first, then clean up.'	1	↑ 2 **13.5%**	3	4	5
2. 'Our goal is to train our people in globalization skills by 1994 but we don't know what the skills are or what percentage of our people are trainable.'	1	↑ 2 **15%**	3	4	5
3. 'There is a major gap between executives who believe that global strategy is understood and middle managers who say they understand it.'	1	2	3 ↑ **60%**	4	5
4. 'Most of our employees do not have a global mindset.'	1	2	3↑ **52.5%**	4	5
5. 'Managing organizational change is a serious challenge for us.'	1	2	3	↑4 **73.5%**	5
6. 'Middle managers, responsible for short-term profits, experience too much pressure and are not able or willing to think ong-term or collaborate globally.'	1	2	3 ↑ **53.5%**	4	5
7. 'Global managers are not born.'	1	2	3 ↑ **60.5%**	4	5
8. 'In global organizations a new kind of leader is required.'	1	2	3	↑ 4 **71.5%**	5

Note: Each response 1–5 was assigned a weight starting with 0 and increasing at intervals of 25. For example, the response of '1' was assigned a zero value, '2' was assigned 25%, '3' was assigned 50% and so on through the number '5'. The number of responses for each category was then multiplied by the assigned weight of the category. For instance, if all 49 responders circled '2', it would be given the weight of 49 × 25% and then divided by the total score for the question.
* The questionnaire is reproduced in full in the Appendix.

business perspective comes from strategic alliances that failed, negotiations that were bungled and bottom-line losses that could be clearly attributed to a lack of competency on the part of the individuals involved. This research is reported from an applied perspective in *Managing Cultural Differences*[6] and other books.

Many of these competencies are not addressed in MBA programs. 'B—minus. That's the mark that B. Joseph White, dean of the University of Michigan Business School, gives other business schools for their efforts in preparing what he calls competent leaders for tomorrow's challenges.'[7]

Finding the right person for the right job has been a longstanding task of management. Now, in the competitive global environment that is rapidly changing and very unpredictable, the task is even more difficult. Many organizations have been successful in determining the critical positions, but they have been less successful in 'distinguishing who will be a star performer from who will be just average or even magical', according to Dr Kenneth Martin of the Hay Group.[8] He also states: 'No company I've ever worked with has any trouble identifying who its best people are. But few can tell you just what it is that makes them the best.'

From this information and a review of over 1000 articles and books that have been published between 1987 and 1993, the 12 organizational and individual competencies required to make globalization work have been drawn up (Fig. 10.1). These competencies will be described and developed in this and the following three chapters.

Attitudes
1. Possesses a global mindset
2. Works as an equal with persons of diverse backgrounds
3. Has a long-term orientation

Leadership
4. Facilitates organizational change
5. Creates learning systems
6. Motivates employees to excellence

Interaction
7. Negotiates and approaches conflicts in a collaborative mode
8. Manages skillfully the foreign deployment cycle
9. Leads and participates effectively in multicultural teams

Culture
10. Understands their own cultural values and assumptions
11. Accurately profiles the organizational and national culture of others
12. Avoids culture mistakes and behaves in an appropriate manner in other countries

Fig. 10.1   Twelve organizational and individual competencies to make globalization work

---

Studies conducted with companies and individuals have demonstrated that organizations and people can successfully change. Self-initiated change ('I want to learn this skill') and professionally facilitated change ('The department will attend a five-day seminar on globalization') have both been successful. How change occurs is not well understood, and this book is not intended to answer the question of *how* organizations and individuals change, or to identify the change methods that have consistently demonstrated successful outcomes. Our purpose is to identify the competencies and to suggest strategies for acquiring them.

Figure 10.2 summarizes the 12 external environmental factors, described in Chapter 2, leading to globalization and the 12 organizational or individual competencies required to succeed in globalization.

Competency 1: Possesses a global mindset

In the play *South Pacific*, Rogers and Hammerstein wrote:[9]

> You've got to be taught to hate and fear
> You've got to be taught from year to year,
> Its got to be drummed in your dear little ear,
>   You've got to be carefully taught.
>
> You've got to be taught to be afraid
> of people's whose eyes are oddly made,
> And people whose skin is a different shade,
>   You've got to be carefully taught.
>
> You've got to be taught before its too late,
>   Before you are six or seven or eight,
> To hate all the people your relatives hate,
>   You've got to be carefully taught,
>   You've got to be carefully taught.

The lyrics state eloquently what we have known for a long time: namely, the basic vehicle of learning has always been, and will continue to be, other humans. At birth, infants are completely dependent on others for survival. In maturing and throughout the socialization process, children learn that the gratification of needs is, to a large extent, dependent on demonstrating 'appropriate' social behavior and on 'inhibiting' aggressive or destructive urges. In groups, whether family, business or other, individual social needs become suggestive to the influence of others, especially those in authority, which may bring about a re-examination of, or changes in, attitudes and behavior.

Attitudes are learned and therefore can be unlearned. A *global mindset* is an attitude: it is not knowledge or information. We learn to be ethnocentric, and we can learn to be global in our perspective.

External Forces

▲ Economies of scale

▲ New and evolving markets

▲ Global sourcing

▲ Reduced tariffs/customs barriers and tax advantages

▲ Homogeneous technical standards

▲ Lowered global transportation costs

▲ Increased telecommunication options at reduced costs

▲ Trend toward homogeneous demand for products

▲ Competition from international competitors

▲ Customer strategy changes from domestic-only to global

▲ Exchange rate exposure

▲ Accelerating rate of technological change

GLOBALIZATION

Vision   Strategy   Structure   Culture

Competencies required to make it work

Attitudes

● Possesses a global mindset

● Has the ability to work as equals with persons of diverse background

● Has a long-term orientation

Leadership

● Facilitates organizational change

● Creates learning systems

● Motivates employees to excellence

Interaction

● Negotiates and approaches conflicts in a collaborative mode

● Manages skillfully the foreign deployment cycle

● Leads and participates effectively in multicultural teams

Culture

● Understands their own culture values and assumptions

● Accurately profiles organizational culture and national culture of others

● Avoids cultural mistakes and behaves in a manner that demonstrates knowledge and respect for the way of conducting business in other countries

Fig. 10.2   Globalization forces and competencies

193

Mindsets

'Mindset' is a word that rarely is used in daily conversation. *Webster's Encyclopedia Unabridged Dictionary of the English Language*, containing over 250 000 entries, does not list it. A smaller Webster's dictionary defines 'mindset' as a 'fixed mental attitude'.

Glenn Fisher's excellent book, *Mindsets: The Role of Culture and Perception in International Relations*,[10] demonstrates the importance of possessing a global mindset to succeed in the globalization process. Individuals working in foreign countries share similar experiences in overseas assignments and must not only meet the requirements of their work assignments, but also be able to adjust to unfamiliar 'attitudes and psychological predispositions'. They must function within the expectations of the host culture. In other words, they must 'work across contrasting mindsets . . . [which] reflect differences in national experience and culture', according to Fisher.

To date, no comprehensive studies have been conducted on the ways in which contrasting mindsets affect international business relationships and transactions. The education of most managers has provided only 'hard' business skills, such as engineering, finance and strategic planning. Fisher suggests the necessity of providing global managers with additional training in the social sciences, as it is not sufficient to provide a person only with facts and information about unfamiliar cultural practices. The explanation of *why* people behave the way they do is more important, because it fosters a deeper understanding, rather than mere acceptance and adaptation.

Fisher's goal is to encourage individuals who find themselves in international settings to be more 'objective' in dealing with 'mismatched mindset', and to 'develop a broader framework in making judgments in international activities'.

Global mindsets

Stephen Rhinesmith correctly postulates that a 'global mindset' is a requirement of a global manager who will guide institutions and organizations into the future. He defines a mindset as:

> a predisposition to see the world in a particular way that sets boundaries and provides explanations for why things are the way they are, while at the same time establishing guidance for ways in which we should behave. In other words, a mindset is a filter through which we look at the world.[11]

Rhinesmith states that people with global mindsets approach the world in a number of particular ways. Specifically they:

1. Look for the 'big picture'; that is, they look for multiple possibilities for any event or occurrence—they aren't satisfied with the obvious.

2. Understand that the rapidly changing, interdependent world in which we are living is indeed complex, and that working in these environments where conflicts need to be managed skillfully is the norm rather than the exception.

3. Are 'process'-oriented; in our experience this is the most important dimension, and the one that is most lacking in individuals who are not globally oriented. Many individuals are unable to understand or are unwilling to learn to 'process', namely to reflect on the 'how' as opposed to the 'what'.

4. Consider diversity as a resource and know how to work effectively in multicultural teams; an ability to collaborate instead of competing is also integral to the person with a global mindset.

5. Are not uncomfortable with change or ambiguity.

6. Are open to new experiences.

Ethnocentricity vs geocentricity

Contrasted to the individual with global mindset is the one who is *ethnocentric*. Ethnocentricity is defined by the *Random House Dictionary* as:

> Belief in the inherent superiority of one's own group and culture; it may be accompanied by feelings of contempt for those others who do not belong; it tends to look down upon those considered as foreign; it views and measures alien cultures and groups in terms of one's own culture.

Levine and Campbell[12] developed a framework illustrating ethnocentrism (Fig. 10.3).

Not only individuals, but also organizations can be ethnocentric. Heenan and Perlmutter state that ethnocentric organizations tend to use home-country personnel in key positions throughout the world, believing they are more intelligent and capable than foreign managers.[13]

Geocentric organizations, on the other hand, attempt to integrate diverse viewpoints through a global systems approach to decision-making.

Attitudes toward themselves and their groups	Attitudes toward others
■ See themselves as virtuous and superior	■ Believe outgroup is inferior
■ See their standards of value as universal and intrinsically true	■ Believe outgroup is weak
■ See themselves as strong	■ Distrust outgroups

Fig. 10.3   Framework of ethnocentrism

In this case, superiority is not equal to nationality, and all groups can contribute to the organization's effectiveness.

The Culture Shock Inventory, developed by W. J. Redden in 1975, was designed to measure individual ethnocentrism, or the degree to which individuals perceived their value system to be appropriate for others.

Attitude change

With globalization, contact between persons from different cultures increases. What happens when this occurs? Do individuals become more global or more ethnocentric?

Following a review of the literature on intergroup contact, Amir concluded that the direction of attitude change, following contact with people who are different, depends largely on the conditions under which the contact has taken place.[14] He indicates that there are 'favorable' conditions, which reduce prejudice, and 'unfavorable' ones, which may increase prejudice.

The favorable condition of 'equal status' as a factor in reducing prejudice was reported by Allport.[15] He pointed out that, for contact between groups to be an element in reducing prejudice, it must be based on 'equal status contact between majority and minority groups in the pursuit of common goals'. Organizations that are globalizing must have common goals.

Summary

For Competency 1, Fig. 10.4 provides an opportunity for readers to reflect on the structure of their company or organization (is it traditional multinational, traditional international or traditional global according to descriptions of these structures in earlier chapters?) and to rate the CEO, corporate staff, subsidiary general manager and staff, as well as all employees in general. We are fully aware there may be great variation among the corporate staff or employees; but what is the central tendency? Or, generally, to what degree do these groups of people possess the competency?

On the basis of our assessment and interpretation of the significant literature on the subject, we have then indicated whether the competency is *essential*, *useful* or *not necessary* for the CEO, corporate staff, subsidiary general manager and staff, and all employees, in order for the transformational goal to be realized and to make globalization work.

	CEO	Corporate staff	Subsidiary general manager and staff	All employees
Your company				

Rate and describe the degree the competency is possessed for each of the categories for your organization·

H = Demonstrates a high degree
S = Demonstrates somewhat
L = Demonstrates to a low degree
N/A = Not applicable for your organization

Transformational goal for structure

	CEO	Corporate staff	Subsidiary general manager and staff	All employees
Worldwide organizational solution	*Essential* For a global vision to be created and implemented	*Essential* To support vision	*Essential* To communicate to employees	*Essential* To support and implement the global strategic vision

Fig. 10.4   Compentency 1: Possesses a global mindset

Competency 2: Works as an equal with persons from diverse backgrounds

> *One of the richest under-utilized resource in America is the talent of its women.*
> HUBERT H. HUMPHREY

This section focuses on working women, since the number of women in the workforce worldwide has dramatically increased since 1950. We are fully aware that diversity in the workforces of many countries is also reflected in a significant increase in the numbers of Third and Fourth World immigrants, the physically challenged, senior citizens and others. Generally, the following workforce trends have been identified:[16]

- By the year 2000, women will comprise just under 50 per cent of the US workforce.

- By the year 2000, non-whites will make up 20 per cent of the US workforce.

- Greater numbers of immigrants are coming to the United States than at any time since World War I.

■ A greater portion of the US workforce is middle-aged, and the workforce is gradually getting older.

The demographics of the workforce in most countries are changing. This is reflected in the development of seminars and workshops on 'cultural diversity' in the United States and other countries. Five years ago these seminars were unheard of, or else, when conducted, they were under the rubric of 'affirmative action'.*

Ian Ross, the president of AT&T Bell Labs, a premier high-tech company with many Nobel Prize Winners as current researchers, has stated that in 1991 over 50 per cent of its employees were born outside the United States.

Changes in the US workforce were discussed in an article entitled 'Future Work'.[17] The authors identified far-reaching changes such as the aging of the workforce and the influx of minorities and women. A manager's ability to anticipate change and its effect on the employees of the organization becomes vital to the competitive survival of the organization. As competition increases, businesses are realizing that workers must be considered assets and not merely fixed costs.

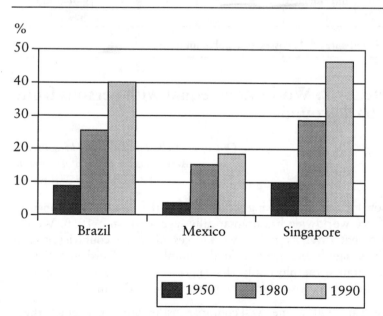

Fig. 10.5 **Increases of Women in the workforce. Percentage of women aged 15 and above who hold positions**

---

* Affirmative action is rooted in US law, which requires organizations to advertise openings and hire without regard to gender, religion or national origin. In some instances quotas are used.

Women in the workforce

As growing numbers of women enter the US workforce, demographers predict the average American woman will have fewer than two children. In 1992, more than 70 per cent of American women held paying jobs. Figure 10.5 shows the significant increase in the percentage of women with paying jobs in Brazil, Mexico and Singapore.

The Conference Board Europe identified similar European demographic trends in a 1991 study of 30 companies with reputations for successfully recruiting, promoting and retaining women.[18] Total European employment for these companies was over 500 000 and more than one-third of these were women. However, only 11 000 of these female employees were managers and around 1300 were in the top 10 per cent of the salary bracket; less than 200 were in the top 5 per cent of the salary bracket, and only 19 were members of boards of directors.

The percentage of women in the workforce shows worldwide increases, as indicated in Table 10.2.

Table 10.2   Women in the workforce

Country	Year	% of women aged 15–64 in workforce
Australia	1990	52.2
Austria	1990	43.0***
Canada	1991	58.2*
Denmark	1990	61.7**
Finland	1991	57.1**
France	1991	44.7**
Germany	1990	45.7**
Italy	1990	32.7**
Japan	1991	50.7**
Mexico	1990	21.6
Netherlands	1991	54.5
Pakistan	1991	14.0
Philippines	1990	47.5
Sweden	1991	54.8
Turkey	1991	34.6
United Kingdom	1990	52.0
United States	1991	55.6**

*   Includes women in the workforce to age 70
**   Includes women in the workforce to age 74
***   Includes women in the workforce to age 80

Source: International Labor Office Yearbook, 1992.

Women in international business

This growing number of women in workforces around the world, combined with expanding globalization among companies, should result in an increased number of women in international business. In fact, the number of international businesswomen *has* grown over the years, but not at a rate consistent with the number of women in the workforces of their respective countries. When it comes to overseas assignments, women face additional barriers. Surprisingly, female managers report that the biggest barriers come from *within* the corporation, rather than from situations actually encountered during foreign assignments.

These barriers stem from upper management's belief that women are not interested in the opportunity of an overseas assignment. Furthermore, according to Nancy Adler and Daphne Israel,[19] corporations often assume that foreigners will be prejudiced against females. The European Conference Board stated: 'The companies may hide behind supposed cultural differences to offer women an uneven chance . . .'[20] Yet, both of these assumptions have been disproved.

Interestingly, the female enrollment in international business programs has been growing. A survey conducted at top management schools found that women are not only interested in international careers, but are slightly more interested than their male counterparts, and that most women found their gender to be more of an advantage than a disadvantage.[21] This is primarily due to their high visibility and their presence in business discussions. The corporations that are reluctant to send females abroad use the excuse that foreign prejudice against women limits their effectiveness and credibility. Given the evidence, prejudices within the company appear to be an even bigger, unaddressed hinderance, not only to working effectively together within a corporation, but also to their international relationships.

The controversy surrounding the capabilities of women in leadership positions appears to have reached a pinnacle. For years, the 'masculinity' of characteristics associated with leadership excluded women from being considered for and assigned to positions of power in the workforce.

Jan Carlzon, the creative president of SAS Airlines, points out that dating back to the agrarian society, women have exhibited leadership qualities in society.[22] Traditionally women have taken care of family and social relationships—an ability that is proving more and more vital to successful leadership.

Numerous publications on the 'art of leadership' stress the importance of effective/open communication within the organization. The better a manager communicates with his or her employees, the more likely they are to work together effectively in performing necessary tasks. The ability to communicate fosters the art of synergy, which allows an organization to reach its full potential and to attain its goals. As a result, organizations that most quickly adapt and adjust themselves to the entrance of women into the workforce place themselves at an advantage when compared with organizations that are reluctant to appoint women to positions of leadership.

However, the stage has been set; what once was exclusively a man's world is now no longer so. In fact, projections suggest that by 2001 one-third of all positions in major companies in the United States will be held by women and one in ten corporations will be under female leadership.

Guidelines for female managers abroad

The difficulties that women may encounter when working on a foreign assignment depend to a certain extent on the social and economic context of the country in which they are conducting business, and also on the individuals with whom they come into contact. Whether a country is liberal toward women's rights or not, individuals within that country vary in their own beliefs about women's roles in organizations. Both the female international manager and the company she represents can take steps to minimize the negative aspects that might be encountered by considering the following guidelines, which have been compiled from interviews with men and women working internationally, and other sources cited throughout this chapter.

1. *Lay the groundwork.*   Don't surprise a client. Before any meeting, regardless of the gender of the participants, provide adequate information to both sides regarding who will be present and what the objectives of the meeting are. Notifying the participants will give the client time to adjust to the prospect of conducting business with a female if it is a new situation for him.

2. *Practice what is preached.*   If a corporation believes that female managers should be treated equally and seriously in business dealings abroad, it should ensure that women are also treated equally and fairly within the organization. Success begins at home. Does your organization believe in the competence of women in positions of leadership?

3. *Consider both women and men for international positions.*   Don't rely on the assumption that women will not want to accept an international position. Ask. Be ready to solve relocation problems just as they would be solved with a male manager.

4. *Provide proper cross-cultural training and preparation courses.*   Orientation is vital to the success of any expatriate operating abroad, male or female. Specific additional assistance for females should include what to expect from male superiors, peers and

subordinates in the respective country. Training and orientation before departure can prepare a woman for success.

5. *Delegate appropriate authority.*   When sending women managers on foreign assignments, give them the same authority to make decisions as any male manager would receive. Women as well as men need the status and perquisites to do their job. If your own organization does not have sufficient confidence in its female managers, why should your business partners?

6. *Be realistic.*   Realize that women managers abroad suffer from the same culture shocks and the same cultural differences that men do. Therefore, it is important to keep expectations reasonable.

The female global manager's role

Just as male international managers can study foreign cultures and initiate appropriate behavior for successful cross-cultural business dealings, female managers can prepare themselves and enact certain behaviors to minimize any hindrances they might encounter while conducting business abroad. Copeland and Griggs recommend the following guidelines for women conducting business overseas:[23]

1. *Realize that often one is crossing cultural barriers.*   A foreign partner may already feel uncomfortable in dealing with someone from another *culture.* Exercising sensitivity and working to build mutual trust should be the first step in creating a professional relationship.

2. *If necessary or appropriate, ask the male business partner if he has ever conducted business with a female.*   This will help to clear the air. Some men are intimidated by a female counterpart. On the other hand, sometimes bringing up the subject helps to establish a good relationship.

3. *Be prepared, and have faith in yourself.*   Plan ahead and think through how to handle uncomfortable situations such as discrimination. Remind your counterpart that a woman is there to conduct business just as a male representative of the organization would.

4. *Act as a model.*   Remember that women are pioneers in this area, and can help educate organizations on the growing importance of women in international business. One woman's behavior and good example can set a precedent for other women to follow. Success stories spread quickly. The more successful women become as international managers, the fewer barriers they will encounter.

Globalization is here to stay and so are women in the workforce. As a result, the presence of businesswomen at the global level will continue to grow. Those organizations that effectively and fairly incorporate both globalization and women managers into their daily activities will reap the biggest profits. In fact, the organizations that utilize the managerial skills of female employees will find themselves with a distinct advantage over the competition. The addition of female managers definitively adds to the diversity and contribution of ideas that develop into successful business strategies.

In the January 1993 issue of *World Executives' Digest* a number of recommendations were identified to help make globalization work. The following five points suggest that women can play a significant role in making globalization successful:[24]

1. *Globalize the organization's vision, strategy, structure, corporate culture and people.*   This includes all women that play a role within the organization. The organization is not truly globalized if only male managers are considered able and willing to assume foreign assignments. Like a car without all of its tires fully inflated, unless all of the employees and managers are globalized, the entire organization will be held back. Globalization involves sharing all aspects of the vision, strategy and corporate culture with everyone, so that together the organization can move forward, using all available energy and talent.

2. *Discern the organization's global strategic vision: is it clearly defined, understood, communicated and accepted throughout the organization?*   This means eliminating any division caused by gender. Discrimination will only hold the group back, whereas the acceptance/promotion of women to management positions can contribute new ideas and approaches to strategy development. Strategy must be explained, emphasized and supported to keep the organization on the path toward achieving goals and turning the corporate vision into reality.

3. *Use management development programs to give an organization's global managers the significant skills and experience they need.*   The skills needed to conduct business in a foreign environment, such as language training, technical know-how, management techniques, bargaining and negotiation strategy, vary little by gender. Thus, the training of male and female managers is essentially the same. It is important, none the less, for organizations to be aware of changing needs for both men and women in the workplace, and these needs must be met in order for employees to effectively do their jobs. The entrance of women into the workforce has changed the elements that corporations need to provide. Now that dual-income families are more common than not, child care and family leave policies are essential for both men and women.

It is not only the role of women that is changing, but also the role of men. Men are assuming a larger role in family matters, which consequently affects a man's relationship to his job. As a result, corporations must re-evaluate the method by which the needs of employees, both male and female, are accommodated. No longer can corporations maintain the status quo and expect employees to excel, even though their personal lives may have changed drastically.

As the family structure changes, so must the organization's structure. Systems such as flex-time, have proven to be a viable means by which to accommodate the needs of both the organization and the employee. The advent of home computers, fax machines and teleconferencing facilities present further opportunities for employees to fulfill their job requirements while taking care of their family.

Respect and understanding on the behalf of the organization for individual needs will foster a loyalty to the organization, especially in hard financial times when the organization may need the understanding and sacrifice of its employees in return.

4. *Use cultural diversity as a resource: it's essential.*   The ascendance of women to leadership positions offers the organization an opportunity to explore new ideas and approaches. Companies that find new, innovative approaches are the ones that are experiencing success today—not the ones that have maintained the status quo. Tom Peters, co-author of *In Search of Excellence*, declares: 'Gone are the days of women succeeding by learning to play men's games. Instead the time has come for men on the move to learn to play women's games.'[25]

5. *Make sure the organization has effective multicultural teams and that communication between units is good.*   As disseminators of information, women managers can facilitate the communication of ideas, impressions and directions in a manner that may not have been as widely utilized in the past when women did not hold managerial or authoritative positions.

Given the historical role of women as facilitators and initiators of family and social relationships, female managers appear to have a natural talent for building relationships. This skill can easily be transferred to the workplace to build strong working relationships among employees and customers. As relationships grow, so does communication, understanding, synergy and, most important, successful results.

Summary

For Competency 2, Fig. 10.6 provides an opportunity for readers to reflect on the structure of their company or organization (is it traditional multinational, traditional international or traditional global according to

	CEO	Corporate staff	Subsidiary general manager and staff	All employees
Your company				

Rate and describe the degree the competency is possessed for each of the categories for your organization.

H   = Demonstrates a high degree
S   = Demonstrates somewhat
L   = Demonstrates to a low degree
N/A = Not applicable for your organization

Transformational goal for structure

	CEO	Corporate staff	Subsidiary general manager and staff	All employees
Worldwide organizational solution	*Essential* To act as a role model for those in the organization	*Essential* To reflect the changing demographics	*Essential* To promote on the basis of competency not gender	*Essential* This is required by changing demographics

Fig. 10.6   Competency 2:   Works as equal with persons from diverse backgrounds.

descriptions of these structures in earlier chapters?) and to rate the CEO, corporate staff, subsidiary general manager and staff, as well as all employees in general. We are fully aware that there may be great variation among the corporate staff or employees; but what is the central tendency? Or, generally, to what degree do these groups of people possess the competency?

Based on our assessment and interpretation of the significant literature on the subject, we have then indicated whether the competency is *essential*, *useful* or *not necessary* for the CEO, corporate staff, subsidiary general manager and staff, and all employees, for the transformational goal to be realized and to make globalization work.

Competency 3: Has a long-term orientation

There are many reasons why companies have not been successful in competing in the global marketplace. One of these reasons is 'short-termism'. Dick Ferry, president and co-founder of Korn/Ferry, addresses this issue:

> Corporate America may talk, on an intellectual level, about what it'll take to succeed in the twenty-first century, but when it gets right down to decision making, all that matters is the next quarterly earnings report. That's what's driving much of the system. With that mind-set, everything else becomes secondary to the ability to deliver the next quarterly earnings push-up. We're on a treadmill. The reward system in this country is geared to the short term.[26]

Research conducted by Michael Porter confirms that in many cases the overwhelming importance of the bottom line and short-term perspective impact many US corporations.[27] Compared with Japanese and Germans, whose cultures and economic systems support long-term investment, American executives, on average, insist on an inflation-adjusted return on investments of 12 per cent or more. This requirement, along with the low percentage of R&D dollars devoted to long-term projects, contributes to an emphasis on short-term profits by US companies. Bonuses and executive compensation packages are also tied to short-term results.

Bennet Harrison poses the question, 'Why do our foreign competitors take a longer view?'[28] His answer: in Germany and Japan, 'cross-ownership' is the norm. *Stakeholders* (customers, suppliers and banks) are closely involved in the operations of the business; by contrast, major *investors* include insurance companies, mutual funds and individuals, who lack in-depth knowledge of companies and industries, and rely on the advice of financial analysts whose recommendations are heavily based upon short-term factors, i.e. quarterly earnings and share price. Other factors include the appointment of corporate directors with little expertise in business and management, whose compensation for these appointments is based upon stock options.

Harrison adds a few other factors to explain the differences between Germany's and Japan's long-term emphasis, such as the rarity of take-overs in these two countries, regulations concerning investment of pension funds and reinvestment of capital gains, and accounting guidelines that support long-term investment.

Example

The cosmetics company Clinique has been remarkably successful in the Japanese market.[29] It was persistent, brash and 'unapologetic', causing a stir in the Japanese market by subscribing to a long-term perspective and challenging the Japanese at marketing.

Clinique became the first cosmetics company to use department stores as its only outlet, rather than selling through specialty cosmetics stores. The American concern argued that it could boost its cosmetics' sales in department stores, since its products were not offered elsewhere as were other manufacturers' offerings. Its strategy was to position itself differently from the Japanese leader, Shiseido, which held considerable strength in its distribution system.

Two other influential factors were good timing and luck, since Japanese women were beginning to shift their preferences to skin care products as opposed to make-up, and Clinique entered the market with products geared specifically to this purpose.

Clinique has managed to capture one-fourth of the department store cosmetics' sales, giving it the top position. Twelve years ago, Shiseido was the market leader with 50 per cent of the market; today, Clinique claims 25–30 per cent, while Shiseido's share has diminished to 15 per cent.

The short-term view also has other implications. For total quality management to work, organizations must take a long-term view and exercise patience. Few dispute the importance of total quality. However, several recent studies on total quality management have questioned the short-term 'quick-fix' mentality of individuals who do not recognize the need for long-term approaches in the implementation of total quality management.

The following example for 'long-termism' was cited by Gary Hamel in his 1993 Executive Focus International presentation:

> Consider the experience of Victor Company of Japan (JVC). Its ancestor was a small company in 1959. So was California-based Ampex. That year, Ampex came out with the first videotape recorder. For $50,000, you could get a refrigerator-sized box that used two miles of 2" tape to get 1/2 hour of black-and-white recording. But JVC eventually took the business away by winning acceptance of its VHS standard. To do that, they had to understand the nature of the opportunity. First they said, 'We would like to give people control over the broadcasters.' Then they built the competencies. Then they tested the viability of the design by going again and again into the marketplace. They introduced a dozen products, all of which failed—but all of which taught them something about the marketplace. Then, setting standards via a coalition, they were finally able to compete for price.
>
> This whole process took 20 years. Compare this with RCA, which spent more than anyone else on video recording technologies—but stopped and started the project every few years, subject to the whims of new CEOs. They went nowhere.[30]

John Huey alludes to the short-term problem from a political perspective. He argues that 'America is at a "critical crossroads",' a time requiring a 'President who is willing to lead,' thereby ensuring that the United States is run by an 'establishment' rather than an 'oligarchy'.[31] In an attempt to differentiate between the two types of government, he defines the two terms as follows:

> *Establishment* an elite group of decision-makers who act in the best interest of the country, confident that they will ultimately prosper in a prosperous country (i.e. Japan).

Oligarchy an insecure elite group that always acts in its immediate self-interest (i.e. Latin American countries).[32]

Institutions that operate on the basis of expediency rarely have a long-term perspective.

Leaders not managers

There is much in the management literature differentiating leaders and managers. Warren Bennis has made significant contributions to this thinking. He states that, 'given the nature and constancy of change and the transnational challenges facing American business leadership, the key to making the right choices will come from understanding and embodying the leadership qualities necessary to succeed in a mercurial global economy.' Simply put, to succeed and thrive in the global marketplace, organizations need a 'new generation of leaders—leaders, not managers'.[33]

Bennis proceeds to differentiate a leader from a manager:

A manager:	*A leader:*
administers	innovates
maintains	develops
focuses on systems/structures	focuses on people
relies on control	inspires trust
takes a short-range view	*adopts a long-range perspective*
asks how and when	asks what and why
keeps his/her eye on the bottom line	keeps his/her eye on the horizon
accepts the status quo	challenges the status quo
is a classic good soldier	is his or her own person
does things right	does the right thing

Also, according to Bennis, of the numerous leaders with whom he has spoken, each share one characteristic: '. . . a concern with a guiding purpose, an overarching vision'. Leaders all possess clear goals, both personal and professional, a strong determination to achieve them and, perhaps most importantly, a long-term orientation.

The long-term perspective was also advocated by Tuttle in a speech to the Motor and Equipment Manufacturers Association encouraging those in business to re-examine 'familiar sacred cows and myths', including the 12-month annual plan, and the belief that new product development can occur over the short term.[34]

The orientation to short-termism is almost an addiction, and is present in most corporations. Long-term orientation is a critical competency to make globalization work.

Summary

For Competency 3, Fig. 10.7 provides an opportunity for readers to reflect on the structure of their company or organization (is it traditional

	CEO	Corporate staff	Subsidiary general manager and staff	All employees
Your company				

Rate and describe the degree the competency is possessed for each of the categories for your organization:

H = Demonstrates a high degree
S = Demonstrates somewhat
L = Demonstrates to a low degree
N/A = Not applicable for your organization

Transformational goal for structure

	CEO	Corporate staff	Subsidiary general manager and staff	All employees
Worldwide organizational solution	*Essential* To accomplish the strategic goals of the organization	*Essential* To monitor the CEO and others preventing a slip into short-termism	*Essential* To work collaboratively for global strategies	*Useful* For quality in performance at all levels

Fig. 10.7   Competency 3: Has a long-term orientation

multinational, traditional international or traditional global according to descriptions of these structures in earlier chapters?) and to rate the CEO, corporate staff, subsidiary general manager and staff as well as all employees in general. We are fully aware there may be great variation among the corporate staff or employees; but what is the central tendency? Or, generally, to what degree do these groups of people possess the competency?

Based on our assessment and interpretation of the significant literature on the subject, we have then indicated whether the competency is *essential*, *useful*, or *not necessary* for the CEO, corporate staff, subsidiary general manager and staff, and all employees for the transformational goal to be realized and to make globalization work.

Notes and references

1. Quoted by Siew Meng Leong and Chin Tiong Tan, 'Managing across borders: an empirical test of the Bartlett and Ghosal (1989) organizational typology', *Journal of International Business Studies*, 24 (3) (1993), p. 449
2. Quoted in Gilbert Fuchsberg, 'Harvard slates broad review of its MBA', *Wall Street Journal*, 17 October 1992.

3. Richard Kirkland, 'Europe's new managers', *Fortune*, 29 September 1986.

4. Brent Ruben, 'The study of cross-cultural competence: traditions and contemporary issues', *International Journal of Intercultural Relations*, 13, (1989), pp. 228–40.

5. See C. K. Prahalad and Yves Doz, *The Multinational Mission: Balancing Local Demands and Global Vision*, Free Press, New York, 1987.

6. Philip R. Harris and Robert T. Moran, *Managing Cultural Differences*, Gulf Publishing Co., Houston, Tex., 1991.

7. Daniel F. Cuff, 'MBA in reality', *New York Times*, 3 May 1992.

8. Kenneth Martin, 'Competencies, not just qualifications', *The Edge*, Hay Group, Spring 1991.

9. From the song 'You've got to be taught' in the play *South Pacific*, music by Richard Rogers, lyrics by Oscar Hammerstein II, 1949.

10. Glenn Fisher, *Mindsets: The Role of Culture and Perception in International Relations*, International Press, Yarmouth, Me, 1988.

11. Stephen Rhinesmith, *A Manager's Guide to Globalization*, Business One Irwin, Homewood, Ill., 1993.

12. R. Levine and D. Campbell, *Ethnocentrism*, John Wiley, New York, 1972.

13. David Heenan and H. Perlmutter, *Multicultural Organizational Development*. Addison-Wesley, Reading, Mass., 1979.

14. Y. Amir, 'Contact hypotheses in ethnic relation', *Psychological Bulletin*, 71 (1969), pp. 319–42.

15. G. Allport, *The Nature of Prejudice*, Addison-Wesley, Reading, Mass., 1954.

16. L. Gardenswartz and A. Rowe, *Managing Diversity*, Business One Irwin, Homewood, Ill., 1993..

17. J. Coates, J. Jarratt and B. Mahaffie, 'Future work', *The Futurist*, May–June, 1991.

18. As reported in Conference Board Europe, 'Europe's Glass Ceiling: Why Companies Profit from a Diverse Work Force', 1991.

19. Nancy Adler and D. Israel, *Women in Management Worldwide*, M. E. Sharp, New York, 1988.

20. Conference Board Europe, op. cit.

21. Nancy Adler, 'Do MBAs want international careers?' Faculty of Management, McGill University, February 1983.

22. Adler, op cit.

23. Lennie Copeland and Lewis Griggs, *Going International*, Random House, New York, 1985.

24. Robert T. Moran, 'Making globalization work', *World Executives' Digest*, January 1993, pp. 16–18.

25. Tom Peters and R. Waterman, *In Search of Excellence*, Harper Row, New York, 1982.

26. Quoted by Warren Bennis, *On Becoming a Leader*, Addison-Wesley, Reading, Mass., 1989, p. 23.

27. Michael Porter, *The Competitive Advantage of Nations*, Free Press, New York, 1990.

28. Bennet Harrison, 'The roots of short-termism', *Technology Review*, October 1992, p.71.
29. T. Watanabe, 'Clinique succeeds while rivals take a powder,' *Los Angeles Times*, 28 July 1992, p. H6.
30. Gary Hamel, 'Pushing the envelope of global strategy and competitiveness', *Executive Focus International: 1993 Executive Forum*, 12 February 1993.
31. J. Huey, 'America at a crossroads', *Fortune*, 19 October 1992, pp. 48–50.
32. Ibid.
33. Warren Bennis, 'Managing the dream: leadership in the 21st Century', *Training*, May 1990, pp. 43–8.
34. Robert P. Tuttle, 'Maintaining competitiveness: get the product on the market', *Vital Speeches*, 15 June 1989, pp. 598–600.

The global manager and change

'Managing organizational change is a serious challenge to us.' Of the executives who responded to the 1993 Thunderbird Survey on issues of globalization, 74 per cent were in agreement with this statement.

The Harvard Business Review World Leadership Survey of approximately 12 000 global managers from 25 countries[1] concludes that change is a part of corporate life.

Jan Timmer, the president of Philips Electronics, who has made major changes in the Dutch company by reducing employment and selling businesses, states: 'You just can't change a deep rooted corporate culture in one or two years. It takes at least five years or longer.'[2]

Percy Barnevik, the CEO of Asea Brown Boveri (ABB) Ltd, puts it this way:

I try to make people at ABB accept that change is a way of life. I often got the question from Swiss and Germans: 'Mr. Barnevik, aren't you happy now? Can't we relax a bit?' They see new targets as a threat or an inconvenience. But I say you must get used to the idea that we are changing all the time.[3]

Drucker, in a similar vein, comments:

Every few hundred years in Western history there occurs a sharp transformation
. . . a divide. Within a few short decades, society rearranges itself—its world view; its basic values; its social and political structure; its arts; its key institutions. Fifty years later, there is a new world. And the people born then cannot even imagine the world in which their grandparents lived and into which their own parents were born. We are currently living through just such a transformation.[4]

This chapter is about change, and the competencies and structures that those responsible for managing global change must have to implement it. Three more competencies required to make globalization work will be identified and described.

Competency 4: Facilitates organizational change

This section will cover two main points: (1) what some academics and business people say about organizational change, and (2) how they recommend managing these changes. We present several perspectives, as it is our belief that no one individual has all the answers, strategies or methods to facilitate change.

Change as a way of corporate life

It is a volatile and unpredictable world. Recently, great optimism abounded in many areas of the world as the walls between countries crumbled (the two Germanys) and new national boundaries were established (the former Soviet Union). Concurrently, there was pessimism as a worldwide recession continued and deepened. General Motors, Kodak, IBM, AT&T, Zerox and General Electric, among others, slashed jobs, and company CEOs and presidents were dumped in unprecedented numbers. Robert Tomasko, in his excellent book *Rethinking the Corporation: The Architecture of Change*,[5] gives many other compelling examples of other organizations.

According to Daniel Nadler, president of Delta Consulting Inc., 'The critical organizational issue has ceased to be stability. It's become change.' Change is here to stay. Chapter 2 outlined the environmental global forces propelling this paradigm shift from stability to change.

What follows are some theories, research and reaction about the uncertain and ever changing environment in which businesses are expected to operate effectively.

At the 1992 Top Management Forum held in Paris, 150 senior executives from Europe and North America met to discuss survival in this extremely competitive world.[6] It was the executives' general consensus that the only survivors will be those who understand and manage change effectively. According to most executives, the ideal organization will be one that 'is strongly decentralized', allowing its subsidiaries the flexibility to manage the local situation. However, the core of the organization must be 'very centralized, to coordinate activities across the globe'.

Speakers and participants in the Third Annual Global Conference on Management Innovation, sponsored by the American Management Association and the Japan Management Association, also agreed that managing strategic change is still a relatively new idea.[7] Many organizations and companies must learn to become more proactive and not simply react to changes in their environment as they have in the past. Effective change begins with the leaders of an organization. To implement new ideas, a leader must 'be willing to accept and live with change', must set the example for other employees to follow (as well as eliminating employees that refuse to follow new directives), and must risk his or her 'own credibility and future'.

Rosabeth Kantor, Barry Stein and Todd Jick, in their book *The Challenge of Organizational Change*,[8] state that the forces for change may be external to the organizations, or 'macroevolutionary' (these forces were outlined in Chapter 2), or internal, or 'microevolutionary'. The internal changes are often a function of growth that may result from internal power struggles between individuals and groups.

Facilitating organizational change

What do the writers of organizational change say about making change happen? Much. The following is a sampling.

Steve Gambrell and Craig Stevens suggest there are three phases of organizational change: what occurs before, during and after changes.[9] They believe that for the change process to be successful an organized plan is necessary throughout each phase of the change process. 'Part of this action plan includes understanding motivations for resistance, differences in employee/management perceptions, and the importance of ongoing communication.'

Before changes occur, Gambrell and Stevens state that to maximize the chances of positive outcome the following skills and techniques should be used:

- Unbiased open-mindedness;

- Good strategic planning abilities;

- Commitment to leadership and team-building skills; and

- A history of commitment and good communications skills.

During the change:

1. Employees must understand why there is a need for change, and this should be communicated to them in a clear and non-threatening manner.

2. When employees are involved in the change process, they adapt more readily and will assume responsibility for the change process.

3. Communication should be a never-ending concern. There will always be room for misinterpretations and gossip. The message should constantly be restated, individually if possible.

4. Understand that change takes time, and success doesn't take place overnight.

André and Sandra Vandermerwe discovered a number of common problems as organizations implement the change processes.[10] The top five dilemmas, mentioned by more than 60 per cent of the respondents in their survey, were:

1. There are human fears regarding discomfort with new roles and responsibilities. (The effective leader will try to foresee these insecurities and build measures into the change process to address them.)

2. There is an air of 'complacency, low sense of urgency'.

3. Companies must allow sufficient time to 'continue business as usual', as well as implement the new measures.

4. Communication from the top levels of management should be directly addressed to lower levels. If information is allowed to filter down, there is a greater propensity for misunderstandings to occur. 'In a major change, you can never over-communicate.'

5. Systems and technology changes should be incorporated into the strategy.

The authors discuss a four-step process for implementing strategic change that incorporates catalysts to foster the changes. The steps are conducted in a process, rather than a linear approach. Each stage works in conjunction with the one that follows it.

The first stage is to monitor the internal and external environments for threats and opportunities. The catalyst for transforming the results of the monitoring/discovery process is 'strategic discomfort'. No change will occur unless the people within the organization feel that change is the only way to preserve the organization. In other words, they must perceive that change is critical to their survival.

The second stage is to create a clear and relevant vision. This vision must be unique, that is, different than any previously introduced. The vision must make sense to the people and give direction to the idea. This is the link between the inspiration and reality. It also requires that someone take responsibility for the entire undertaking and 'walk the talk'.

In the third stage, internal systems must be set up to give people the authority to implement the change. Motivation and support are key. To facilitate this, leaders should be designated to oversee the project. The people need to be 'energized and mobilized'.

The final phase is to monitor the process and give the responsible individuals the ability to make the necessary modifications that are based upon what they have learned through the process. Control is not the desired function: keeping the project on track is. It is essential at this point to keep the momentum and enthusiasm going.

André and Sandra Vandermerwe assert that there are three main speeds of strategic change: 'crisis change, reactive change, and anticipatory change'. In crisis change it is necessary to minimize the time allowed for completion of the project, while in reactive change some condition is driving the change, but there is sufficient time to analyze the possible responses. The need for anticipatory change, like reactionary change, is difficult to convey to individuals reluctant to leave their comfort zones. It is the most difficult to justify, since there are no immediate threats facing the organization. The authors suggest allowing for more time than is considered necessary to implement changes, to give people a chance to 'adjust to new ideas, roles and relationships'. Their research revealed that every situation differed and there was no single method for implementing strategic change.

Perhaps the clearest and therefore the most useful ideas on change are contained in the Pritchett and Pound booklet, *The Employee Handbook of Organizational Change.*[11] First, the authors dispel the myths about change such as:

Myth	Reality
■ It will go away.	■ It won't.
■ My job is the same.	■ You need to change too.
■ Problems prove that changes are harmful for the organization.	■ Problems are part of the change process.
■ I'm not in a position to make a difference.	■ You are part of the solution or part of the problem.
■ They don't know what they are doing.	■ Some mistakes are inevitable.

They also make some recommendations about being a change agent:

- Be positive

- Take ownership of the changes

- Select your battles

- Be tolerant of mistakes

- Practice stress management

Ruth Hooper and Ian Oliphant-Thompson write that organizational change is occurring at such a rapid pace and frequency that, if not managed skillfully, it could upset the entire organizational structure.[12] Before beginning any such changes, it is important to understand not only the company's corporate culture, but also the employee's belief and value system. The word 'change' alone can invoke feelings of fear and frustration.

The authors suggest two ways to change culture:

1. '[A]ddress the issue of organizational values and allow people to understand the nature of the business they are working in.'

2. '[P]hysically change people's behavior.' For example, rotate people within the company, form teams, begin training and personal development programs.

A critical and final step in the change process is having top managers set the example. They should be encouraging and helpful to others, as opposed to 'managing'. Knowing where the points of resistance are originating will enable management to turn negative energy into positive energy.

The following are a few questions that Hooper and Oliphant-Thompson recommend asking when determining whether change is necessary:

1. What is the size of the problem? Is it very serious?

2. What is the source of the problem? Is it personal or organizational?

3. Is this a temporary or permanent problem, and will it reoccur?

4. What are the causes of the problem, not the symptoms?

James Belasco compares developing organizations to the way an 'old, slow elephant' is taught to 'dance'.[13] Organizations must be able to identify a vision, then empower the individuals within to work towards goals. But he believes vision alone is inadequate; the people responsible for turning it into a reality must wholeheartedly support the vision.

The most important task is to create a sense of urgency, or 'fire', compelling people to change their behavior. Belasco speaks of showing employees a 'promised land' that demonstrates a better future if change is implemented today.

He also believes that leaders must lead through demonstration, encouraging employees and reinforcing the desired behavior. To ensure their support, a leader must convey belief and sincerity in the project and be certain that all understand the vision. Maintaining the sense of urgency is as important as 'generating specific, concrete actions that support the vision'.

In an excellent essay in the *Harvard Business Review*, Michael Beer and others discuss 'the fallacy of programmatic change'.[14] A study of organizational change at six major corporations revealed that, in attempting to cope with changing competitive pressures, many managers devise corporate-wide programs, such as new mission statements and quality circles. They make two fundamentally incorrect assumptions: (1) that the presence of comprehensive programs will automatically bring about the necessary changes, and (2) that employees will adapt their behavior to the new 'formal structures and systems'. The companies that did make successful changes tended not to pursue a structured approach; rather, the changes began in subsidiary divisions or plants and were inspired and promoted by general managers.

The authors assert that the best way to implement change is to provide general direction for the company but leave specific decisions to the individual divisions. If employees find themselves in new challenging situations that impose new demands on 'roles, responsibilities, and relationships', they will be impelled to change their 'behaviors and attitudes to survive'.

Beer *et al.* state that there are three interconnected elements that are necessary for implementing corporate changes: 'coordination, commitment and competencies'. Unsuccessful change programs can work against the company by weakening its credibility. Buzzwords are used so freely that they often 'become a substitute for detailed understanding of the business'.

The authors suggest a six-step program to implement change successfully. Companies should focus on 'task alignment', which they define as 'reorganizing employee roles, responsibilities, and relationships to solve specific business problems':

1. Involve employees in clearly defining the problem requiring attention.

2. Involve employees in developing a new organizational structure.

3. Provide strong leadership to persuade all employees to follow the new vision. Give employees training and support to enable them to implement new strategies, and reinforce strategies by moving/ eliminating people who don't fit with the new activities.

4. Allow each department to find its own solution for reaching the new goals. People will be more committed if they develop their own guidelines.

5. Institute formal 'policies, systems, and structures' *after* employees have become committed.

6. Monitor and revise strategies if necessary to maintain momentum.

In conclusion, the authors state:

> Companies need a particular mind-set for managing change: one that emphasizes process over specific unit-by-unit learning process rather than a series of programs, and acknowledges the payoffs that result from persistence over a long period of time as opposed to quick fixes.

Patricia Craig also discusses why many companies that try to introduce organizational changes have difficulty implementing these changes successfully.[15] She believes it is because organizations fail to consider the management and information process modifications needed to complement the changes in structure and work processes. Unless clear messages are conveyed about the corporate values (accomplished through management and information processes), employees will not change the way in which they have approached their work in the past. Stated differently, the corporate culture does not change to support the new structure. To bring corporate culture in line with the company's new requirements, management can 'use the elements of organizational design as levers'. Changes in the organization structure, work processes and management and information processes and systems can be coordinated to alter employees' traditional behaviors.

The existence of corporate culture has been acknowledged for many years, but only recently have scholars and managers attempted to identify viable methods for modifying it. Although every operation has unique characteristics, organizations that display the following features tend to be successful at implementing new strategies:

- A clear vision, followed consistently in all activities

- Clear communication and reinforcement of that vision

- Understanding of the company's core competencies

- A horizontal management structure, and team focus

- Effective performance measures

Jack Welsh summarized his perspective on change as follows:

> When I try to summarize what I've learned since 1981, one of the big lessons is that change has no constituency. People like the status quo. They like the way it *was*. When you start changing things, the good old days look better and better . . . You've got to be prepared for massive resistance. Incremental change doesn't work very well in the type of transformation GE has gone through. If your change isn't big enough, revolutionary enough, the bureaucracy can beat you.[16]

In managing change and attempting to regain competitiveness, most organizations are 'rightsizing'. This is occurring in the United States, Asia and Western Europe, which is in its worst recession since World War II. 'Rightsizing', of course, is a euphemism for downsizing. However, 'downsizing' is demoralizing and re-engineering or doing better what you have done before is insufficient. Very successful organizations (Wal-mart and the Merck/Medco Agreement) are re-inventing strategy and are growing differently. This can be accomplished only through a sophisticated organizational perspective on change.

In summary, the authors cited above all believe we can condense what many organizational change experts espouse into the following guidelines:

- Create a vision.

- Communicate the vision.

- Involve everyone.

- Process the implementation.

The vision is then recreated, as change is inevitable. This is illustrated in Fig. 11.1.

No writer or speaker on contemporary business issues today would dispute the notion that the paradigm has shifted from stability to change.

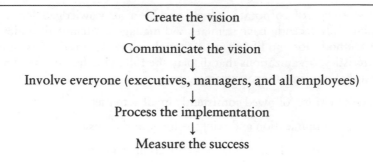

Create the vision
↓
Communicate the vision
↓
Involve everyone (executives, managers, and all employees)
↓
Process the implementation
↓
Measure the success

Fig. 11.1   Guidelines to achieving organizational change

Summary

For Competency 4, Fig. 11.2 provides an opportunity for readers to reflect on the structure of their company or organization (is it traditional multinational, traditional international or traditional global according to descriptions of these structures in earlier chapters?) and to rate the CEO, corporate staff, subsidiary general manager and staff, as well as all employees in general. We are fully aware there may be great variation among the corporate staff or employees; but what is the central tendency? Or, generally, to what degree do these groups of people possess the competency?

Based on our assessment and interpretation of the significant literature on the subject, we have then indicated whether the competency is *essential*, *useful* or *not necessary* for the CEO, corporate staff, subsidiary general manager and staff, and all employees, for the transformational goal to be realized and to make globalization work.

	CEO	Corporate staff	Subsidiary general manager and staff	All employees
Your company				

Rate and describe the degree the competency is possessed for each of the categories for your organization:

H   = Demonstrates a high degree
S   = Demonstrates somewhat
L   = Demonstrates to a low degree
N/A = Not applicable for your organization

Transformational goal for structure

	CEO	Corporate staff	Subsidiary general manager and staff	All employees
Worldwide organizational solution	*Essential* Change is a permanent way of organizational life	*Essential* Resisters of change will not survive	*Essential* To link interdependently to corporate global strategy	*Essential* All employees must be involved in the change process

Fig. 11.2   Competency 4: facilitates organizational change

Competency 5: Creates learning systems

Peter Senge said it best in his book, *The Fifth Discipline*: 'The organizations that will truly excel in the future will be the organizations that discover how to tap people's commitment and capacity to learn at *all* levels in an organization.'[17]

The following is a case study of a non-learning organization in a global context.[18]

Case study

Several long conversations I've had recently with a European executive have made me acutely aware of two major cross-cultural organizational problems. The first is the inability of many companies to make use of new expertise developed by individuals in the firm. The second is the rather serious re-entry problems experienced by many expatriates following a successful international experience.

My friend is 51 years old. He has worked for one of the largest chemical companies in Europe for more than 25 years. He joined the company as a young chemical engineer, completed his apprenticeship and accepted a position as a sales representative in Australia. He lived there until his return to Europe five years ago.

After his first five years in Australia, he was appointed president of a small subsidiary. Though the European parent company has a policy of job rotation every three years, no replacements were available, so he was happy to stay on in Australia working for various subsidiary companies.

By the end of his Australian stint, he was a member of many of the most important boards in the country. By all obvious measures, he was a success. The companies he managed flourished, and several of them were sold at considerable profit. Yet during his long spell in Australia, he never once had a performance appraisal and never knew clearly how his work was viewed by his superiors in Europe.

When he was eventually replaced in Australia by another European, he was brought home and given a job that he has found to be neither satisfying nor challenging. He has specific responsibilities related to overseas assignments in one country. Ironically, his immediate boss has never lived outside his native country.

The executive's case highlights the tragic inability of many large organizations to handle their people well and to integrate their individual learning into the organization. What is most surprising to me is the executive's claim that since his return he has never been consulted about Australia by anyone in his company.

He knows the country well—his company has large investments there, not all of them going so well today. He believes that his replacement is not doing well and that two or three of the Europeans assigned there should be reassigned. The trouble is that all are 'being propped up,' he says by someone in the European headquarters.

But the real problem, as this case illustrates, is what to do with these people when they eventually return to Europe.

Unfulfilled aspirations

Optimizing individual employee and organizational needs has long been a management problem. Developing and maintaining relevant competencies within a work setting has been equally challenging.

The executive's many years of successful service in Australia show that he has learned from his experience. The pity is that his organization has not benefited from the experience, as the barriers for organizational learning appear to be too large. His learning is not being integrated in the organization or being passed on. It would appear in such cases that each person fails or succeeds by a trial-and-error method.

The ability of an organization to transfer learning from the individual is even more important now for another reason, namely, the accelerating changes in the environment.

Until a few years ago, the problems and challenges associated with returning home were rarely considered. Now, re-entry for both the individual and the organization is often the most difficult phase in the cycle of international life.

The re-entry process begins overseas with psychological withdrawal of the expatriate faced with returning home. Upon return, re-entry shock may occur for six months or more, as the person struggles to adjust himself again to the life style and tempo of the changed home and organizational cultures. Apart from the challenge of establishing home and family life is the issue of a new assignment in the parent company or organization.

For many expatriates, it is a time of crisis and trauma, the last stage of the culture shock process. For executives who are sensitive and become absorbed in the host culture, the experience abroad can be especially profound, causing them and members of their families to review their lives, values, attitudes—to assess how they became what they are.

It prompts others to want to change their life styles. The return home becomes the opportunity to carry out these aspirations. Many wish to apply the new self-insights and to seek new ways of growing and contributing to their company.

Unfortunately, recent research on the return of corporate employees from abroad strongly suggests that managerial skills gained overseas are not perceived as valuable and are underutilized by the organization.

In fact, one study found that persons who came back from assignment abroad and did not apply their acquired skills were those who were evaluated most highly by their managers. An unexpected finding? For me it was a shock.

I recently asked a group of 20 expatriates if they had debriefed after their experience overseas or even been consulted on their companies' situation in that country. All answered 'no.' What a loss.

The sad lesson for organizations is that if they are unable to transfer the know how and benefit from the overseas experience of their executives, they are doomed to become prisoners of their own environment.

Andrew Kupfer states the problem a little differently.[19] He argues that companies intending to widen their business operations should look to the 'veterans' for guidance. These veterans bring experience and an understanding of the relationship between worldwide manufacturing, labor and quality. 'Once established overseas, a good global competitor knows how to assimilate the best aspects of local practice', states Kupfer. A veteran seeks to broaden strategies beyond the domestic market and ascertain whether to offer standard products in all markets or to adapt the products to local needs. Often these products and practices that began as ideas in a distant global market are imported into the domestic business culture or market.

As companies rely on their veterans to transcend markets and country borders and teach the corporation about their reality, the new role of leadership must be to create learning systems that enliven and inspire the corporation in dynamic ways.

In the past, the traditional style of leadership was embodied by the person who gave clear direction, made decisions based on good problem-solving skills, and then energized or possibly manipulated a commitment to a common goal. Our understanding of leadership has developed beyond these parameters.

Similarly, the respect and understanding of those who work with us and for us has dramatically changed. Hopefully, we no longer view the workforce as powerless, lacking the intelligence to initiate change or the stamina to see it to fruition. We are on the brink of creating learning systems that regard interdependence and collaboration as necessities.

According to Senge, the role of leadership in creating these systems is that of designer, steward and teacher.[20] The most neglected and least developed aspect of leadership is that of designer, a designer responsible for the quiet, substantive work of a corporation's vision, strategies and systems. 'Designing is by its nature an integrative science because *design requires making something work in practice*.' The vision, strategy and systems that are created and shared should empower all employees to learn how to integrate these into their particular jobs, thereby increasing the productivity of the entire company. To effectively design the vision and strategy, and initiate a learning process, the leader must thoroughly understand how the organization communicates and learns at present, so that insightful and innovative changes in the existing system can be realized.

It is important to remember, as the designer of a learning system, that individuals will be open to learning new skills as long as they can connect them to a need. Also, they will learn what they need to know, not what someone thinks they need to know.

A leader must be not only a designer, but also a steward of the learning process. In addition to designing and understanding how the organization can evolve, he or she must see how the organization contributes to the global picture.

In creating learning systems, the leader must be the teacher. Senge believes that 'leaders of learning organizations must do more than just formulate strategies to exploit emerging trends. They must be able to help people understand the systemic forces that shape change. It is not enough to intuitively grasp these forces.' Leaders must help others see the bigger picture and cannot just impose their strategies and vision. Concurrently, and perhaps most importantly, leaders must 'foster learning' continually for all employees.

Summary

For Competency 5, Fig. 11.3 provides an opportunity for readers to reflect on the structure of their company or organization (is it traditional multinational, traditional international or traditional global according to descriptions of these structures in earlier chapters?) and to rate the CEO, corporate staff, subsidiary general manager and staff, as well as all

	CEO	Corporate staff	Subsidiary general manager and staff	All employees
Your company				

Rate and describe the degree the competency is possessed for each of the categories for your organization:
H   = Demonstrates a high degree
S   = Demonstrates somewhat
L   = Demonstrates to a low degree
N/A = Not applicable for your organization

Transformational goal for structure

	CEO	Corporate staff	Subsidiary general manager and staff	All employees
Worldwide organizational solution	*Essential* To gain commitment toward excellence for all	*Useful* To facilitate constant improvement	*Essential* Global expertise and expense must be shared	*Useful* For the required constant improvement and commitment to excellence

Fig. 11.3   Competency 5: Creates learning systems

employees in general. We are fully aware there may be great variation among the corporate staff or employees; but what is the central tendency? Or, generally, to what degree do these groups of people possess the competency?

Based on our assessment and interpretation of the significant literature on the subject, we have then indicated whether the competency is *essential*, *useful* or *not necessary* for the CEO, corporate staff, subsidiary general manager and staff, and all employees, for the transformational goal to be realized and to make globalization work.

Competency 6: Motivates employees to excellence

The pronoun test

An operative word in American organizations for the past several years is 'empowerment'. 'Our employees are empowered', says an executive from a Fortune 500 company that is in significant trouble. 'Our employees are empowered', says an executive from a different Fortune 500 company, this one thriving in turbulent times. Perhaps an important difference between the two organizations may be determined by what Robert Reich calls the 'pronoun test':

> For six months now I've been visiting the workplaces of America, administering a simple test. I call it the 'pronoun test.' I ask front-line workers a few general questions about the company. If the answers I get back describe the company in terms like 'they,' or 'them,' I know it's one kind of company. If the answers are put in terms like 'we,' or 'us' I know it's a different kind of company.
>
> It doesn't much matter what's said about the company. Even a statement like 'they aim for high quality here' suggests a workplace that hasn't yet made the leap into true high performance. It isn't yet achieving ever higher levels of quality, productivity and service. Only 'we' companies can do this.[21]

Yuzo Yasuda describes how Toyota, over the past 40 years, has used its 'Creative Idea Suggestion System' to collect over 20 million ideas for the improvement in its operations.[22] Although the concept was originally borrowed from the United States, Toyota's system differs in that its main aims are to promote a personally satisfying company culture and to improve the management of the business. (Suggestion systems in the United States seem to be used for different reasons—mainly for saving or making money.)

Through its adoption of the Creative Suggestion System, Toyota has been able to achieve continuous improvement in its production and management functions. Employees are encouraged to think of ways to make their jobs more efficient. First, a problem and its cause(s) are identified. The employee then proposes a solution to the problem based on careful observation. 'Experimentation is a key to the Toyota suggestion system philosophy. The company wants employees to want to make suggestions, so the system is designed for a high rate of success', says Yasuda. All suggestions must be formulated outside of regular working hours, and before a suggestion is submitted for review the employee may 'test' the solution on a limited basis to determine if it is useful.

Once a proposal has been submitted to management, it goes through a thorough but quick evaluation. Suggestions are accepted or rejected by a subcommittee set up specifically for that purpose. Larger incentive awards are determined by a team of senior executives known as the Corporate Idea Committee. A good suggestion system requires commitment in both time and other resources. Managers must provide a stimulating and open environment in which their employees feel comfortable to make suggestions. Positive feedback is very important, and managers are taught to never respond to a suggestion negatively; instead, they should work with the employee to refine a rough idea or even draft a totally new suggestion for improvement. A primary advantage of such a system is that it involves all levels of an organization in the problem-solving process.

George Land and Beth Jarman address the challenge of getting a large organization to pull its employees together to work toward a common goal.[23] They recommend following the principles of 'Future Pull'. The task will then become easier and should result in greater trust and loyalty of the employees. Future Pull has several components:

1. *Know your purpose and vision.*   A vision is the bigger picture. In other words, what is the company's ultimate goal and purpose for its employees? This should relate to the employees and not to the product.

2. *Commit to achieve your vision and purpose.*   'Actions speak louder than words.' The leader and members of top management must be committed to the vision and must reinforce it on a daily basis with their actions.

3. *Abundance is nature's natural state.*   When the vision is embraced and the employees have been empowered, it follows that the rewards will also be there.

4. *Make the world a better place by living according to shared values.*   Team-building is almost always a key component. Expand the vision externally to customers—not just employees.

The famous former football player, Fran Tarkenton, and his co-author have written an excellent book on motivation.[24] 'People don't change their behavior unless it makes a difference to them to do so.' This statement is the premiss of Tarkenton's system for motivating people. He argues that managers must stop focusing on the workers' attitudes and start focusing on their behavior. Once the *consequences* of a behavior are changed, the behavioral and attitudinal changes are not far behind. Three rules of human behavior are outlined:

1. Behavior that is reinforced by positive consequences tends to continue or improve.

2. Behavior that is demotivated by negative consequences tends to decrease.

3. Good, productive behavior that goes unnoticed tends to decrease over time.

Of the three, the first and last are the most important ways to motivate people. Tarkenton sees a problem in American management, in that it does not like to reward people for doing what they are paid to do. He suggests using the PRICE motivation system:

- *P = Pinpointing.*   Identify the behavior to be changed and set specific objectives. This should be done by setting objectives with the help of the employee(s) involved.

- *R = Recording.*   In this step progress is monitored, letting employees know where they stand. It provides constant feedback which should motivate them to do better.

- *I = Involvement.*   Employees need to take part in the decision-making process if they are expected to give their best work to a project or process.

- *C = Consequences.*   Positive reinforcement is the best consequence of good behavior and a motivator to help employees do their best.

- *E = Evaluation.*   It is important to track progress toward objectives and identify what worked and what didn't.

Finally, managers must be willing to let their employees take risks.

In the March 1991 issue of *Executive Excellence*, John Naisbitt and Patricia Aburdene link the new leadership qualities with the motivation of employees.[25] They state that the successful leader is not only an effective manager but also someone who inspires and motivates all employees to become effective managers and leaders on their own. This is accomplished by giving them responsibility and authority, or by empowering employees. Providing flexibility and guidance are also key factors. When these attitudes pervade the workplace, loyalty and commitment will be achieved. The leader then can continue to look into the future and establish new goals to work toward.

In global companies, the complexity of motivating employees to excellence is increased. To whom do they give their allegiance? Robert Reich asks 'Who is them?'[26] He defines 'them' as the growing group of global managers. Their allegiance is not to any particular nation or culture, but to the success of their company. Each decision is based on what will lead to corporate success rather than on loyalty to their home country. In other words, the global manager will do whatever is necessary to maximize performance. In recent years, part of this strategy has involved acquiring companies based in many different areas of the world. The goal is to meet the needs of many culturally different and cost-conscious customers. As a consequence, the global manager must seek the highest-quality skills and materials for the most cost-effective price.

What does the global manager call home? Reich believes for the global manager home is anywhere in the world. The location of the company headquarters is not of importance. The truly successful companies are like chameleons and meld into their surroundings. Local nationals are hired and given substantial autonomy, and local governments work hand-in-hand with the company.

Motivating employees to excellence is a task of the leaders of global organizations. Figure 11.4 outlines our perspective on how essential or useful this competency is for the various structures and levels of individuals.

Summary

For Competency 6, Fig. 11.4 provides an opportunity for readers to reflect on the structure of their company or organization (is it traditional multinational, traditional international or traditional global according to descriptions of these structures in earlier chapters?) and to rate the CEO,

	CEO	Corporate staff	Subsidiary general manager and staff	All employees
Your company				

Rate and describe the degree the competency is possessed for each of the categories for your organization:

H   = Demonstrates a high degree
S   = Demonstrates somewhat
L   = Demonstrates to a low degree
N/A = Not applicable for your organization

Transformational goal for structure

	CEO	Corporate staff	Subsidiary general manager and staff	All employees
Worldwide organizational solution	*Essential* All employees must be empowered	*Essential* To accomplish required quality standards	*Essential* To empower in appropriate ways all employees	*Essential* To 'walk the talk' and strive for excellence

Fig. 11.4   Competency 6: Motivates employees to excellence

corporate staff, subsidiary general manager and staff, as well as all employees in general. We are fully aware there may be great variation among the corporate staff or employees; but what is the central tendency? Or, generally, to what degree do these groups of people possess the competency?

Based on our assessment and interpretation of the significant literature on the subject, we have then indicated whether the competency is *essential*, *useful* or *not necessary* for the CEO, corporate staff, subsidiary general manager and staff, and all employees for the transformational goal to be realized and to make globalization work.

Notes and references

1. Rosabeth Kantor, 'Transcending business boundaries: 12,000 world managers view change', *Harvard Business Review*, May–June 1991.
2. See William Erickson, 'How hard it is to change culture', *Fortune*, October 1992.
3. Percy Barnevik, quoted in 'Mr Barnevik, aren't you happy now?', *Business Week*, 27 September 1993, p. 128.

4. Peter F. Drucker, *Post-Capitalist Society*, HarperCollins, Harper Business, New York, 1993.
5. Robert M. Tomasko, *Rethinking the Corporation: The Architecture of Change*, American Management Association, New York, 1993.
6. See Joshua Greenbaum, 'View from the top: survival tactics for the global business arena', *Management Review*, October 1992, pp. 49–53.
7. See Martha Peak, 'Managing for radical change', *Management Review*, February 1993.
8. Rosabeth Kantor, Barry A. Stein and Todd D. Jick, *The Challenge of Organizational Change*, Free Press, New York, 1992.
9. Steven W. Gambrell and Craig A. Stevens, 'Moving through the three phases of organizational change', *International Management*, July/August 1992, pp. 4–6.
10. André Vandermerwe and Sandra Vandermerwe, 'Making strategic change happen', *European Management Journal*, June 1991, pp. 174–80.
11. Price Pritchett and Ron Pound, *The Employee Handbook of Organizational Change*, Pritchett Publishing Company, Dallas, Tex., 1990.
12. Ruth Hooper and Ian Oliphant-Thompson, 'A change for the better . . . ?', *Management Services*, 36, 6 (1992), pp. 28–9.
13. James Belasco, *Empowering Change in Your Organization: Teaching the Elephant to Dance*, Crown Publishers, New York, 1990.
14. Michael Beer, Russell A. Eisenstat and Bert Spector, 'Why change programs don't produce change', *Harvard Business Review*, November/December 1990, pp. 158–66.
15. Patricia Plessinger Craig, 'Effective organizational change: pushing the right levers', *The Planning Forum Network*, January 1993, p. 5.
16. Quoted in A. Lad Bergin and Ellee Koss, *Transformation to High Performance*, SRI International, Report no. 823, Summer 1993.
17. Peter M. Senge, *The Fifth Discipline*, Doubleday Currency, New York, 1990.
18. By Robert T. Moran from the 'Cross-Cultural Contact' column in *International Management*, January 1988, p. 74.
19. Andrew Kupfer, 'How American industry stacks up', *Fortune*, 9 March 1992, pp. 30–46: a review article of ten-year activity.
20. Senge, op. cit.
21. Robert Reich, 'Pronoun test is key to kind of workplace', *Arizona Republic*, 2 August 1993, p. A9.
22. Yuzo Yasuda, *40 Years, 20 Million Ideas*, Productivity Press, Cambridge, Mass., 1991.
23. George Land and Beth Jarman, 'Future Pull', *The Futurist*, July/August 1992, pp. 25–7.
24. Fran Tarkenton with Tad Tuleja, *How to Motivate People*, Harper and Row, New York, 1986.
25. John Naisbitt and Patricia Aburdene, 'New leadership', *Executive Excellence*, March 1991, pp. 10–12.
26. Robert B. Reich, 'Who is them?' *Harvard Business Review*, March/April 1991, pp. 77–88.

The global manager acting skillfully

In today's slimmer, flatter, leaner companies, greater precision is demanded in fitting people to jobs ... and to aim for tighter selection and longer preparation of executives to be sure of appropriate abilities and skills ... the days when multinational companies like SKF could employ and train large numbers of able executives on the principle that a few would rise to the top, while all eventualities would be covered are not going to return.

Business Europe, 20–26 September 1993

This chapter develops more fully an earlier theme of this book—that the global manager must think both globally and locally as well as behave appropriately. Three competencies required to make globalization work will be described. Figures 12.4, 12.6 and 12.7 will give readers an opportunity to rate their organizations and to compare this rating to the transformational goal.

Mercedes-Benz announced at the end of September 1993 that it will be building an assembly plant in a small town in Alabama. In the press releases, it was stated that 34 states and over 100 communities had negotiated for this relationship. Japanese companies are building plants in Southeast Asia, the United States and Europe. European and US companies are present in most parts of the globe. Some US companies are even returning to Vietnam. The United States, Mexico and Canada have signed a free trade agreement. The euphoria for the global marketer has not diminished, and the negotiating competencies needed to succeed are increasing.

Competency 7: Negotiates and approaches conflicts in a collaborative mode

The material describing this competency is drawn from many excellent sources but primarily from *Managing Cultural Differences*,[1] *Getting your Yen's Worth: How to Negotiate with Japan*,[2] *Dynamics of Successful International Business Negotiations*,[3] *Managing Cultural Synergy*[4] and *Developing the Global Organization*.[5]

To make globalization work, we need to negotiate and approach conflicts collaboratively. Skillful international business negotiators *know* more than, and *behave* (act) differently from non-skillful negotiators.

What skillful negotiators know

Skillful international negotiators know that culture plays an important role in international negotiations

'Negotiation is a process in which two or more entities come together to discuss common and conflicting interests in order to reach an agreement of mutual benefit.'[6] In international business negotiations, there are cultural differences in most aspects of the negotiation process. The following examples of variations from a number of cultures are taken from *International Negotiations: A Cross-Cultural Perspective.*[7]

1. *Cultural conditioning.* This considers the way negotiators view the nature of the negotiation process itself. American negotiators are often frustrated because their counterparts do not enter into the expected give-and-take, which is typically experienced in domestic or labor–management negotiations in the United States.

2. *The use of a mediator.* For many cultures, such as the Japanese, open disagreement is be avoided. When there are conflicts in a negotiation situation, a third party is often used to assist in the negotiation process.

3. *Trusting the other party.* American negotiators usually begin a negotiating session by trusting each other until it is shown that such trust is unfounded. However, the French are more inclined to mistrust until trust is proven.

4. *The importance of protocol.* Negotiators from some countries are selected for their skillful rhetoric or their connections rather than for their business or negotiating competency.

5. *Selection of the negotiation team.* In the United States, negotiators are selected primarily on the basis of technical competence. However, in other societies people who do not have a high degree of technical expertise may be chosen to negotiate, because the members of a negotiation team are selected on the basis of personal power or authority.

Skillful international negotiators are aware of their cultural baggage

Most negotiations are difficult and frustrating. When the negotiations take place between people from different cultures and miscommunication can occur because of language problems, it is indeed challenging to negotiate long-term relationships of mutual benefit. The difficulties arise partly because of the cultural baggage individuals bring to the negotiating situation.

John Graham and Roy Herberger suggest a combination of characteristics that American negotiators typically use which typify the Western 'John Wayne' style of negotiating:[8]

- I can go it alone.

- Just call me John. (Americans value informality.)

- Pardon my French. (Americans have historically not set a high priority on learning foreign languages.)

- Get to the point. (American and some other Western cultures like to get to the heart of the matter very quickly.)

- Lay your cards on the table. (Americans expect honest information at the bargaining table.)

- Don't just sit there: speak up. (Americans do not deal well with silence during the negotiating process.)

- Do not take 'no' for an answer. (Persistence is highly valued by Americans.)

Skillful international negotiators profile accurately their negotiating counterparts

Negotiation is a cyclical process, and within the process there are four identifiable components that are essential to understanding how to profile one's negotiating counterparts:[9]

1. *Policy*—the negotiating policy of each party. Policy defines the vital interests of a business and describes the customary course of action used to protect and promote those interests.

2. *Interaction*—how each party will try to persuade the other during the negotiation. This refers to the period of information exchange during which the negotiators propose offers and counteroffers.

3. *Deliberation*—how each party earns the other's trust and on what each party will base its decisions. This is the process by which the negotiators evaluate the interaction, and adjust their understanding of their counterpart's requirements.

4. *Outcome*—how agreement is reached. This refers to the final understanding reached by the parties.

These four components of the negotiation process establish a framework in which global business negotiators can make decisions and take appropriate actions before, during and after negotiations, by enabling them to predict and interpret the actions of their negotiating counterparts.

Process component	Component variable(s)
Policy	1. Basic concept of negotiation
	2. Selection of negotiators
	3. Role of individual aspirations
	4. Concern with protocol
	5. Significance of type of issue
Interaction	6. Complexity of language
	7. Nature of persuasive argument
	8. Value of time
Deliberation	9. Basis of trust
	10. Risk-taking propensity
	11. Internal decision-making systems
Outcome	12. Form of satisfactory agreement

Fig. 12.1   Components of the negotiation process
(Source: R. T. Moran, P. R. Harris and W. G. Stripp, *Developing the Global Organization*, Gulf Publishing, Houston, Tex., 1993. Reproduced with permission).

Figures 12.1 and 12.2 illustrate the process components and the component variables.[10] By selectively categorizing information under each of the 12 variables listed in Fig. 12.1, skillful negotiators can develop a profile that shows the counterpart's philosophy of negotiation—who the negotiators are and why they were selected; what the negotiators want for themselves; how they will act and expect others to act; what kind of things are most important to them; how they will try to persuade others verbally and nonverbally; how they will use the time and how long they expect negotiations to take; what makes them trust someone; how they handle risk; who makes the decisions and how the decisions are made; and what form of agreement they expect.

Skillful negotiators understand these variables and the ranges of negotiating behavior. By understanding the possible alternatives, a skillful negotiator is able to adjust according to each global negotiating situation.

Skillful international negotiators can switch styles when negotiating[11]
To be skillful, effective and successful in one's own culture by being assertive, quick and to the point is one thing; to be equally successful in another culture, perhaps by being unassertive, patient and somewhat indirect, is another mode entirely—like handling two swords a the same time (Nitoryu style), a skill made famous by the seventeenth-century Japanese samurai, Miyamoto Musashi.

Yo Miyoshi, president of H. B. Fuller Japan Co. in Tokyo, says he modifies his behavior to suit his audience. 'When I discuss something with the head office in the United States, I try to be Western. But when I deal

Variable	Negotiator's profile range	
Basic concept of negotiation	Strategic	Synergistic
Selection of negotiators	Technical ability	Social skills
Role of individual aspirations	Organization	Self
Concern with protocol	Formal	Informal
Significance of type of issue	Substantive	Relationship-based
Complexity of language	Verbal	Nonverbal
Nature of persuasive argument	Logic	Emotion
Value of time	Strict	Relaxed
Basis of trust	Law	Friendship
Risk-taking propensity	Cautious	Adventurous
Internal decision-making systems	Authoritative	Consensus
Form of satisfactory agreement	Explicit	Implicit

Fig. 12.2 Framework for global business negotiations
(*Source*: R. T. Moran, P. R. Harris and W. G. Stripp, *Developing the Global Organization*, Gulf Publishing, Houston, Tex., 1993. Reproduced with permission).

with my people in the company here, I am Oriental or Japanese.' Miyoshi is able to shift his style, or to handle two swords at the same time. He had to learn this behavior. In negotiating situations, global negotiators who are able to make style switches like Yo Miyoshi will be more effective negotiators and managers.

We all have our own basic personality characteristics, the sword that made us successful—our aggressiveness and competitiveness, for example. But in another culture the second sword we are expected to carry might be characterized by quite different qualities, such as gentleness, cooperativeness, followership, indirectness and a commitment to relationships.

The global manager and conflict[12]

Conflict is an important subject for research and discussion. Traditionally, social scientists who have studied conflict have been aware of its destructive element, which was observed in wars, strikes, family disruption and disharmony. However, conflict is present in all organizations and, if managed well, serves useful purposes. Rensis Likert states: 'The strategies and principles used by a society and all its institutions for dealing with disagreements, reflect the basic values and philosophy in that society.'[13]

Like the word 'culture', there is no single agreed-upon definition for 'conflict'. Kenneth Thomas, an expert on the management of conflict says: 'Conflict is the process that begins when one party perceives that the other has frustrated, or is about to frustrate, some concern of his.'[14] This frustration may result from actions ranging from intellectual disagreement to physical violence. The skillful management of conflict is a major issue at the personal and organizational level.

Many global managers view conflict as healthy, natural and an inevitable part of all relationships. The idea of dissent has a strong tradition in Western history. When faced with a problem, some cultures like to get to the bottom of it quickly and directly.

Global managers and negotiators need to devise effective mechanisms for dealing with conflicts that cross cultures. Thomas and Kilmann suggest a two-dimensional framework (Fig. 12.3), with one dimension being the cooperative–uncooperative striving to satisfy the other's concern, and the second being the degree to which one assertively pursues one's own concerns.[15]

In Fig. 12.3 the assertive style is competitive and attempts to satisfy one's concerns at the expense of the other. The cooperative style (2) attempts to satisfy the other's concerns but not one's own. A compromising style (3) is a preference for achieving moderate, but incomplete, satisfaction of both parties. A collaborative style (5) attempts to fully satisfy the concerns of both parties (the most synergistic), and the avoidance style (1) indicates an indifference to the concerns of either party.

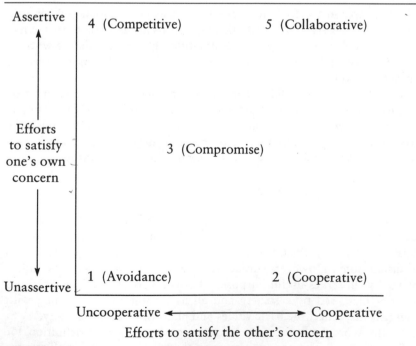

Fig. 12.3   Mechanism for conflict resolution
(*Source*: adapted from Thomas and Kilmann)

Effective global managers must be able to achieve a synergistic solution, diagnosing problems accurately and managing a strategy for conflict. The facts, as perceived by both parties, and the values and cultures are crucial to the synergistic solution.

We end with a quotation from *Managing Cultural Synergy*.

> The very differences in the world's people can lead to mutual growth and accomplishment that is more than the single contribution of each party to the intercultural transaction.
>
> We can go beyond awareness of our own cultural heritage to produce something greater by cooperation and collaboration. Cultural synergy builds upon similarities and uses differences resulting in more effective human activities and systems. The very diversity of people can be utilized to enhance problem solving by combined action.[16]

Summary

For Competency 7, Fig. 12.4 provides an opportunity for readers to reflect on the structure of their company or organization (is it traditional multinational, traditional international or traditional global according to descriptions of these structures in earlier chapters?) and to rate the CEO, corporate staff, subsidiary general manager and staff, as well as all employees in general. We are fully aware there may be great variation among the corporate staff or employees; but what is the central tendency? Or, generally, to what degree do these groups of people possess the competency?

Based on our assessment and interpretation of the significant literature on the subject, we have then indicated whether the competency is *essential*, *useful* or *not necessary* for the CEO, corporate staff, subsidiary general manager and staff, and all employees, for the transformational goal to be realized and to make globalization work.

	CEO	Corporate staff	Subsidiary general manager and staff	All employees
Your company				

Rate and describe the degree the competency is possessed for each of the categories for your organization:

H　= Demonstrates a high degree
S　= Demonstrates somewhat
L　= Demonstrates to a low degree
N/A = Not applicable for your organization

Transformational goal for structure

	CEO	Corporate staff	Subsidiary general manager and staff	All employees
Worldwide organizational solution	*Essential* To create the future together as partners	*Essential* 90% of negotiating is intra-company and great skill is required	*Essential* To work collaboratively with global headquarters	*Useful* To create a healthy work environment

Fig. 12.4　Competency 7: Negotiates and approaches conflicts in a collaborative mode

Competency 8: Manages skillfully the foreign deployment cycle

It has been estimated that American corporations and government spend about $50 billion each year in education and training. The goal is to improve the performance of the individual, thus enhancing the operating performance of a company or the government.

Jay Duffy, manager, employee development, for a division of a large global company, believes training may be a solution if one of the following four situations exists:[17]

1. A gap exists between the skill level and the current position requirement.

2. The tasks of a present position need to be performed differently.

3. The job has changed or will change.

4. Future positions may require different or additional skills.

The gap between job requirements and the skill of the employee was demonstrated in research conducted and reported by Kathleen Miller,[18] among others.

In the past, Miller states, workers learned their trade when young, and performed the same job throughout their life. Today this is no longer true. Between 1979 and 1984, an estimated 5.1 million Americans lost their jobs because their skills were no longer needed. This created a problem not only for those that became unemployed, but for the employers who no longer had an adequately trained workforce. Most companies are realizing that, to meet the needs of the changing global economy, they must retrain their employees.

To avoid the costs of retraining, many employers tried firing and then hiring new employees with the appropriate skills. This proved to be not only expensive but also demoralizing for the organization. The problem of developing retraining programs was then addressed.

The difficulty of adequately preparing people for working internationally is even greater. It was expressed in the following way by a human resource executive of a Fortune 100 company during a speech in September 1992: 'Our goal is to train our people in globalization skills by 1994, but we don't know what the skills are or what percentage of our people are trainable.'

Hari Bedi, a columnist for *Asian Business*, sees a similar gap in Asia as applied to managing in a multicultural environment:

> An ability to manage in a multicultural environment is critical to success in international business today.
>
> Globalisation of business exists side by side with cultural enclaves, creating a dichotomy that affects people both personally and professionally. But unfortunately there is no organised corporate effort in Asia to prepare managers to cope with the problem.
>
> It's high time that a few large companies took the lead to sponsor an institute, which could offer suitable programmes on a regular basis.[19]

It is our perspective that *the most important training required today, and in the near future, will be to develop to a high degree the 12 competencies identified in this book.*

More companies are beginning to try to prepare their people adequately for overseas work. In the past, there was no preparation beyond 'Are you technically competent and willing to go?'

In an earlier book, Harris and Moran outlined in great detail the what, how, when and why of an effective transition and foreign deployment process.[20] Bren White,[21] Stewart Black, Hal Gregersen and Mark Mendenhall,[22] as well as Stephen Rhinesmith[23] and others, have further developed these concepts as applied to a changing global environment.

The necessity of effective preparation for global assignments and an effective global deployment process is demonstrated by research on

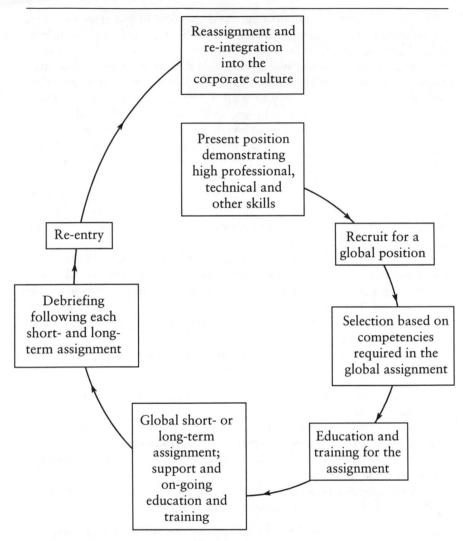

Fig. 12.5   The global deployment process: best practices

Canadian technical advisors by the Canadian International Development Agency. The book, *Cross-Cultural Effectiveness*,[24] found an important interaction between overseas effectiveness and overseas satisfaction.

In terms of overseas effectiveness, the study found that: 65 per cent of the technical advisers were neither effective or ineffective, 20 per cent were highly effective and 10 per cent were very ineffective. However, no matter how effective or ineffective they were, 75 per cent were satisfied, 10 per cent were neutral and 15 per cent were highly dissatisfied with their assignments.

The importance of skillfully managing the selection, preparation, support and re-entry processes is outlined in Fig. 12.5.

In developing a foreign deployment system, Harris and Moran[25] provide an overview of the many considerations, starting with the entry to and exit from another culture. These include:

- Selection and preparation of human resource training staff
- Recruitment of global candidates
- Selection of personnel for global service
- General cultural or area training
- Specific culture and language training
- Pre-logistical preparation and departure
- On-site orientation and briefings
- Culture shock/adjustment skill development
- Overseas monitoring and support
- Acculturation and integration, personally and professionally, in the new assignment
- Re-entry preparation
- Exit-transition
- Re-entry shock
- Readjustment
- Reassignment and re-integration in the organization

Where the cultural differences between one's home culture and the host culture are very different, it becomes all the more crucial for companies, organizations and government agencies to provide an effective relocation system.

Ernest Gundling states: 'Japan bound U.S. managers have to be turned upside down and shaken gently, so that their cultural assumptions won't get in the way of working with the Japanese.'[26] Gundling believes that Japanese and American cultures vary significantly, and that care should be taken to ensure that the training program meets the participant's expectations, and that adequate instruction and exposure to Japanese norms is provided.

First, the trainer should establish her or his credibility to the participant. This is necessary to 'gain trust and build rapport'. Second, participants should be briefed on key concepts and background information so that they have the proper tools. This is also the time for the trainer to determine the person's previous experience and knowledge of the Japanese culture. In the third phase, the trainees participate in simulations of typical business situations. They should understand the 'how to', the 'why' and the 'how not to' of working effectively with the Japanese. Next, the trainer must be attuned to the stress experienced by the trainees as they experiment with their newly acquired cultural knowledge. They must strive to provide positive feedback. The final step in the training process is to solicit feedback. This enables the trainer to identify strengths and weaknesses and to improve the training design.

Selecting the right person

Black, Gregersen and Mendenhall[27] state the importance of finding the right people for international assignments. They found that US firms often choose people for overseas assignment without selecting them carefully enough, and that they rely more on technical competence than on any of the other competencies. Similar problems in the selection process for overseas assignment are found in Japan, Europe and Scandinavia.

Those responsible for global assignments consider many criteria, but the following selection factors are the ones that Black *et al.* believe are the most predictive of expatriate success:

1. *Strategic factors*—ability of the firm to determine strategy of international assignment: why is the expatriate being sent?

2. *Professional skills*—direct professional knowledge of the job and understanding of problems to be solved

3. *General managerial skills*—knowing how to deal with interpersonal conflict and resolution

4. *Communication skills*—ability to communicate effectively in other cultures and have an interest in developing significant relationships with host country nationals

5. *Individual characteristics*—being open to exploring the host culture and not evaluating everything on a right-or-wrong basis

6. *Gender-related factors*—need for US firms to pay attention to the gender of the potential candidate: although fewer than 15 per cent of US human resource directors acknowledge that they intentionally select males, in reality they seem to do so more than 95 per cent of the time.

Education and training for the assignment

After the selection process, global education and training orientation is needed to help persons both think globally and locally and to act appropriately. Individual learning packages for the employee and the employee's family, plus adequate language and technical training designed to fit each individual, are essential. These programs should include general culture orientation, language skill orientation, culture-specific orientation, training and learning, and job orientation.

Gary Fontaine has developed a total management strategy for mastering international assignments.[28] The strategy encompasses all facets of the overseas assignment, from the screening and self-selection of candidates through orientation and training, to providing for organizational and social support of the candidate and his or her family. He differentiates between orientation and training as between supplying information and developing skills. An organization must develop orientation programs that will enable a positive, successful overseas experience for its employees.

Orientation programs

Orientation programs provide information about the international assignment itself and about the host culture. The information provided typically falls into three broad categories. *Background information* includes the history, geography, politics and social culture of the foreign environment. *More extensive orientation programs* will provide information on the literature, economic system, current events, important people, science and industry, religions, holidays and language(s) of the country. *Practical information* will include things such as the cost of living, social customs, exchange rates, security, health and law, housing and schools, currency, transportation, telephones, time zones and the measurement system. Information necessary to make the international transition, such as regulations regarding passports, visas, work permits, health, tax and legal clearances and how to send funds, must be provided by the organization and in many cases should be taken care of by the organization. The employee should also be aware of the exact job assignment, what is required and how he or she will be evaluated.

The family of the assigned employee should also be involved in the orientation process. Spouses should receive all of the above information (as well as information about obtaining employment for him- or herself), while children, depending on their ages, should be told about some of the school and cultural issues that will impact them.

Re-entry

After the expatriate has lived abroad and is ready to return home, the final step in the process of foreign deployment is the re-entry preparation. Many expatriates who have lived abroad for long periods of time often experience difficulty in returning. Living abroad causes people to change and re-examine their lives. People who have expanded their horizons, become more cosmopolitan, and changed their global outlook sometimes undergo very serious personal crises. It is critical, therefore, for an organization to provide support upon return.

Black *et al.* found three basic areas where expatriates must readjust: to their new jobs and work environment, to communicating with home-country co-workers and friends, and to the general living environment (food, weather, housing, transportation, schools, etc.).[29]

In general, most current literature on education and training is just beginning to place greater emphasis on re-entry training. Firms have become concerned about cross-cultural training before sending an employee abroad, but until recently they have often neglected to retrain and re-integrate expatriates in an effective manner upon their return to the home country.

Summary

For Competency 8, Fig. 12.6 provides an opportunity for readers to reflect on the structure of their company or organization (is it traditional multinational, traditional international or traditional global according to descriptions of these structures in earlier chapters?) and to rate the CEO, corporate staff, subsidiary general manager and staff, as well as all employees in general. We are fully aware there may be great variation among the corporate staff or employees; but what is the central tendency? Or, generally, to what degree do these groups of people possess the competency?

Based on our assessment and interpretation of the significant literature on the subject, we have then indicated whether the competency is *essential*, *useful* or *not necessary* for the CEO, corporate staff, subsidiary general manager and staff, and all employees for the transformational goal to be realized and to make globalization work.

	CEO	Corporate staff	Subsidiary general manager and staff	All employees
Your company				

Rate and describe the degree the competency is possessed for each of the categories for your organization:

H   = Demonstrates a high degree
S   = Demonstrates somewhat
L   = Demonstrates to a low degree
N/A = Not applicable for your organization

Transformational goal for structure

	CEO	Corporate staff	Subsidiary general manager and staff	All employees
Worldwide organizational solution	*Useful* To support the efforts of the training department	*Essential* To ensure proper selection and training of all persons	*Essential* To adequately train key employees	*Not necessary for success*

Fig. 12.6   Competency 8: Manages skillfully the foreign deployment process cycle

Competency 9: Leads and participates effectively in multicultural teams

> *My worst experiences at Thunderbird were the project teams I had to participate in.*
> Recent Master of International Management graduate

> *The teams I was a member of were the best learning experiences I've ever had.*
> Another recent Master of International Management graduate

> *Every morning in Africa, when a gazelle wakes up, it knows that it must run faster than the fastest lion or it will be killed. Every morning that a lion wakes up, it knows that it must run faster than the slowest gazelle or it will starve.*

> *Moral: It doesn't matter whether you are a*
> *lion or a gazelle. When the sun comes up,*
> *you had better be running.*
>
> *Translate that to human terms and you can*
> *begin to understand why we think of cross-*
> *functional teams not in terms of 'a program,'*
> *but in terms of 'survival.'*
> ROBERT HERSHOCK
> *Planning Forum Network*, September 1993[30]

'High performance teams', 'team work', 'worldwide global product teams' and other words expressing similar ideas are commonplace in the management literature today. Stories of teams producing remarkable accomplishments are well known. Well functioning teams can increase productivity and creativity.

However, functioning skillfully on a team is a learned skill. The Conference Board addresses the problem:

> The CEO must be fully committed to globalization and must actively and persistently drive the globalization process. Chief executive commitment is more important than international experience and background. It is essential that the CEO understands the issues (e.g. culture, human resources, empowerment) and translates commitment into actions. Words alone will not drive the process.
>
> Second, a core team of managers with an international background must be available in the organization before anything can happen. These managers must bring international culture and international experience to energize the globalization process.
>
> The process of building an international team large enough to permeate the entire organization is long and arduous. It requires years of training, attention to recruiting, career development, and job rotations through foreign assignments.[31]

The role of multicultural teams in the globalization process is well recognized.

Stages of team development

A team is an interdependent group of individuals who generally agree on a goal and the way they will accomplish their objective. In the process of accomplishing goals, teams go through four stages, according to Glenn Parker and others:[32]

1. *Forming.* Group members are unclear on the purpose of the team and use this time to become more familiar with new teammates.

2. *Storming.* Characterized by conflict, in this stage members express frustrations and concerns about their purpose and learn to deal with differences in order to accomplish their goals.

3. *Norming.*   If they have successfully completed the storming stage, members now become more comfortable working with each other and with the group's methods for dealing with conflict.

4. *Performing.*   Team members are now ready to get down to the task at hand. They understand the rules and roles of the team and begin to emphasize achieving results.

Team player styles also significantly effect group makeup. 'The contributor' is task- and result-oriented, with a heavy emphasis on information-gathering. 'The collaborator' is concerned about the team's mission and tends to focus on the big picture. 'The communicator' is interested in maintaining good relationships between all team players and wants to make sure that all members are heard and valued. 'The challenger' is problem-oriented and is not afraid to question the wisdom of the group.

Effective teams are characterized by people of diverse backgrounds, talents and personalities. Team members are interdependent, and they all agree on a common goal and the best way to achieve that goal.

A dictionary describes a team as a number of persons working in some joint action. The more people have in common, the easier it is to develop a team.[33] When one crosses cultures and tries to assimilate outsiders into a team, team development becomes more complicated—even when all the team members are employed by the same global organization. By understanding organizational and group dynamics, team leaders are better able to create consensus among divergent persons.

There are significant differences between the productivity of homogeneous and heterogeneous teams. Cultural diversity within teams increases potential productivity. It also increases the complexity of the process. Thus, culturally diverse teams have potential for higher productivity than culturally homogeneous groups, but greater risk of loss arising from a faulty process.

Nancy Adler suggests that a team's productivity can best be described by the following formula:[34]

Actual productivity = Potential productivity
              — losses due to faults in how the teams work together

A team's productivity is related to its task, resources and process, and the task is the first important determinant of productivity. Research has shown that *diverse groups are better suited for specialized tasks, whereas homogeneous groups are better suited for routine repetitive tasks.* This is important to remember when choosing team members.

Excellent resources, including instruments, learning aids and simulations on team development, can be found in Chapter 3, 'Cross-Cultural Team Development', in Moran *et al.*'s *Developing the Global Organization.*[35] Price Pritchett and Ron Pound's *Team Reconstruction: Building a High Performance Work Group During Change*[36] will also be of value.

Summary

For Competency 9, Fig. 12.7 provides an opportunity for readers to reflect on the structure of their company or organization (is it traditional multinational, traditional international or traditional global according to descriptions of these structures in earlier chapters?) and to rate the CEO, corporate staff, subsidiary general manager and staff, as well as all employees in general. We are fully aware there may be great variation among the corporate staff or employees; but what is the central tendency? Or, generally, to what degree do these groups of people possess the competency?

Based on our assessment and interpretation of the significant literature on the subject, we have then indicated whether the competency is *essential, useful,* or *not necessary* for the CEO, corporate staff, subsidiary general manager and staff, and all employees, for the transformational goal to be realized and to make globalization work.

	CEO	Corporate staff	Subsidiary general manager and staff	All employees
Your company				

Rate and describe the degree the competency is possessed for each of the categories for your organization:
H   = Demonstrates a high degree
S   = Demonstrates somewhat
L   = Demonstrates to a low degree
N/A = Not applicable for your organization

Transformational goal for structure

	CEO	Corporate staff	Subsidiary general manager and staff	All employees
Worldwide organizational solution	Essential Leadership changes require CEO to demonstrate team player characteristics	*Essential* To accomplish the goals of a transformational organization	*Essential* Worldwide product and project team are increasingly important	*Essential* With changes in the make-up of the workforce, employees must be trained to work with others

Fig. 12.7   Competency 9: leads and participates effectively in multicultural teams

Notes and references

1. Philip R. Harris and Robert T. Moran, *Managing Cultural Differences*, 3rd edn, Gulf Publishing, Houston, Tex., 1991.
2. Robert T. Moran, *Getting your Yen's Worth: How to Negotiate with Japan, Inc.*, Gulf Publishing, Houston, Tex., 1987.
3. Robert T. Moran and William G. Stripp, *Dynamics of Successful International Business Negotiations*, Gulf Publishing, Houston, Tex., 1991.
4. Robert T. Moran and Philip Harris, *Managing Cultural Synergy*, Gulf Publishing, Houston, Tex., 1982.
5. Robert T. Moran, Philip R. Harris and William G. Stripp, *Developing the Global Organization*, Gulf Publishing, Houston, Tex., 1993.
6. Harris and Moran, op. cit., p. 56.
7. Glenn Fisher, *International Negotiations: A Cross-Cultural Perspective*, Intercultural Press, Yarmouth, Me, 1980.
8. John Graham and Roy Herberger, 'Negotiators abroad—don't shoot from the hip', *Harvard Business Review*, July–August 1983, pp. 160–8.
9. Moran and Stripp, op. cit., p. 91.
10. See also Stephen Weiss and William G. Stripp, *Negotiating with Foreign Businesspersons*, New York University Graduate School of Business Administration, Monograph no. 89-9, 1985.
11. This section is taken from a column by Robert T. Moran, 'Handling two swords at the same time', *International Management*, July 1986, p. 56.
12. This section is taken from the material on conflict in Moran and Harris, op. cit.
13. Rensis Likert and J. G. Likert, *New Ways of Managing Conflict*, McGraw-Hill, New York, 1976.
14. Kenneth Thomas, *Conflict and Conflict Management*, University of California at Los Angeles, Working Paper no. 74-3, 1974.
15. This section is taken from one based on material by Thomas and Kilmann in the book by Moran and Harris, op. cit., p. 67.
16. Moran and Harris, op. cit., p. 303.
17. In Joyce Goetano and Aleta Richards, '100 percent polyurethane quality newsletter', Miles Inc., December 1992.
18. Kathleen Miller, *Retraining the American Workforce*, Addison-Wesley, Reading, Mass., 1989.
19. From Hari Bedi, 'A faculty of good feelings', *Asian Business*, August 1993, p. 4.
20. From Harris and Moran, op. cit., Chapter 7, 'Managing transitions and foreign deployment'.
21. Bren White, *World-Class Training*, Odenwald Press, Dallas, Tex., 1992.
22. J. Stewart Black, Hal B. Gregersen and Mark E. Mendenhall, *Global Assignments*, Jossey-Bass, San Francisco, 1992.
23. Stephen H. Rhinesmith, *A Manager's Guide to Globalization*, Business One Irwin, Homewood, Ill., 1993.

24. Daniel J. Kealy, *Cross-Cultural Effectiveness: A Study of Canadian Technical Advisors Overseas*, Canadian International Development Agency, Quebec, 1990.
25. From Harris and Moran, op. cit., p. 234.
26. Ernest Gundling, 'Japan-bound training', *Training & Development*, July 1992, p. 41.
27. Black, Gregersen and Mendenhall, op. cit.
28. Gary Fontaine, *Managing International Assignments*, Prentice-Hall, Englewood Cliffs, NJ, 1989.
29. Black *et al.*, op. cit.
30. Robert J. Hershock, 'Cross-functional teams: the driving force for change', *The Planning Forum Network*, 6, 7 (September 1993), p. 4.
31. Conference Board, *Corporate Strategies for Global Competitive Advantage*, Conference Board, New York, 1992.
32. Glenn M. Parker, *Team Players and Teamwork*, Jossey-Bass, San Francisco, 1990.
33. Moran, Harris and Stripp, op. cit.
34. Nancy Adler, *International Dimensions of Organizational Behavior*, Kent Publishing, Boston, Mass., 1986.
35. Moran *et al.*, op. cit.
36. Price Pritchett and Ron Pound, *Team Reconstruction: Building a High Performance Work Group during Change*, Pritchett Publishing, Dallas, Tex., 1992.

The global managers' understanding of national and organizational culture and avoiding cultural errors

CHAPTER

13

*'It's not possible to be a global citizen,'
Robert Moran says. 'I'm not even sure its an
ideal to strive for. Most effective business
people are deeply Japanese, profoundly
American,' Moran says. 'They know what
that means and can make the appropriate
adjustments to work effectively in other
systems.'*
USA Today,
14 September 1993[1]

The French philosopher–mathematician Pascal said many years ago: 'There are truths on this side of the Pyrenees that are falsehoods on the other.' This metaphor for national boundaries sums up the challenge facing global managers when they attempt to conduct business outside their home ground. This chapter considers culture as an important ingredient in making globalization work. The last three competencies are described.

Competency 10: Understands their own culture, values and assumptions

'Know thyself'
Socrates

Global managers from one country have to work and negotiate with their global counterparts regularly. A common requirement is that they must each be able to communicate effectively and work with individuals who have been socialized in a different cultural environment, and whose customs, values, lifestyles, beliefs, management practices and other important aspects of their personal and professional lives are different.

A European executive during a personal conversation said, 'I can't think of any situation in my 25 years of international experience when international business was made *easier* because people from more than one country were participating.' A global manager must be aware of the many beliefs and values that underlie his or her own country's business practices, management techniques and strategies.

Figure 13.1 illustrates how values and beliefs from one culture and alternative aspects from another influence the management functions.

251

Aspects of US culture*	Alternative aspect	Examples of management function affected
The individual can influence the future. (Where there is a will there is a way.)	Life follows a course and results are beyond the work of the individual.	Planning and scheduling
The individual can change and improve the environment.	People are intended to adjust to the physical environment rather than to alter it.	Organizational environment morale, and productivity
We must work hard to accomplish our objectives (Puritan ethic).	Hard work is not the only prerequisite for success: wisdom, luck and time are also required.	Motivation and reward system
Commitments should be honored. (People will do what they say they will do.)	A commitment may be superseded by a conflicting request, or an agreement may only signify intentions and have little or no relationship to the capacity of performance.	Negotiating and bargaining
The best qualified persons should be given the positions available.	Family considerations, friendship and other considerations determine employment practices.	Employment, promotions, recruiting, selection and reward
Company information should be available to anyone who needs it within the oragnization.	Withholding information to gain or maintain power is acceptable.	Organization, communication, managerial style
Each person is expected to have an opinion and to express it freely even if his/her views do not agree with his/her colleagues.	Deference is to be given to persons in power or authority and to offer judgment that is not in support of the ideas of one's superiors is unthinkable.	Communications, organizational relations
Competition stimulates high performance.	Competition leads to disharmony.	Career development and marketing
A person is expected to do whatever is necessary to get the job done. (One must be willing to get one's hands dirty.)	Various kinds of work are accorded low or high status and some work may be below one's 'dignity' or place in the organization.	Assignment of tasks, performance, and organizational effectiveness
Persons and systems are evaluated.	Persons are evaluated but in such a way that individuals not highly evaluated will not be embarrassed or caused to 'lose face'.	Rewards and promotions performance evaluation and accountability

*Aspect' here refers to a belief, value, attitude or assumption that is part of the culture in that it is shared by a large number of persons in that culture.

Source: Adapted from P. R. Harris and R. T. Moran, Managing Cultural Differences, Gulf Publishing, Houston, Tex., 1991. Reproduced by permission.

Fig. 13.1 US values and alternative values

The order of the values and the sequence is not important; nor are the values or aspects of culture listed mutually exclusive. This list illustrates how cultural differences in attitudes, values, assumptions, personal beliefs, interpersonal relationships and social and organizational structure affect the traditional management functions of decision-making, promotion, recruitment and development, organizing, planning and motivation, among others.

Given these differences, and their profound effect upon the performance of each management function, the global manager must have a high degree of cultural self-awareness to be able to accept and understand the *relativity* of culture. There is no absolute or correct way of doing anything.

Summary

For Competency 10 Fig. 13.2 provides an opportunity for readers to reflect on the structure of their company or organization (is it traditional multinational, traditional international or traditional global according to descriptions of these structures in earlier chapters?) and to rate the CEO, corporate staff, subsidiary general manager and staff, as well as all employees in general. We are fully aware there may be great variation among the corporate staff or employees; but what is the central tendency? Or, generally, to what degree do these groups of people possess the competency?

Based on our assessment and interpretation of the significant literature on the subject, we have then indicated whether the competency is *essential*, *useful*, or *not necessary* for the CEO, corporate staff, subsidiary general manager and staff, and all employees, for the transformational goal to be realized and to make globalization work.

	CEO	Corporate staff	Subsidiary general manager and staff	All employees
Your company				

Rate and describe the degree the competency is possessed for each of the categories for your organization:

H   = Demonstrates a high degree
S   = Demonstrates somewhat
L   = Demonstrates to a low degree
N/A = Not applicable for your organization

Transformational goal for structure

	CEO	Corporate staff	Subsidiary general manager and staff	All employees
Worldwide organizational solution	*Essential* To avoid imposing one's values and work synergistically	*Essential* To listen and accept the perspective of subsidiaries	*Essential* To develop the required global relationship	*Essential* To support the global mindset useful for all employees

Fig. 13.2   Competency 10: Understands their own culture, values and assumptions.

Competency 11: Accurately profiles the organizational culture and national culture of others

Corporate culture is the way of life of an organization. The best recent book on the subject is John Kotter and James Heskett's *Corporate Culture and Performance*. In their recent studies of many large organizations, they concluded:

1. Corporate culture can have a significant impact on a firm's long-term economic performance.

2. Corporate culture will probably be an even more important factor in determining the success or failure of firms in the next decade.

3. Corporate cultures that inhibit strong long-term financial performance are not rare; they develop easily, even in firms that are full of reasonable and intelligent people.

4. Although tough to change, corporate cultures can be made more performance-enhancing.[2]

It is debated how, and to what extent, a corporate culture can be modified to fit a global organization's vision and strategy. Most writers agree that it is possible but debate the process.

Culture and nations

The declining competitiveness of many US and European organizations and the success of Japanese companies in the 1970s and 1980s has stimulated an analysis of Japanese organizations to determine, among other things, 'Why are so many enormously successful?' and 'Can we integrate aspects of their corporate and material cultures into our own?'

George C. Lodge and Ezra Vogel state that every country has an ideology—that is, 'a set of beliefs and assumptions about values that a nation holds to justify and make legitimate the actions and purposes of its institutions'.[3] Nations are successful when their ideologies are adaptable and coherent. When there is a large gap between a country's ideology and its practice, there are problems.

Japan and the United States are good examples. No one denies the economic miracle of Japan. Few, if any, had forecast it. General Douglas MacArthur on 21 September 1945 said: 'Japan will never again become a world power . . . Japan industrially, commercially, militarily and every other way is in a state of complete collapse.' He was wrong.

An important event that occurred over 100 years ago may suggest how the Japanese respond to their environment. It may give us a clue to the adaptability of their ideology.

For most of its history, Japan maintained a policy of isolation. This was enforced strictly during the Tokugawa regime from 1600 to 1854. Exceptions were trade with the Dutch on an island close to the city of Nagasaki in southern Japan. Japan also had some contacts with Korea and China.

In the early nineteenth century, ships from Britain and other countries were permitted to enter Japanese ports for water and supplies. This practice continued until 1825, when the Tokugawa military government ruled that foreign ships should not be given assistance and should be driven away from the shores of Japan. In 1842 this law was repealed, and Japan once again gave food, water and fuel to foreign vessels.

By 1852, however, the United States wanted more. The US President sent a mission to Japan, led by Commodore Matthew Perry, to establish a trade and navigation treaty. Perry had several specific objectives. He wanted to force the Japanese to receive a letter from the US President in a place besides Nagasaki, to impose the image of a strong America on Japan and to negotiate a treaty quickly.

Perry arrived near Tokyo with four warships and demanded a meeting. Despite delaying tactics on the part of the Japanese, they eventually received Perry and accepted the letter from President Fillmore. Perry departed, and returned three months later, with seven warships, to receive the answer of the military government.

The Japanese agreed to most of the demands. They showed prudence in resigning themselves to the inevitable, adapting their 'ideology' to the events that were acting on their environment.

Given the history of the Japanese from that time to the present, can one not say that there may be something cultural, perhaps unique, in the people that allows them to adjust their ideology to fit varying circumstances? Recent history certainly has shown this to be true, with the Japanese adapting to changes in remarkably successful and profitable ways.

Contrast this with the seeming inability of the United States to do the same. From its beginnings over 200 years ago, the United States has professed an ideology based on individualism. Americans fought a revolution to preserve democracy, and they resent control and interference, especially by government.

They believe that all persons are created equal and strive through law to promote equal opportunity. They idealize the self-made man who rises from adversity. 'Doing you own thing' expresses the belief in being able to control one's destiny.

Americans also believe that, with determination, anyone can accomplish what he or she sets out to do, thus fulfilling the individual's potential. This individualism, historically, has worked and been good for the United States.

But, looking to the present, and to the future, might there not be 'community' needs of the individual? Are there external forces now influencing the environment of Americans that necessitate the adjustment of the ideology to fit the present needs?[4]

The same question is discussed by Joel Kotkin in *Tribes: How Race, Religion and Identity Determine Success in the New Global Economy*.[5] His premiss is that, as ideologies collapse, tribal interest increases as people seek 'definition for the collective past'. These global tribes are 'well adapted to succeed within today's progressively more integrated world-wide economic systems.' He includes Jews, British, Japanese, Chinese and Indians as principals in this grouping. In other words, as national boundaries break down, ethnic groups will seek others of their same cultural background anywhere in the world, and not just within their business community or country.

What is national culture? A short definition is 'the total way of life of a people'. This implies that culture is stable but never static and that it changes over time.

'Don't underestimate how different European business conduct is . . . Europeans may even speak flawless English. But our business cultures are very different.'[6]

Dr Geert Hofstede, a European, has conducted some very significant research with business applications on the 'mapping' or 'management conceptions' or 'software' of national cultures. In his books, *Culture's Consequences: International Differences in Work-Related Values*[7] and *Cultures and Organizations: Software of the Mind*,[8] he identifies four dimensions of national culture.

The first *power distance* indicates 'the extent to which a society accepts that power in institutions and organizations is distributed unequally'. The second, *uncertainty avoidance*, indicates 'the extent to which a society feels threatened by uncertain or ambiguous situations'. *Individualism* is the third dimension and refers to a 'loosely knit social framework in a society in which people are supposed to take care of themselves and of their immediate families only'. *Collectivism*, the opposite, occurs when there is a 'tight social framework in which people distinguish between in-groups and out-groups; they expect their in-group (relatives, clan, organizations) to look after them, and in exchange for that owe absolute loyalty to it'.

The fourth dimension is *masculinity* with its opposite pole, *femininity*. This dimension expresses 'the extent to which the dominant values in society are assertiveness, money and things, not caring for others, quality of life and people'.

For a thorough understanding of this work, Hofstede's books are crucial. However, the importance can be illustrated by Fig. 13.3. The position of 50 countries and three regions is shown on the Power Distance and Individualism–Collectivism indexes.

Hofstede has shown a way of mapping national cultures. Other writers, such as Harris and Moran,[9] Kluckhohn and Strodtbeck[10] and Hall and Hall,[11] have approached the same subject, but not as systemically or thoroughly. One of the most important competencies in making globalization work is the ability to accurately profile organizational culture and national culture.

Summary

For Competency 11 Fig. 13.4 provides an opportunity for readers to reflect on the structure of their company or organization (is it traditional multinational, traditional international or traditional global according to descriptions of these structures in earlier chapters?) and to rate the CEO, corporate staff, subsidiary general manager and staff, as well as all employees in general. We are fully aware there may be great variation among the corporate staff or employees; but what is the central tendency? Or, generally, to what degree do these groups of people possess the competency?

Based on our assessment and interpretation of the significant literature on the subject, we have then indicated whether the competency is *essential*, *useful* or *not necessary* for the CEO, corporate staff, subsidiary general manager and staff, and all employees, for the transformational goal to be realized and to make globalization work.

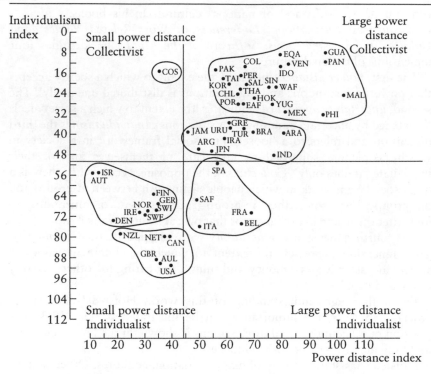

Fig. 13.3   Power, distance and individualism: collectivism index *Source*: Geert Hofstede, *Cultures and Organizations: Software of the Mind*, McGraw-Hill, Maidenhead, Berks, UK. 1991. Reproduced by permission.

Abbreviation	Country or region	Abbreviation	Country or region
ARA	Arab-speaking countries (Egypt, Iraq, Kuwait, Lebanon, Libya, Saudi Arabia, United Arab Emirates)	ISR	Israel
		ITA	Italy
		JAM	Jamaica
		JPN	Japan
		KOR	South Korea
ARG	Argentina	MAL	Malaysia
AUL	Australia	MEX	Mexico
AUT	Austria	NET	Netherlands
BEL	Belgium	NOR	Norway
BRA	Brazil	NZL	New Zealand
CAN	Canada	PAK	Pakistan
CHL	Chile	PAN	Panama
COL	Colombia	PER	Peru
COS	Costa Rica	PHI	Philippines
DEN	Denmark	POR	Portugal
EAF	East Africa (Ethiopia, Kenya, Tanzania, Zambia)	SAF	South Africa
		SAL	Salvador
		SIN	Singapore
EQA	Equador	SPA	Spain
FIN	Finland	SWE	Sweden
FRA	France	SWI	Switzerland
GBR	Great Britain	TAI	Taiwan
GER	Germany FR	THA	Thailand
GRE	Greece	TUR	Turkey
GUA	Guatemala	URU	Uruguay
HOK	Hong Kong	USA	United States
IDO	Indonesia	VEN	Venezuela
IND	India	WAF	West Africa (Ghana, Nigeria, Sierra Leone)
IRA	Iran		
IRE	Ireland(Republic of)	YUG	Yugoslavia

	CEO	Corporate staff	Subsidiary general manager and staff	All employees
Your company				

Rate and describe the degree the competency is possessed for each of the categories for your organization:

H   = Demonstrates a high degree
S   = Demonstrates somewhat
L   = Demonstrates to a low degree
N/A = Not applicable for your organization

Transformational goal for structure

	CEO	Corporate staff	Subsidiary general manager and staff	All employees
Worldwide organizational solution	*Essential* To understand the mental map and management concepts of others	*Essential* To work skillfully with diversity	*Essential* To understand mental map and management conceptions of others	*Useful* To work effectively with different viewpoints

Fig. 13.4   Competency 11: Accurately profiles the organizational culture and national culture of others

Competency 12: Avoids cultural mistakes and behaves in a manner that demonstrates knowledge of and respect for other countries

Jack Condon and Fathi Yousef many years ago wrote:

> Many people believe that the language of gestures is universal. Many people believe that one picture is worth a thousand words, the implication being that what we see is ever so much clearer than what is said. Many people believe that communication means speaking and that misunderstandings only occur with speaking. Many people believe that smiling and frowning and clapping are purely natural expressions. Many people believe that the world is flat.[12]

Skillful international managers have learned to see the world differently and to understand the way others manage and do business. This implies that there is no single way of doing anything and that no one culture is perfect or complete in all aspects. Successful communication with other cultures means not judging customs, rituals or ways of doing business as ridiculous, or inferior to one's own. A Swedish executive of a large multinational corporation expressed it this way: 'We Swedes are so content with the quality of our products and the Swedish way, that we forget that 99 per cent of the rest of the world isn't Swedish.'

Examples of cultural mistakes

In February 1977, US President Jimmy Carter was in Mexico to 'build bridges' and 'mend fences'. Mexico had recently discovered large amounts of oil. President José López Portillo was the first speaker. 'Let us seek only lasting solutions—good faith and fair play. Nothing that would make us lose the respect of our children,' he said. On hearing López Portillo's remarks, Carter didn't use his prepared speech, but chose to answer spontaneously. He said:

> We both have beautiful and interesting wives, and we both run several
> kilometers everyday. As a matter of fact, I told President López Portillo that I
> first acquired my habit of running here in Mexico City. My first running course
> was from the Palace of Fine Arts to the Majestic Hotel where me and my family
> were staying. In the midst of the Folkorico performance, I discovered that I was
> afflicted with Montezuma's revenge.[13]

As it turned out, stating that he had Montezuma's revenge (diarrhea) was not funny at all. In light of what he wanted to accomplish—'building bridges'—the remark was entirely inappropriate.

Dan Quayle, as Vice-President of the United States, made an official visit to Asia in 1989. The *New York Times International* reported the following penchant to filter impressions through his 'America is best' perspective.

> He said he found Australia 'fascinating' because it was so much like America.
> He found Indonesia daunting because of its many languages and large
> population.
>
> In American Samoa, after he was given a ceremonial drink called Ava made
> from the kava root by tribal high chiefs, Mr Quayle told reporters that 'it tasted
> like a laxative.'[14]

The *Jakarta Post*[15] had a front page story that began:

> 'Quayle Arrives Behind Schedule' along with a picture of the Quayles going into
> their meeting with the Indonesian Vice President, Sudharmono, almost two
> hours late on Sunday, at 9:30 P.M. instead of the originally scheduled 7:45 P.M.
>
> The paper speculated that perhaps there had been a problem with Air Force
> Two on the flight from Australia to Indonesia, since there had been reports of a
> flicker of light in the engine on the flight from Sydney to Fort Douglas, where the
> Quayles relaxed over the weekend at a luxurious resort with golf, tennis, and
> diving.

The truth was, the plane was fine. The Vice President was late because he could not drag himself away from the Great Barrier Reef.

When United Airlines bought the Asia Pacific routes from Pan Am in 1987, John Zeeman, the executive vice-president for marketing and planning, acknowledged in a speech examples of the numerous cultural mistakes that United Airlines made and learned from.

- The map we inserted into our sales promotion brochure left out one of Japan's main islands.

- Our magazine ad campaign, 'We Know the Orient', listed the names of Far Eastern countries below pictures of local coins. Unfortunately, the coins didn't match up with the countries.

- I leave to your imagination how Chinese businessmen felt taking off from Hong Kong during the inauguration of our concierge services for first-class passengers. To mark the occasion, each concierge was proudly wearing a white carnation . . . a well-known oriental symbol of death.

- Perhaps the most embarrassing mistake was our inflight magazine cover that showed an Australian actor, Paul Hogan, wandering through the Outback. The caption read, 'Paul Hogan Camps it Up.' Hogan's lawyer was kind enough to phone us long-distance from Sydney to let us know that 'camps it up' is Australian slang for 'flaunts his homosexuality.'[16]

The concept of low-context and high-context communication was an issue when President Clinton met President Boris Yeltsin in Vancouver in April 1993. Some notes in Russian from one of Mr Clinton's meetings with Mr Yeltsin became public. Mr Clinton was quoted as telling his Russian counterpart that 'yes' often meant 'no' when spoken by the Japanese. A spokesperson for Mr Clinton had a great deal of difficulty explaining this remark, although the Japanese politely accepted the US explanations.

US baseball players in Japan also experience the difficulty of communications as related by Robert Whiting. The story is told about a US player in Japan who was knocked down by the opposing pitcher of the Orions:

> Tony Solaita of the Nippon Ham Fighters paid a call on the Lions' catcher during pregame batting practice. The catcher was Japanese, so Solaita was forced to converse with him through the interpreter assigned to him by his employers.
>
> 'Listen, you no good SOB,' Solaita growled, 'if you have a pitcher throw at my head again, I'll bleeping kill you!'
>
> The interpreter did not turn a hair. 'Mr. Solaita asks that you please not throw at his head anymore,' he translated. 'It makes his wife and children worry.'[17]

Another example of a serious cultural error concerns AT&T, who recently had to apologize for a cultural mistake they made. It seems they used a monkey to depict Africans. The drawing 'shows characters on several continents talking on the phone. All are human except the one in Africa, which is a monkey.'[18] AT&T told the NAACP and others that the drawing was done by a freelance artist, but it had been passed by AT&T editors. A cultural mistake.

The above examples illustrate errors that can be attributed to cultural arrogance or ignorance. In David A. Ricks's book[19], business blunders in marketing, translation, management, finance, law, production and other areas of commercial transactions are identified. Roger E. Axtell's *Do's and Taboos around the World*[20] also discusses many taboos in various countries. These books are useful guides for developing this competency.

Before assessing this competency, it is important to state loudly and clearly that it is our experience, supported by long discussions with many global mangers as well as research, that *not only American globals make cultural mistakes: Japanese, French, German, Swedes, Chinese, Mexicans and globals from all other countries also make them.* Improvement is required of all to make globalization work.

Summary

For Competency 12 Fig. 13.5 provides an opportunity for readers to reflect on the structure of their company or organization (is it traditional multinational, traditional international or traditional global according to descriptions of these structures in earlier chapters?) and to rate the CEO, corporate staff, subsidiary general manager and staff, as well as all employees in general. We are fully aware there may be great variation among the corporate staff or employees; but what is the central tendency? Or, generally, to what degree do these groups of people possess the competency?

Based on our assessment and interpretation of the significant literature on the subject, we have then indicated whether the competency is *essential*, *useful*, or *not necessary* for the CEO, corporate staff, subsidiary general manager and staff, and all employees, for the transformational goal to be realized and to make globalization work.

	CEO	Corporate staff	Subsidiary general manager and staff	All employees
Your company				

Rate and describe the degree the competency is possessed for each of the categories for your organization:
H = Demonstrates a high degree
S = Demonstrates somewhat
L = Demonstrates to a low degree
N/A = Not applicable for your organization

Transformational goal for structure

	CEO	Corporate staff	Subsidiary general manager and staff	All employees
Worldwide organizational solution	*Essential* For successful intercultural interactions	*Essential* For successful intercultural interactions	*Essential* For successful intercultural interactions	*Essential* For successful intercultural interactions

Fig. 13.5 **Compentency 12: Avoids cultural mistakes and behaves in a manner that demonstrates knowledge of and respect for other countries**

Notes and references

1. Quoted by Del Jones in 'More business travelers going global', *USA Today*, 14 September 1993, p. 1E.
2. John P. Kotter and James L. Heskett, *Corporate Culture and Performance*, Free Press, New York, 1992.
3. George C. Lodge and Ezra F. Vogel (eds.), *Ideology and National Competitiveness: An analysis of nine countries*. Harvard Business School Press, Boston, 1987.
4. See Robert T. Moran, 'Japan's remarkable ability to adapt to the real world', *International Management*, May 1988, p. 77.
5. Joel Kotkin, *Tribes: How Race, Religion and Identity Determine Success in the New Global Economy*, Random House, New York, 1992.
6. Robert McGarvey, 'Global connections', *US Air Magazine*, June 1993.
7. Geert Hofstede, *Culture's Consequences: International Differences in Work-Related Values*, Sage, Beverly Hills, Cal., 1980.
8. Geert Hofstede, *Cultures and Organizations: Software of the Mind*, McGraw-Hill, Maidenhead, Berks (UK), 1991.
9. Philip R. Harris and Robert T. Moran, *Managing Cultural Differences*, Gulf Publishing, Houston, Tex., 1991.

10. F. Kluckhohn and F. Strodtbeck, *Variations in Value Orientations*, Row, Peterson, Evanston, Ill., 1961.
11. Edward T. Hall and Mildred Reed Hall, *Hidden Differences: Doing Business with the Japanese*, Anchor Press, Garden City, NY, 1987.
12. Jack Condon and Fathi Yousef, in an introduction to *Intercultural Communication*, Bobbs-Merrill, Indianapolis, Ind., 1988.
13. *New York Times*, 15 February 1977.
14. *New York Times International*, 8 May 1989.
15. *Jakarta Post*; quoted in the *New York Times International*, 8 May 1989.
16. In a speech by John Zeeman entitled 'What United Airlines is learning in the Pacific', 14 November 1987, given before the Academy of International Business, Chicago.
17. R. Whiting, *You Gotta Have Wa*, Macmillan, New York, 1989.
18. 'AT&T offers apology for African depiction', *USA Today*, 18 September 1993.
19. David Ricks, *Blunders in International Business*, Blackwell Business, Cambridge, Mass., 1993.
20. Roger E. Axtell, *Do's and Taboos around the World*, John Wiley, New York, 1987.

Afterword

Our goal, stated in the Introduction, was to write about:

'competition, global changes, vision, structure, strategy, organizational change, competencies required to succeed in a complex business world—in a style that is simple, practical and useful, yet, when appropriate, grounded in theory and sound academic and business practices.'

Now that you, our reader, have come this far, we hope we have succeeded even to a modest degree.

The Questionnaire

*Questionnaire sent by the American Grad-
uate School of International Management
to 88 members of Thunderbird's World
Business Advisory Group, January 1993*

The research

'Globalization' may be the most frequently used word to describe the corporate strategy of the 1990s.

This questionnaire, being completed by senior executives of many of the world's largest companies, is designed for two purposes. First, to identify environmental, leadership, and organizational factors that would necessitate strategic and structural change in organizations. Second, to identify problems in implementing global strategies.

This research will be reported in the book *The Global Challenge: Building the New Worldwide Enterprise* to be published by McGraw-Hill in 1994 and co-authored by Robert Moran and John Riesenberger. All executives who respond to the questionnaire will receive a summary report in April 1993. We believe this data will not only be of interest to you but of use in your globalization challenges as well.

Your responses will be anonymous. Questionnaires are numbered for purposes of mailing respondents a summary in April.

We thank you.

ROBERT T. MORAN, PhD
Professor of International Studies
  and Director of the Program in
  Cross-Cultural Communication

JOHN R. RIESENBERGER
Executive Director, Strategic
  Marketing Services
The Upjohn Company

Please return your completed questionnaire within one week to:

ROBERT T. MORAN
American Graduate School of International Management
15249 N. 59th Ave.
Glendale, AZ 85306–6000

Please indicate the extent to which each of the following quotations from senior executives of large global companies applies to your organization.

		Does not apply				*Applies*
1.	'We decided to globalize first, then clean up.'	1	2	3	4	5
2.	'Our goal is to train our people in globalization skills by 1994, but we don't know what the skills are or what percentage of our people are trainable.'	1	2	3	4	5
3.	'There is a major gap between executives who believe that global strategy is understood and middle managers who say they understand it.'	1	2	3	4	5
4.	'Most of our employees do not have a global mindset.'	1	2	3	4	5
5.	'Managing organizational change is a serious challenge for us.'	1	2	3	4	5
6.	'Middle managers, responsible for short-term profits, experience too much pressure and are not able or willing to think long-term or collaborate globally.'	1	2	3	4	5
7.	'Global managers are made, not born.'	1	2	3	4	5
8.	'In global organizations a new kind of leader is required.'	1	2	3	4	5

Other comments: _____

_____

_____

_____

_____

9. The identification and learning of skills is crucial in an organization that is globalizing successfully. Based on your own experience, please complete the grid below.

Check if skill or competency is required of:

Skills	CEO or managing director	Head-quarters staff	Profit centre managers	Subsidiary managers
1. Understands overall corporate mission				
2. Has lived and worked overseas				
3. Long-term overseas business experience				
4. Second language competency				
5. Third language competency				
6. Degree in international business				
7. Significant understanding of other business cultures				
8. Is a skillful international business negotiator				
9. Is an effective bridge between headquarters and subsidiaries				
10. High interest in working in a global environment				
11. Is flexible				
12. Can tolerate ambiguity				

Please review the chart and circle the five most important skills for the CEO, headquarters' staff, profit center managers and the subsidiary managers.

10. Many organizations, as they begin globalization, select domestic employees as key people in this process. Please list the skills or traits that these persons now need to acquire to successfully meet the challenge of globalization.

1. _____
2. _____
3. _____
4. _____
5. _____

Other Comments: _____

_____

Thank you.

We would like to identify how you view your industry in terms of globalization. For each question, please indicate how important each factor was five years ago (1988), how important it is now (1993), and how important it will be, in your opinion, five years from now (1998), by circling the appropriate number.

				Your Industry		
11.	Economies of scale			1988	1993	1998
			Low	1	1	1
			importance	2	2	2
				3	3	3
			High	4	4	4
			importance	5	5	5
12.	New and evolving markets			1988	1993	1998
			Low	1	1	1
			importance	2	2	2
				3	3	3
			High	4	4	4
			importance	5	5	5
13.	Global sourcing			1988	1993	1998
			Low	1	1	1
			importance	2	2	2
				3	3	3
			High	4	4	4
			importance	5	5	5
14.	Reduced tariffs/customs barriers and tax advantages			1988	1993	1998
			Low	1	1	1
			importance	2	2	2
				3	3	3
			High	4	4	4
			importance	5	5	5

15.	Trend toward homogeneous		1988	1993	1998
	technical standards	Low	1	1	1
		importance	2	2	2
			3	3	3
		High	4	4	4
		importance	5	5	5
16.	Lowered global		1988	1993	1998
	transportation costs	Low	1	1	1
		importance	2	2	2
			3	3	3
		High	4	4	4
		importance	5	5	5
17.	Increased telecommunication		1988	1993	1998
	options at reduced costs	Low	1	1	1
		importance	2	2	2
			3	3	3
		High	4	4	4
		importance	5	5	5
18.	Trend toward homogeneous demand		1988	1993	1998
	for products	Low	1	1	1
		importance	2	2	2
			3	3	3
		High	4	4	4
		importance	5	5	5
19.	Competition from international		1988	1993	1998
	competitors	Low	1	1	1
		importance	2	2	2
			3	3	3
		High	4	4	4
		importance	5	5	5
20.	Customer strategy changes		1988	1993	1998
	from domestic-only to global	Low	1	1	1
		importance	2	2	2
			3	3	3
		High	4	4	4
		importance	5	5	5
21.	Exchange rate exposure		1988	1993	1998
		Low	1	1	1
		importance	2	2	2
			3	3	3
		High	4	4	4
		importance	5	5	5

22. Accelerating rate of technological change

		1988	1993	1998
Low importance		1	1	1
		2	2	2
		3	3	3
High importance		4	4	4
		5	5	5

The final section of questions is for classification purposes only.

1. Please indicate the size of your organization:
(number of employees)

Fewer than 100 _____ 100–500 _____ 501–2500 _____
2501–5000 _____ 5001–10 000 _____ More than 10 000_____

2. Company classification:
(check one)

Manufacturing (industrial)	_____	Manufacturing (consumer)	_____
Services	_____	Finance	_____
Real estate	_____	Insurance	_____
Merchandising/retailing	_____	Government	_____
Utilities	_____	Transportation	_____
Construction/engineering	_____	Communications	_____

Other (*please specify*) _____

3. Please indicate your organization's percentage of sales in each area:

Home country _____%
International _____%

4. What is your position within the organization?

CEO/CFO _____ Chairperson _____ President _____
Managing director _____ Vice-president _____
Other (*please specify*) _____

5. How long have you been with your present organization?

Less than 1 year	_____	Between 16 and 20 years	_____
Between 1 and 5 years	_____	More than 20 years	_____
Between 6 and 10 years	_____		
Between 11 and 15 years	_____		

6. How long have you been in your present position?

Less than 1 year	_____	Between 16 and 20 years	_____
Between 1 and 5 years	_____	More than 20 years	_____
Between 6 and 10 years	_____		
Between 11 and 15 years	_____		

Selected bibliography

Bartlett, Christopher A. and Sumantra, Ghoshal, *Managing Across Borders: The Transnational Solution*, Harvard Business School Press, Boston, Mass., 1989.

Below, Patrick J., Morrisey, George L. and Acomb, Betty L. *The Executive Guide to Strategic Planning*, Jossey-Bass, San Francisco, 1987.

Berry, Thomas H., *Managing the Total Quality Transformation*, McGraw-Hill, New York, 1991.

Bowles, Jerry and Hammond, Joshua, *Beyond Quality: How 50 Winning Companies Use Continuous Improvement*, Putnam's Sons, New York, 1991.

Campbell, Andrew and Young, Sally, *Do You Need a Mission Statement?* Special Report no. 1208, The Economist Publications, London, 1990.

Capra, Fritjof and Steindl-Rast, David, *Belonging to the Universe*, Harper Collins, New York, 1992.

Crosby, Philip B., *Quality is Free*, McGraw-Hill, New York, 1979.

—— *Quality without Tears*, McGraw-Hill, New York, 1984.

Davidson, William H. and Malone, Michael S., *The Virtual Corporation*, Harper Collins, New York, 1992.

Dobyns, Lloyd and Crawford-Mason, Clare, *Quality or Else: The Revolution in World Business*, Houghton Mifflin, Boston, Mass., 1991.

Drucker, Peter F., *Managing for the Future*, Truman Talley Books/Dutton, New York, 1992.

Dudley, James W., *1992—Strategies for the Single Market*, Kogan Page, London, 1989.

Fombrun, Charles J., *Turning Points: Creating Strategic Change in Corporations*, McGraw-Hill, New York, 1992.

Goldratt, Eliyahu M. and Cos, Jeff, *The Goal—A Process of Ongoing Improvement*, North River Press, Croton-on-Hudson, NY, 1986.

Hammer, Michael and Champy, James, *Reengineering the Corporation*, Harper Collins, New York, 1993.

Harrington, H. James, *Business Process Improvement: The Breakthrough Strategy for Total Quality, Productivity and Competitiveness*, McGraw-Hill, New York, 1991.

Harris, Philip R. and Moran, Robert T., *Managing Cultural Differences*, Gulf Publishing Co., Houston, Texas, 1991.

Hiam, Alexander, *Closing the Quality Gap: Lessons from America's Leading Companies*, Prentice-Hall, Englewood Cliffs, NJ, 1992.

Huge, Ernest C., *Total Quality: An Executive's Guide for the 1990's*, Business One Irwin, Homewood, Ill., 1990.

Juran, Joseph M., *Juran on Leadership for Quality: An Executive Handbook*, Free Press, New York, 1989.

Macdonald, John and Piggott, John, *Global Quality*, Mercury Books, London, 1990.

Meyer, Christopher, *Fast Cycle Time: How to Align Purpose, Strategy and Structure for Speed*, Free Press, New York, 1993.

Mizuno, Shigeru, *Company-wide Total Quality Control*, Asian Productivity Organization, Tokyo, 1990.

Nanus, Burt, *Visionary Leadership*, Jossey-Bass, San Francisco, 1992.

Ouchi, William G., *The M-Form Society*, Addison-Wesley, Reading, Mass., 1984.

Pattison, Joseph, *Acquiring The Future*, Dow Jones-Irwin, Homewood, Ill., 1990.

Porter, Michael E., *Competitive Strategy*, Free Press, New York, 1980.

—— (ed.), *Competition in Global Industries*, Harvard Business School Press, Boston, Mass., 1986.

Prahalad, C. K. and Doz, Yves L., *The Multinational Mission*, Free Press, New York, 1987.

Primozic, Kenneth, Primozic, Edward and Leben, Joe, *Strategic Choices: Supremacy, Survival or Sayonara*, McGraw-Hill, New York, 1991.

Pucik, Vladimir, Tichy, Noel M. and Barnett, Carole K. (eds), *Globalizing Management: Creating and Leading the Competitive Organization*, John Wiley & Sons, New York, 1992.

Quinn, James Brian, *Intelligent Enterprise*, Free Press, New York, 1992.

Rhinesmith, Stephen, *A Manager's Guide to Globalization,* Business One Irwin, Homewood, Ill., 1993.

Robert, Michel, *The Strategist CEO*, Quorum Books, New York, 1988.

—— *Strategy Pure and Simple*, McGraw-Hill, New York, 1993.

Steiner, George A., *Strategic Planning*, Free Press, New York, 1979.

Thurow, Lester, *Head to Head: The Coming Economic Battle among Japan, Europe and America*, William Morrow, New York, 1992.

Tomasko, Robert M., *Rethinking the Corporation: The Architecture of Change*, AMACOM, New York, 1993.

Tregoe, Benjamin B. and Zimmerman, John W., *Top Management Strategy*, Touchstone, New York, 1980.

Wall, Bob, Solum, Robert S. and Sobol, Mark R., *The Visionary Leader: From Mission Statement to a Thriving Organization, Here's Your Blueprint for Building an Inspired, Cohesive Customer-Oriented Team*, Prima Publishing, Rocklin, Cal., 1992.

Walton, Mary, *The Deming Management Method*, Perigree, New York, 1988.

Yip, George S., *Total Global Strategy: Managing for Worldwide Competitive Advantage*, Prentice-Hall, Englewood Cliffs, NJ, 1992.

Index